INCREDIBLY STRANGE!

INCREDIBLY STRANGE!

RIPLEY
PUBLISHING

a Jim Pattison Company

PUBLISHING

Publisher Anne Marshall
Editorial Director Rebecca Miles
Editorial Assistant Charlotte Howell
Text Geoff Tibballs
Interviews Jo Wiltshire
Proofreader Judy Barratt
Researchers James Proud, Charlotte Howell
Indexer Hilary Bird
Art Director Sam South
Project Designer Rocket Design (East Anglia) Ltd
Cover Design Michelle Canatella
Reprographics Juice Creative

Executive Vice President Norm Deska
Vice President, Archives and Exhibits Edward Meyer

Published by Ripley Publishing 2010
Ripley Publishing, Suite 188, 7576 Kingspointe Parkway,
Orlando, Florida 32819, USA

2 4 6 8 10 9 7 5 3 1

Copyright © 2010 by Ripley Entertainment Inc.
All rights reserved. Ripley's Believe It or Not!, and Ripley's,
Believe It or Not! are registered trademarks of Ripley
Entertainment Inc.

ISBN 978-1-893951-62-4

Some of this material first appeared in *Ripley's Believe It or
Not! The Remarkable...Revealed*

Library of Congress Cataloging-in-Publication Data
   Ripley's believe it or not! : incredibly strange! / [text, Geoff
Tibballs ; interviews, Jo Wiltshire].
     p. cm.
Includes index.
ISBN 978-1-893951-62-4
1. Curiosities and wonders. I. Tibballs, Geoff. II. Wiltshire, Jo.
AG243.T3985 2009
001.9--dc22
                          2009039571

Manufactured in Chaiwan, Hong Kong in November/2009
by Print Plus Limited
1st printing

First published in Great Britain in 2010 by
Random House Books, Random House, 20 Vauxhall Bridge
Road, London SW1V 2SA

www.rbooks.co.uk

Addresses for companies within The Random House Group
Limited can be found at www.randomhouse.co.uk/offices/htm

The Random House Group Limited Reg. No. 954009

A CIP catalogue record for this book is available from the
British Library

ISBN 9781847946294 (UK)

CONTENTS

RIPLEY'S WORLD

In December 1918, while working as a sports columnist for the New York Globe, Robert Ripley created his first collection of odd facts and feats.

The cartoons, based on unusual athletic achievements, were submitted under the heading "Champs and Chumps," but his editor wanted a title that would describe the incredible nature of the content. So, after much deliberation, the title was changed to "Believe it or Not!" The cartoon was an instant success and the phrase "believe it or not" soon entered everyday speech.

Ripley's passion was travel and by 1940 he had visited no fewer than 201 countries. Wherever he went, he searched out the bizarre for inclusion as his syndicated newspaper cartoons, which had begun to reach worldwide distribution, being translated into 17 different languages and boasting a readership of 80 million people. During one trip he crossed two continents and covered over 24,000 mi (39,000 km) "from New York to Cairo and back" to satisfy his appetite for the weird.

At the height of Ripley's popularity his cartoons reached an audience of over 80 million people.

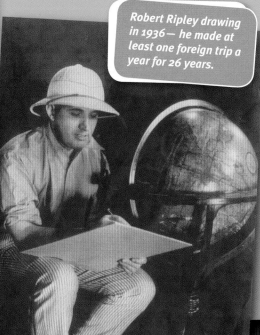

Robert Ripley drawing in 1936— he made at least one foreign trip a year for 26 years.

In 1923 Ripley met religious ascetics of the Sadhus in southeast Alipore, India. This group of Hindus are so devout that some will sit on a bed of nails, or stand up for the whole of their lives.

Robert Ripley spent a lot of his life on board ships sailing to different parts of the world on his search to discover the weird and wonderful.

Ripley's Legacy Lives On

Although he died in 1949 (after collapsing on the set of his weekly television show) his "Believe it or Not!" cartoons are still produced on a daily basis—just as they have been everyday since 1918—making Ripley's the longest running syndicated cartoon in the world.

Intrepid researchers follow in Robert Ripley's footsteps, continually scouring the world and enabling Ripley's to remain the undisputed king of the strange and unbelievable. With a huge computer database of incredible facts, people, and events, a massive photographic archive, and a warehouse stuffed with unique exhibits, Ripley's is able to present a celebration of the amazing diversity of our world, without ever passing judgment. From the outset, Robert Ripley encouraged his dedicated readers to submit material and photographs—a tradition that exists to this day. His weekly mailbag sometimes exceeded 170,000 letters! The one man who started it all was once commemorated in his hometown church of Santa Rosa, California. The entire church was made from a single giant redwood tree.

Thousands of telegrams and letters like these were sent to Ripley at the height of his popularity. People hoped to feature in his famous cartoon strips with their unbelievable stories. Between 1929 and 1931 Ripley received so many letters addressed with unusual codes and signs that the Postmaster General stopped delivering them because it took too long to decipher them.

Ripley's now has many museums around the world. This one in Ocean City hosts authentic shrunken heads, the world's rarest egg, and two-headed animals.

A portrait of Robert Ripley made out of 10,000 gumballs, which believe it or not, if you wanted to, would take 27 years to chew!

Ripley's cartoons are still produced every day without fail. This colour strip is a modern-day version produced in 2004.

Ripley's—**Believe It or Not!**

BUSINESS CARD KING!

YEAR-OLD GREG SAPERSTEIN HAS A COLLECTION OF OVER 15,000 BUSINESS CARDS FROM AROUND

NOT A TOY, BOY!

IN 1988, A ROCKET FUEL PLANT IN NEVADA CAUGHT FIRE AND EXPLODED WITH SUCH FORCE THAT IT REGISTERED 3.5 ON THE RICHTER SCALE AT AN EARTHQUAKE MONITORING STATION HUNDREDS OF MILES AWAY!

IN NOVEMBER 2005,

BELIEVE OR

IT WAS ONCE BELIEVED THAT COULD BE CURED BY DRINKIN

9

Lonely Curiosities

Despite 37 museums worldwide jam-packed with Ripley artifacts, there are approximately 12,500 more in the Ripley warehouse in Orlando, Florida.

Ripley's has been expanding at a phenomenal pace over the last couple of years, opening museums in London, New York, San Antonio, and Bangalore, India, with a further four set to open shortly. Their goal is to gain 1,000 new exhibits a year, that's three a day! And they have certainly been achieving it.

Archivist Edward Meyer has been looking after these "lonely curiosities" for 31 years, and is sure they will find a home sooner rather than later.

He says: "Nothing is intentionally 'locked away'. Everything we acquire will eventually be displayed, but we are always buying faster than we are building, so some things do sit around the warehouse for a while." Acquiring exhibits has become so popular that 50 per cent of new acquisitions are brought to Meyer rather than him seeking them out.

The Ripley warehouse in Orlando, Florida, is approximately the size of an American football field and can hold 9,000 exhibits! This means it will inevitably continue to host many of the world's believe it or not exhibits that we may never see. Looks like Ripley's will have to build even more museums—where to this time?

This two-headed calf is known by Ripley's as a "Prank of Nature." With two sets of everything the heads even had two separate personalities, believe it or not!

Ripley's holds the largest collection of shrunken heads in the world with a total of 120, 40 of which are stored in the Ripley warehouse. All of the heads originally came from one tribe, the Shuar-Jivaro tribe in Ecuador, and are worth up to $50,000 at auction. As well as shrunken heads, Ripley's also has two shrunken torsos in its collection!

This two-trunked elephant was found in Zimbabwe, Africa, in 2004 and was kept in the warehouse for a while. The Ripley team was actually looking for an albino giraffe when locals informed them about the amazing elephant. It was a male bull about three to four years old, and weighed several tons—the head alone weighed over 1,000 lb (450 kg) and measured 9 x 9 ft (3 x 3 m). After several tests in New York, including one for DNA, both trunks were found to be real and fully functional. The only one in the world, the elephant is now on display in the San Antonio Museum, Texas.

Just a small section of the vast Ripley warehouse in Orlando, Florida, the home to thousands of Ripley exhibits.

FISHY TALES

Florida-based artist Juan Cabana creates his own fantastic mermaids and sea monsters from fish and animal remains.

He wraps fish and animal skins around steel, plastic, and fiberglass frames, often adding alligator claws for the hands and monkey skulls for the heads. One of his biggest creations—a mermaid nearly 7 ft (2.1 m) long—had the body of a 100-lb (45-kg) grouper.

His interest began several years ago when he acquired an old Japanese-made Feejee mermaid on the Internet auction site eBay. "Just holding the mermaid, I felt the energy and power. I was hooked and decided to continue the tradition of making these creatures." At first he tried to copy the originals, but then developed his own style.

The shape and size of each creature depends on the materials he has available. "I don't kill any fish or animals. I get my fish skins from a local market, where they would otherwise be thrown away. At first I was revolted by handling fish skins, but gradually I got used to them. I also had to learn taxidermy."

Each mermaid can take weeks to build. "Rather than looking fresh and alive, my creations are supposed to look old, mummified, and withered, as if they had been found washed up on a beach. I invent a story for each mermaid, saying that I found it on a particular beach rather than just saying I made it."

One of Cabana's mermaids is seen here looking as if it had washed up on a beach.

Lighter Lit!

The government building in Astana, Kazakhstan, known by locals as "The Cigarette Lighter" because of its shape, caught fire on May 30, 2006.

Hebrew Coin

After shopping at her local supermarket in Sumter, South Carolina, Lynn Moore noticed something odd in her change. She knew it wasn't a penny, but she was very surprised to hear the news from a coin expert that the coin was probably from ancient Hebrew society, and was minted around 135AD.

Hamster Home

In May 2006, as revenge for a practical joke, Luke Trerice's friends turned his apartment, in Olympia, Washington, into a giant hamster cage! The cage featured an exercise wheel that was 6 ft (1.8 m) in diameter, shredded newspaper on the floor, and a huge water bottle. In 2004, Trerice wrapped his friend's apartment contents in aluminum foil!

Boy Racer

An 11-year-old boy from Independence, Missouri, took his parents' 1995 Chevrolet and drove 200 mi (322 km), reaching speeds of 85 mph (137 km/h) before running out of gas and accidentally locking the keys in the car.

Missed Monolith

A 44-year-old Australian man was arrested for drunk-driving in March 2006 after asking police the way to Uluru—when he was parked just 330 ft (100 m) away from it, with his headlights pointing straight at it. The Uluru landmark, also known as Ayers Rock, rises 1,115 ft (340 m) above the Australian desert and is 6 mi (9.6 km) around.

Hound Hairpieces

Ruth Regina of Miami, Florida, runs a boutique that sells wigs for dogs whose owners want them to look sexy! Among her most popular lines are the "Yappy Hour" (a fluff of curls) and the "Peek a Bow Wow," which falls down over part of the dog's face, apparently giving a stylish look reminiscent of 1940s movie star Veronica Lake.

Heavy Sleepers

A pair of Serbian gas-station attendants on night shift slept while thieves broke into their office in 2006 and escaped with a safe weighing 700 lb (317 kg). Although the gang had to rip the safe from the wall and drag it out of the building, the theft was not discovered until the morning shift arrived.

Rickshaw Robot

Over the last 26 years Wu Yulu, a Chinese farmer from Beijing, has built 25 robots out of scrap metal, screws, nails, and wire from garbage dumps. Some models light cigarettes, others serve tea, and this particular one, which took him a year to build, pulls rickshaws. "Humanoid robot rickshaw" stands 6 ft (1.8 m) high and has ping-pong eyes and a sponge mouth. There is a steering wheel on the rickshaw with a button that controls the robot's movement. Powered by electricity, it is capable of moving forward and backward for 6 hours covering 5 mi (8 km), taking 30 to 40 steps a minute.

Bar Horse

Peggy, the carthorse, regularly joins her owner Peter Dolan for a pint of beer and pickled-onion potato chips at the Alexandra Hotel in Jarrow, England. She used to be tied up with a long rope outside the pub, but one day followed her owner into the bar and stayed for a drink.

Hospital Wedding

Rev. Don Hoover of Lincoln, Illinois, conducted the marriage of Janel Hoover and Ed Tibbits at the hospital emergency room where he'd been taken after developing severe leg cramps.

Anger Bar

A new bar that has opened in the Chinese city of Nanjing allows stressed-out customers to unleash pent-up anger by attacking staff, smashing glasses, and generally causing mayhem! The Rising Sun Anger Release Bar employs 20 strong young men as "models" for customers to punch and scream at.

Splashed Cash

When Vanisha Mittal married Amit Bhatia in Paris, France, her father, billionaire industrialist Lakshmi Mittal, rented the Tuileries Garden at Versailles and Louis XIV's chateau for a wedding celebration that cost $60 million.

Cheesy Attraction

U.S. Navy Petty Officer Mike Evans opened a bag of Cheetos and discovered a giant cheese snack the size of a lemon. He then donated the cheesy lump to the town of Algona, Iowa, to be used as a tourist attraction.

Pet Soup

A 2006 survey showed that one in three dog owners in South Korea enjoys boshintang soup, which is made from dog meat. It is said to aid stamina and virility.

Pancake Folly

A man from Bensalem, Pennsylvania, who robbed a bank in 2006 and escaped with around $4,000, was caught when he stopped for pancakes. Police said the man might have got away with the raid on a Bank of America branch had he not stopped for a snack at the nearby Sunrise Diner.

Alcoholic Lake

Following a malfunction at a nearby distillery in June 2006, Bracholinksie Lake in Wielkopolska, Poland, was reported to have concentrations of vodka as high as 30 percent.

Kitchen Trap

A Czech man avoided jail for four years by hiding under the floorboards in his mother's kitchen. Police finally caught up with him on a surprise visit to the house when they spotted him trying to slide through a trap door into a vacant cellar.

Ghostly Driver

A Tennessee man was ticketed for five driving violations ten days after he died.

Hefty Hero

When a teenage cyclist was trapped under a car in Tucson, Arizona, in July 2006, he was saved by a strong bystander who lifted the car right off the ground. At 6 ft 4 in (1.93 m) tall and weighing 300 lb (136 kg), Tom Boyle raised the Chevrolet Camaro single-handedly, allowing the driver to haul the injured cyclist clear.

Cat with 12 Claws

This five-month-old cat called Bigfoot from Brooklet, Georgia, has six claws on each of its front feet. It was born to normal parents.

Cat Killer

A woman from Miami Gardens, Florida, had been searching for her one-year-old Siamese cat for two days in 2005 when her son discovered a bulging python slithering in the family's backyard. An X ray on the snake showed that it had indeed eaten a cat.

Minnow Mystery

Biologists at the University of Manchester found this duck egg in a small pond in the French Alps. They noticed something moving inside and, when they cracked open the shell, discovered three live minnows! They were baffled as to how the minnows got there as there appeared to be no crack in the egg.

Celebrity Delusion

A Canadian drunk driver escaped conviction in 2006 because he believed Shania Twain was helping him to drive. The 33-year-old man was arrested for speeding in downtown Ottawa, but a judge ruled him not criminally responsible because he suffered from delusions that female celebrities were communicating with him telepathically.

Gold Digger

When his gold detector picked up a signal near the front patio of his home in Montclair, California, in 2006, 63-year-old Henry Mora started digging. He intended excavating only a few feet but, as the detector kept bleeping, Henry kept digging. Eventually, worried authorities were forced to stop him after he created a hole 60 ft (18 m) deep! He admitted he had got "carried away."

Flute Melted

A Swedish orchestra playing instruments carved from ice had to abandon a 2006 concert after the flutist's warm breath caused her flute to melt! Tim Linharts had made functioning flutes, violins, and a double bass out of ice for the performance in a large igloo in the town of Pitea.

Excused Duty

A 103-year-old Canadian woman was excused from serving her jury duty in 2006 because it would have interfered with her afternoon nap. Phyllis Perkins from Saskatoon, Saskatchewan, asked to be excluded on the grounds that she needed her regular daytime doze.

Parking Fine

A Florida motorist finally paid his parking fine—60 years after getting it. William Fogarty, now 87, received the ticket in Norfolk, Virginia, in May 1946. He bought a $1 money order to pay the fine, but forgot to send it off. When he was clearing out an old box in 2006, he found the money order and mailed it.

Fake Crash

A California man staged a fake plane crash in his own garden—as a Halloween stunt! Complete with false human legs sticking out the bottom, the scene was so realistic it even fooled the police. Inspired by the TV series Lost, Steve Chambers picked up the parts of a G3 Gulfstream jet from the factory in Van Nuys where he works as an aviation mechanic. He sealed off the site with yellow caution tape and added a sign reading: "Do not enter: Under investigation."

WINTER BLUES

In 2006, Dr. Alex Bobak converted the waiting room in his London surgery into a beach to help patients beat the winter blues.

He transformed the space into a Caribbean-style paradise where waiting-room chairs were swapped for sun loungers, palm trees, sand, and sun. Several light-therapy lights were brought in to replicate the sun's rays.

Pink Handcuffs

In 2005, police officers in Maricopa County, Arizona, began using fluorescent pink handcuffs when making arrests!

Surprise Catch

In August 2005, Alan Chaplaski, a fisherman from Stonington, Connecticut, was trawling for shrimp when he snagged a U.S. Navy nuclear submarine 362 ft (110 m) long!

Pizza Hero

While dressed in cape and tights as superhero "Luke Pie-Rocker" for his pizza delivery job, Cameron Evans of Minneapolis, Minnesota, foiled a purse snatching in June 2006.

Seeing Double

Retired lifeguard Michael Morris from Cornwall, England, got more than he bargained for when making an omelet for his lunch one day in April 2006. Cracking a particularly large egg into a bowl (hoping he'd maybe bought a double-yolker), Morris was amazed when a smaller egg fell out. His egg-within-an-egg has been described as extremely rare by experts.

Slim Chance

A prisoner dieted his way to freedom in Australia by squeezing through a narrow gap after losing more than 30 lb (13.6 kg). He had weighed 154 lb (70 kg) when jailed in 2003, but because he had slimmed down to 124 lb (56 kg) in the intervening two years, he was able to escape through a space he had chiseled between the wall and the bars on his cell window.

High Dining

A group of 22 Belgian chefs took part in an extreme dining experience in Brussels in April 2006. Strapped into racing-car seats, they enjoyed a three-course meal while suspended from a crane 165 ft (50 m) high above the streets of Belgium's capital city.

Faked Death

A woman from Des Moines, Iowa, allegedly faked her own death to avoid paying parking fines. She apparently wrote her own obituary, made to look like a page from the website of the Des Moines Register, and forged a letter informing a judge that she had died in a car crash. But was caught out after she was given yet another parking ticket just a month after her "death."

Dog Distraction

Police in Stockton-on-Tees, England, investigated a bizarre burglary in 2006 in which one of the thieves pretended to be a dog. Two men barged into a house owned by a brother and sister in their nineties, and while one of the thieves distracted the couple by dropping to his knees, crawling around on all fours and barking like a dog, his accomplice grabbed the woman's purse.

Snake Stowaway

Like most people returning from vacation, following a 2006 trip to the Philippines, Helga Gurnsteidl from Nuremberg, Germany, put her dirty clothes in the washing machine. When she took her clean clothes out of the washing machine, however, she found a snake in them. Amazingly, the green ring snake—a rare Filipino native—had survived the flight to Germany as well as the spin cycle in the washer.

Flock Of Seagulls

A flock of several hundred gull-like shearwaters crashed into a fishing boat for half an hour off the coast of Alaska in the early hours of August 30, 2006. More than 1,600 bird carcasses were found washed up on the nearby shores of the town of Unalaska over the next two days. Flocks of shearwaters can number a million birds and some species are attracted to lights on boats.

Wedding Fraud

A Japanese man and woman were sent to prison in 2006 for falsely claiming that he was of royal descent and for staging a lavish wedding to collect gift money from unsuspecting guests. They had apparently swindled more than $25,000 in gift money from 61 guests at their 2003 wedding reception.

Baby Names

A Belgian couple expecting their 15th baby put an ad in an Antwerp newspaper because they had run out of ideas for names. Brigitte Dillen and Ivo Driessens had given all of their children names ending in a "y" but after Wendy, Cindy, Jimmy, Brendy, Sonny, Sandy, Purdy, Chardy, Yorry, Yony, Britney, Yenty, Ruby, and Xanty, they were unable to come up with any new suggestions.

Trash Find

Dropping off his household trash at a dump site, Michael Hoskins of Danville, Virginia, spotted a pile of old books waiting to be thrown away. Among them he discovered a 188-year-old King James Bible, one of less than half a dozen copies belived to be in existence.

Charity Reception

A scorned bride canceled her September 2006 wedding and turned the reception into a charity event. After learning that her fiancé had been cheating on her, Kyle Paxman decided to salvage something positive from the disappointment by inviting 125 women and making the reception at Lake Champlain, Vermont, a charity benefit for Care USA.

Golf Shame

A caddy at a golf course in Long Island, New York, was awarded $34,000 in a sexual harassment lawsuit in 2006 after he was ridiculed by his boss for losing two golf matches to a woman.

Rooster Silenced

In 2006, a Scottish council sought an Anti-Social Behaviour Order on a rooster that crowed too early and too loudly. Since Charlie's crowing apparently exceeded the 30-decibel limit set by the World Health Organization, Borders Council demanded that his owner, Kenneth Williamson, keep the bird silent between 11 p.m. and 7 a.m.

Simple Explanation

When water suddenly began spouting from the base of a statue of the late Pope John Paul II in his hometown of Wadowice, Poland, in 2006, people flocked from all over the country to drink from the "miracle fountain." But the suggestion of divine intervention was shattered when city council officials revealed that it was they who had installed a pipe beneath the statue so that the water would make it look prettier.

Piece of Mind

Sambhu Roy of India survived an electrical accident with severe burns to his skull. His scalp was completely burned and several months later, reportedly, a piece of his skull fell off. The inner covering of the skull was unaffected and new bone had grown and pushed the dead skull out. Sambhu has kept the old piece of skull as a personal trophy.

Biting the Bullet

A 73-year-old Inuit woman was hospitalized in Nome, Alaska, after an abdominal X ray revealed that her appendix was filled with buckshot. Doctors said Inuits hunt so many ducks and geese for food that some of the buckshot remains in the cooked meat and is then eaten and digested.

Alien Visitor

When the International Bird Rescue Research Center in Cordelia, California, treated an injured duck in May 2006, an X ray revealed what looked like the face of ET in the bird's stomach. The Center planned to auction the "unbelievable" X ray to raise funds.

Drank Coins

Gigi Florin of Romania was hospitalized after swallowing 120 coins washed down with wine—the result of a bet he made with a friend. He thought the wine would help digest the coins, but then collapsed.

Knife Swallower

Mao Kyan from Chendu in China had a 3-in (7.6-cm) knife stuck in his throat for eight months. He had swallowed the knife during a police raid on his flat to avoid being charged with possessing a weapon.

Close Shave

A 61-year-old Mesa, Arizona, man was shot in the face while sleeping. He didn't realize what had happened until three days later when the bullet showed up in an X ray.

Unusual Diet

Dr. F. Durga swallowed all of these metal objects, which included a fish hook, three pocket knives, five rifle shells, 17 horseshoe nails, a collection of coins and keys, and various pieces of broken glass. He underwent surgery in 1908 to remove the items from his stomach.

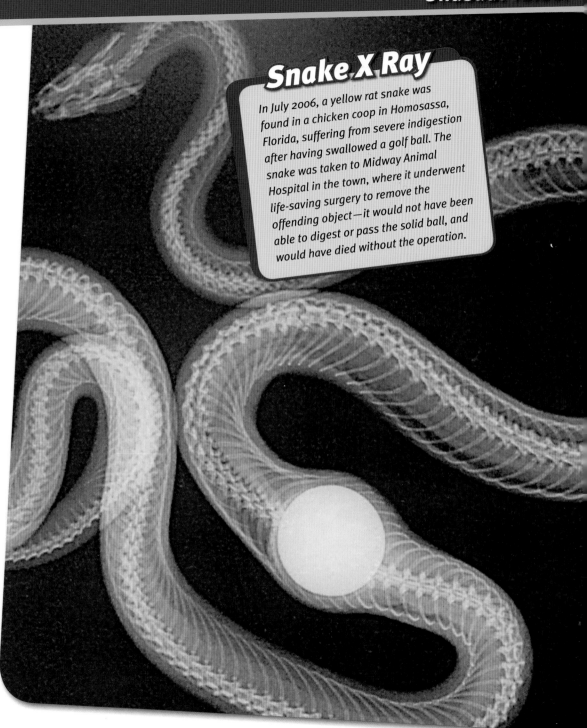

Snake X Ray

In July 2006, a yellow rat snake was found in a chicken coop in Homosassa, Florida, suffering from severe indigestion after having swallowed a golf ball. The snake was taken to Midway Animal Hospital in the town, where it underwent life-saving surgery to remove the offending object—it would not have been able to digest or pass the solid ball, and would have died without the operation.

STOMACH FOR A FIGHT

EXTREME HEARTBURN FORMULA

IN DEPTH

Sonya Thomas is America's competitive eating champion, calling herself the Black Widow. She weighs just 99 lb (45 kg), but has managed to put away 46 mince pies in ten minutes and 52 hard-boiled eggs in just five!

How did you start competitive eating?

I eat more than normal people, so I thought it might be something I'd be good at. I won a qualifier for the annual July 4 contest three years ago at Nathan's Famous Hog Dogs on Coney Island, New York. In the final I ate 25 hotdogs with buns in 12 minutes—a new women's record.

Were you a big eater as a child?

I was born and grew up in South Korea, and only emigrated to America when I was 26. I didn't eat a lot as a child because we were so poor.

Do you feel ill after a contest?

No—an average contest consumption will only be about 9 lb of food in 10 or 12 minutes—that's not enough to fill me up!

Do you have any special training or techniques?

I do daily aerobic exercise and eat one big, but healthy, meal a day. I drink a lot of water or diet cola with it—maybe 20 glasses—to expand my capacity. And before a big contest, I find out what food it will be and practice eating it at speed.

Why do you call yourself the "Black Widow?"

Eating contests are traditionally all male, and the Black Widow is a female spider that kills and eats her mate! When I started to rank higher and higher in the contests, the men said: "How can a little woman do that?" I kept beating them and eventually they respected me.

You are only 5 ft 5 in with a tiny frame— have you got an unusual digestive system?

Most top eaters are not heavy—skinny people have less fat to restrict the stomach. You need a large throat, or esophagus, to get the food down, a strong jaw for chewy foods, and a big stomach capacity. Mine holds 18 to 20 lb of food.

Is it dangerous—and how do you avoid putting on weight?

I don't gain weight because I only eat like that once in a while. During contests, there is a danger of choking, but every sport has its injuries. There are always medical people standing by.

What are your favorite contest foods?

Oysters—46 dozen in 10 minutes. Seafood is the easiest. 11 lb of cheesecake in nine minutes was one I'm proud of, as well as 46 crab cakes in 10 minutes and 162 buffalo wings in 12 minutes.

Is there anything you won't eat?

I didn't eat any meat until I was 21. I still don't like it much—especially pork. And I don't like anything too unusual, like frogs' legs! But I don't think about how it tastes—I just think about winning.

How long will you carry on—and what would you like to eat next?

I hold 27 records, but I will carry on as long as my body can do it. I manage a fast-food restaurant— perfect for me! But I want to increase my speed. I want to try sushi, and after that noodles—I think they would go down quickly!

Burning Heart

To demonstrate his love for his girlfriend, Hannes Pisek made a huge heart out of 220 burning candles on the floor of his apartment in Hoenigsberg, Austria. Sadly, while he was collecting his girlfriend from work, his burning heart set fire to the apartment. He not only lost his home but also his girl who promptly went back to live with her parents.

Poor Planning

Two thieves from Cincinnati, Ohio, might have got away with stealing a flat-screen TV measuring 55 in (1.4 m) wide from a store in Middletown, Ohio—if only they had brought a bigger getaway car. Instead they made their escape in a tiny Mercury Sable with the TV hanging out of the open rear door, and were quickly spotted by police.

Time Capsule

A message in a bottle that had remained hidden in a wall at Quonset Naval Air Station, Rhode Island, for 65 years was finally unearthed in 2006. It had been written in 1941 by two carpenters who were part of a civilian army hired to build military bases in the area. The message asked, "Will this bottle see the sun?" With its discovery came the answer.

It's Fish Again!

In 1941, Adolph Flashner was known as "King of the Sea," because he ate fish at every single mealtime, including breakfast. He also claimed never to have eaten meat in his life.

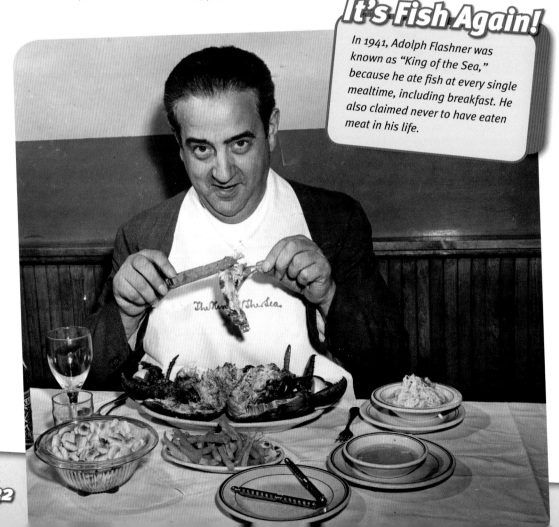

Milk for the Gods

August 2006 saw Hindu temples across northern India thronged with devotees all coming to see statues of the gods Shiva, Ganesh, and Durga purportedly drinking spoonfuls of milk that were offered to them. At the Shiva temple in Lucknow, priest Sudhir Mishra said that 21 pt (10 l) of milk had been offered to a statue of Shiva and that all of it had been drunk by the god. Indian government scientists said that the milk had disappeared because it had effectively been absorbed by the statue, but this did not stop the rush of pilgrims to the temples.

Tongue Vision

Although he has been blind since birth, Mike Ciarciello can "see" through his tongue. In 2006, researchers at Canada's University of Montréal mounted a small camera on his forehead, which sent electrical impulses about what it saw to a small grid placed on his tongue. As a result, he was able to walk through a tricky obstacle course without a cane. "It's a concept in which you replace a sense that was lost by another one that is there," explained supervising neuropsychologist Maurice Ptito. "They sense the world through their tongue, and that gives them the feeling of seeing. You don't see with your eyes. You see with your brain."

Life Saver

A police officer in Serbia, saved an old lady's life after she accidentally swallowed a set of false teeth while eating a sandwich. The passing policeman thought the woman had choked on the sandwich, but when he squeezed her diaphragm the pair of dentures flew out of her mouth.

Parking Row

A street parking attendant in Rio de Janeiro, Brazil, was charged in 2006 with sawing a woman in two over a parking-space dispute. Police said the man murdered the 51-year-old businesswoman following an argument after she had parked her car in a prohibited spot.

Too Realistic

Responding to a call from a park ranger reporting a hostage situation, Colorado police arrested a number of suspects, only to discover that they were actors making a crime movie. Larimer County deputies handcuffed crew members and pointed a rifle at actor Chris Borden.

Car Chase

The driver of a stolen BMW led police on a 370-mi (595-km) car chase across southwestern Australia, driving up to 110 mph (177 km/h). He stopped only when he ran out of gas.

Football Frenzy

When Chicago Bears beat Green Bay Packers 26–0 in their September 2006 season opener, it cost Bears' fan Randy Gonigam $300,000 in free furniture. Gonigam, owner of a store in Plano, Illinois, had offered customers free furniture up to $10,000 a head if the Bears achieved a shutout against the Packers. With 206 customers taking up the offer, it was a good job he had taken out $300,000 insurance to cover himself.

Old Address

Shot in the head during a robbery, Larry Taylor of Georgia then walked 2 mi (3.2 km) so he could die at his mother's house—only to find that she had moved. Larry ultimately survived the ordeal.

Vodka Pipeline

In 2004, smugglers were caught bringing vodka into Lithuania from neighboring Belarus through a pipeline that was an amazing 2 mi (3.2 km) long.

Miraculous Recovery

A dog in California was run over, shot, and frozen—but still lived! Dosha, a ten-month-old of mixed breeding, first ran into trouble when she was hit by a car near her owner's Clearwater home. To put her out of her misery, a police officer shot her in the head and, presumed dead, she was put in a freezer at an animal control center. Then, two hours later, a veterinarian opened the door to the freezer and was amazed to see Dosha standing upright in a plastic orange bag, the equivalent of a human body bag.

In Like Flint

Nicky Killeen's Weimaraner, Flint, fell on a 3-in (8-cm) stick that became lodged behind his eye next to his brain in 2006. Nicky, from Essex, England, didn't see the incident but noticed that Flint's eye was swollen. A local veterinarian initially prescribed the dog anti-inflammatory medication and antibiotics. When the treatment had no effect, Flint had a scan, which revealed the large splinter. It had just missed Flint's arteries, eyeball, nerves, and brain. The splinter was removed, and Flint suffered no ill effects from his ordeal.

LETTER MANIA

At the height of Robert Ripley's popularity, he received thousands of letters from around the world every week telling him of unbelievable facts that the writers hoped might be included in his famous cartoon strip. Over a period from 1929–31, many of these arrived addressed in a highly unusual fashion.

Letters were written in all languages and dialects. They included a letter addressed in Runic code—the language of the ancient Vikings—and one addressed to simply *"Believe It or Not!"* written in the old Confederate Civil War Code. Others were written in shorthand, numeric codes, sign language, and Indian signs, and some had a rip on the front of the envelope to indicate "Rip"–ley. Some bore only question marks, and many had rippling lines drawn across them—indicating a "ripply" river.

In April 1930 the U.S. Postmaster General said that the Post Office would cease to deliver the coded letters to Ripley because postal clerks had had to devote too much time to deciphering the codes!

Wow, Alice!

This kitten with two faces was born in Inverness, Florida, in July 2006. She was inspected by veterinarian Dr. Wade Phillips who reported that she had two mouths, both of which were fully functional, two noses, and four eyes. Her owner, Brandy Conley, gave her two names: "Wow," for everyone's first reaction on seeing her, and "Alice," after rock star Alice Cooper. Sadly, Wow Alice did not survive.

Pilot Stranded

Half an hour from the end of a flight from Ottawa to Winnipeg in 2006, the plane's pilot took a toilet break, only to find himself locked out of the cockpit on his return. After he had banged on the cockpit door for 10 minutes, the crew were forced to remove the faulty door from its hinges in order to let him back in.

$10,000 Tip

For Hutchinson, Kansas, restaurant waitress Cindy Kienow, three years of attentive service to a customer paid off in spectacular fashion in 2006 when he left her a $10,000 tip on a $26 dinner—that's more than 38,000 percent of the cost of the meal! Miss Kienow said the regular was always a generous tipper. "He said, 'This will buy you something kind of nice, huh?' And I said, 'Yeah, it will.' I didn't know what to say."

Girl Talk

CNN viewers were able to listen to news presenter Kyra Phillips' private cell-phone conversation about her family in 2006 after she forgot to switch off the microphone she was wearing when she went to the washroom. Her thoughts on her "passionate" husband and "control freak" sister-in-law were broadcast live, and drowned out a speech by President George W. Bush.

Litter Spill

A major road in California had to be temporarily closed in 2006 after a truck carrying ten tons of cat litter overturned and spilled its load. It took four hours to clean up the mess, spread across two lanes of the Golden State Freeway in Sun Valley.

Skunk Deterrent

In order to keep trespassers out of condemned buildings, Richland County deputies in South Carolina use simulated skunk odor as a deterrent.

In a Flap

The escape of a chicken from a farm in Nuberg, South Carolina, in 2006 caused widespread damage to an adjoining property. Six large cows on the neighboring farm were spooked by the flapping chicken and stampeded out of their barn, half demolishing the building and knocking down several sections of fence.

Petite Pub

Measuring just 8 x 8 ft (2.4 x 2.4 m), the recently opened Signal Box Inn at Cleethorpes, Lincolnshire, England, is not a pub for large parties. A former railway signal box, it has space for only four stools and standing room for another two customers.

Forgery Failed

A man in Thunder Bay, Ontario, Canada, was arrested for forging a prescription in 2004 after the pharmacy staff decided it was too legible and called the police.

Birthday Escape

In Kolasin, Montenegro, a prisoner broke out of jail in 2006 by overpowering guards and scaling a wall 10 ft (3 m) high... just to wish his girlfriend a happy birthday. After going straight to her house and passing on the greetings, he turned himself in to police. He claimed he had been forced to escape because he hadn't been allowed to use the prison phone.

Perky Pensioner

A 75-year-old woman chased after a middle-aged man who stole her purse and when she caught up with him, she gave him $3! Betty Horton of South Salt Lake, Utah, said the man had apologized to her, saying he was broke. So after giving him a sound telling off, she handed him some spare change.

Can Mountain

In 2005, a man in Ogden, Utah, had his house cleaned after amassing 70,000 empty beer cans collected over eight years of living alone.

Old Noodles

Noodles unearthed on an archeological site in Lajia, China, in 2005 are reckoned to be about 4,000 years old. Unlike modern noodles, which are made from wheat flour, these were made using grains from millet grass and are thought to have been buried during a catastrophic flood.

Finger Clue

After breaking into a leisure center in Hamburg, Germany, Michael Baumgartner fled when police arrived—but a ring on his index finger caught on a metal fence and tore his finger off. The severed finger was found by police at the scene and matched to his prints on their database.

House Dumped

Littering reached a whole new level along a highway in Tampa, Florida, when someone discarded the complete second floor of a three-bedroom, two-bathroom house beside U.S. Highway 301.

Tank Ride

In 2006, a man drove a 12-ton tank through the historic town center of Hradec Kralove in the Czech Republic—just to buy his kids ice cream. Miroslav Tucek said he had to use the armored personnel carrier, which he bought from the Czech Army, because his car had broken down. He told police it was too far to walk from his home and he had promised his children they could have an ice cream.

Skin Portrait

This portrait of Sara Fernandez is a painting with a difference, for it has been painted on the surgically removed skin of her mother. Angie Hernandez from Tucson, Arizona, had a tummy tuck in March 2006, and decided to put her skin to this unusual use. The skin, which measures 7 x 9 in (18 x 23 cm), was professionally cured before Angie's brother, Reuben Daniell, painted the portrait. It should last forever.

Black-and-White Twins

At odds of around a million to one, these two bonny babies are actually twins. Conceived naturally, Alicia and Jasmin Singerl from Queensland, Australia, have a mixed-race mother and a white father. In most cases, the eggs from a mixed-race woman will be a mix of genes for both black and white skin but, occasionally, the eggs carry genes for predominantly one skin color. This is what happened with the twins' mother—twice over and at the same time!

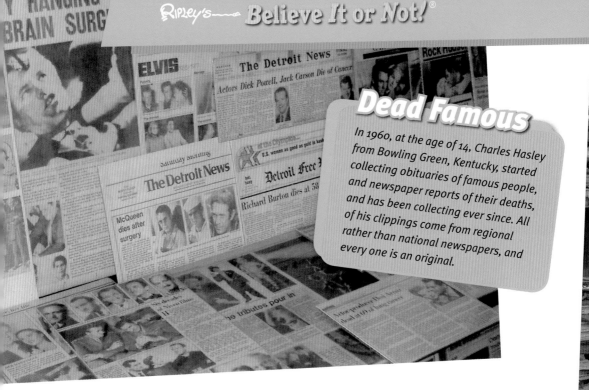

Dead Famous

In 1960, at the age of 14, Charles Hasley from Bowling Green, Kentucky, started collecting obituaries of famous people, and newspaper reports of their deaths, and has been collecting ever since. All of his clippings come from regional rather than national newspapers, and every one is an original.

Nutty Professor

In January 2006, a harassed professor of history at a Canadian University offered automatic B-minus grades to any students in his overcrowded class if they would simply go away. Twenty of the 95 accepted.

Lucky Shot

A 54-year-old man was shot in the abdomen during a robbery in Bakersfield, California, in February 2006, but during surgery doctors found a tumor that otherwise would not have been identified until much later.

Wife Sold

Unable to settle a $3,500 debt, a Romanian man handed over his wife as repayment instead. Emil Iancu signed a document stating that his wife Daniela would live with elderly creditor Jozef Justien Lostrie. Far from being insulted, Mrs. Iancu was delighted by the new arrangement, as she said she no longer had to tidy up after her lazy husband.

Grave Concern

In 2006, Yahaya Wahab received a phone bill for $218 trillion from Telekom Malaysia for recent calls that had been made—on the line of his dead father! After initially giving him ten days to pay up or face prosecution, the company agreed to look into the matter.

Lucky Beggar

His marriage proposal rejected, an angry lover tossed the engagement ring in a beggar's bowl. The recipient, Tim Pockett, who plays the penny whistle for loose change in Shropshire, England, could not believe his luck when the diamond solitaire white-gold ring landed in his collection pot. The spurned suitor had told him: "That will keep you going for a couple of days."

Newspaper Addict

Feng Yi from the southern Chinese city of Hefei has collected more than 800,000 copies of 6,000 different types of newspaper from around the world. He plans to open a museum in his hometown to house his collection.

Bog Jog

A jogger who took a wrong turn during a 2006 lunchtime run in Florida ended up stuck in a swamp for four days. Training for the Baltimore Marathon, 62-year-old Eddie Meadows left his desk at the University of Central Florida's research park every lunchtime to jog around the campus. But on this occasion he got lost, fell into a bog, and survived only by sipping water from the swamp.

Pig Pong

The entire village of Elsa in southern Germany was flooded by pig manure when a storage tank with a capacity of 63,400 gal (240,000 l) burst in February 2006.

Suspicious Minds

Texas farmers near the Mexican border have erected ladders to allow illegal immigrants to climb over their fences. The move was designed to stop them cutting holes in the fences, which allowed the farmers' cattle to escape. However, most of the illegal immigrants have apparently been ignoring the ladders because they think it's a trick!

Octopus Wrestling

Eric Morris of Port Orchard, Washington, regularly wrestles giant Pacific octopuses in Puget Sound and at the World Octopus Wrestling Championships each year in Tacoma, Washington.

Elderly Robber

A 79-year-old woman was arrested in Chicago, Illinois, in 2006 after she tried to hold up a bank at gunpoint. Brandishing a toy gun and demanding $30,000 cash, she told the cashier she wasn't able to speak very loudly because she had just come from the dentist.

Emergency Landing

In September 2006, a light airplane made an emergency landing on a busy street in the heart of Montréal, Canada. The Cessna's engine had cut out during an aerial tour of the city, forcing the pilot to touch down safely on Parc Avenue, a main north–south thoroughfare, in front of dozens of baffled onlookers. The only damage was to a street sign clipped by one of the plane's wings.

The Weigh Inn

In March 2006, the Ostfriesland Hotel in Germany began charging visitors by how much they weigh.

Weird Theft

In May 2006, thieves in Germany stole an entire roller coaster! The Big Dipper, weighing 20 tons and worth $25,000, disappeared from a truck that had stopped at a car park on its way to a funfair near Bischofsheim.

Tree-Mendous Office

Davison Design and Development, a product design company based in Pittsburgh, Pennsylvania, has provided its employees with a tree house, the insides of a robot, and a pirate ship as creative spaces within which to work, known as "Inventionland." The tree house is actually an area of trees, the first of which is about 20 ft (6 m) in diameter. It has a tunnel carved into it, through which workers pass on their way across a bridge of water to get to the elevated "house" standing 15 ft (4.5 m) high. A porch in the tree house overlooks a lake and a waterfall.

Health Hazard

In Greater Manchester, England, in 2006, an office floor collapsed under the weight of a boardroom table during a meeting of 21 health-and-safety officers.

Drill Stylist

A man in Edmonton, Alberta, Canada, partially scalped his girlfriend by attempting to "style" her hair with a power drill—a technique he said he had learned about on TV.

Doggy Nuptials

A female Great Dane and male Pug dog had their union blessed by Rev. Charlotte Richards in the petal-strewn Little White Wedding Chapel in Selfridge's department store in London, England, in April 2005. The bride wore a white lace veil and white paw bands.

Hard Kick

During the 2006 World Cup in Germany, two Austrian men were arrested for placing concrete-filled soccer balls around Berlin with signs that encouraged people to kick them.

Titanic Wedding

David Leibowitz and Kimberly Miller of New York City were married in a submersible that was resting on the bow of the sunken ship *Titanic*.

In the Pink

Brumas, a healthy nine-year-old white cat from Devon, England, has inexplicably turned pink. Brumas went for a stroll one day in 2005 and came home with bright pink fur. He was checked out by a veterinarian, who told his owners that the cat was healthy and that the cause of the color change was not toxic. He also told them that it had not been caused by paint, leaving them mystified as to what had really happened.

CAN YOU SEE IT?

Spider-face

This spider with markings on its back resembling a human face was found in the city of Wujiaqu in northwestern China in April 2006.

Jesus Tile

This image of Jesus was spotted on the bathroom wall of a house in Essex, England, in 2005. It appeared on one of a panel of randomly patterned tiles in the home of retired city worker, Philomena Risat.

Hearing Voices

A Japanese man was arrested in 2006 after making 37,760 silent calls to directory enquiries because he enjoyed listening to the "kind" voices of female telephone operators. He made up to 905 calls a day.

Tree Dweller

An Indian man has spent 50 years in a tree after a row with his wife. Gayadhar Parida, now 84, took to staying in a mango tree after the quarrel and, although he moved trees when his original tree house was destroyed in a storm, he has steadfastly refused to return to the family home in Kuligaon, Orissa. He accepts food offered to him by family members but comes down only to drink water from a pool.

Lost Ring

Mrs. Caroline Scufaca of Canon City, Colorado, was understandably upset on losing her wedding ring in 1923. She had to wait 15 long years before the ring turned up in her garden—on a carrot!

Mom on Strike

Fed up with her unruly, untidy children, a single mother from London, Ontario, Canada, announced in September 2006 that she was going on strike. Mother-of-three Roxanne Toussaint erected a tent and a sign on her front lawn that read "Mom On Strike" and refused to do any further housework until the kids signed a written pledge promising to help out more.

Guard Bait

After robbing a Jersey City, New Jersey, bank of more than $4,000 in May 2006, a thief slowed down a pursuing security guard by throwing $20 bills to the ground. As the guard stopped to pick up $1,500 in dropped notes, the robber was able to make his escape.

Dracorex Hogwartsia

When the children's museum of Indianapolis, Indiana, had the chance to name a newly discovered species of dinosaur, they referenced Hogwarts, the fictional wizard's school attended by Harry Potter.

Court Ruling

Believing that posing for photos is sinful, Canada's small Hutterite religious community managed to win a court ruling in May 2006 to acquire drivers' licences without identity pictures.

Holy Ultrasound

Studying the latest ultrasound picture of her unborn son, 20-year-old Laura Turner of Warwickshire, England, was amazed to see that it appeared to show an image of Jesus in a shroud.

Edible Weapon

In December 2004, a man from Oklahoma was charged with assault after trying to stab another man with a pork chop!

Gravedigger Buried

A 62-year-old gravedigger from Nieuwleusen, the Netherlands, had a lucky escape in 2006 after accidentally burying himself. A trailer containing the earth he had removed tipped over and fell back into the grave, knocking him over and covering him completely. Fortunately, a colleague managed to scrape away the soil from the gravedigger's face so that he could breathe until rescued.

Dutch Dilemma

Police officers from Bristol, England, were forced to learn Dutch in 2006 because three dogs they recruited from Holland did not respond to commands in English.

Cigarette Break

A hospital patient in Berlin, Germany, was stuck in a broken elevator for more than three days in 2006 after sneaking out of bed for a cigarette. Severely dehydrated, 68-year-old Karlheinz Schmidt was finally found after technicians were called to repair the elevator—80 hours after he first got into it.

Jumbo Jam

A 40-ft (12-m) long water-spewing mechanical elephant weighing 42 tons, as much as seven African elephants, brought the center of London, England, to a standstill in May 2006. The princely pachyderm was part of a four-day street theater performance by a French arts company. The elephant, made largely of wood, consisted of hundreds of moving parts, and was operated by more than ten puppeteers using hydraulics and motors.

Fall Guy

A retired Polish schoolteacher went to the hospital hoping to be given painkillers to relieve his headache, but instead doctors pulled a 5-in (13-cm) knife blade out of his head. The knife had pierced Leonard Woronowicz's skull when he had fallen over a stool in his kitchen. All he noticed was a small gash on his head, so he put a bandage on it. He wasn't even suspicious when he couldn't find the kitchen knife the following day.

Insurance Claim

English insurance company Norwich Union reached a settlement in 2006 with one of its employees, Linda Riley, over her workplace injuries. Ironically, she had tripped over a pile of claim forms in the office.

2,000 Years Too Late

A German art student joined the Chinese terracotta army in the city of Xi' an almost 2,200 years too late! Pablo Wendel donned a costume that matched uniforms worn by the soldiers buried in the tomb of Emperor Qin Shihuangdi, who ruled between 221 and 210BC. He slipped past security at the museum and into the pit where 2,000 warriors are on display. Security staff took a few minutes to find him standing still among his fellow warriors.

Gator God

This alligator belonging to Michael Wilks from Salem, Wisconsin, clearly has the letters "G O D" marked on its side. The letters became visible once the gator reached three years of age.

"Minor" Offence

In May 2006, police in Vancouver, British Columbia, Canada, arrested a 14-year-old boy and two 13-year-olds for robbing seven banks!

Porsche Prank

Greg Good, the Carolina Panthers fan who dresses up as Catman at the football team's home games, was excited at the prospect of winning a Porsche in a TV station's competition, but it turned out that the prize was a toy Porsche. When station bosses realized that the on-air practical joke had backfired on them badly, they presented Good with a pickup truck as consolation prize.

Hot Pants

Fleeing after robbing a Bank of America branch in Tampa, Florida, in 2006, a man stuffed the bag of cash down his pants. The chemical dye included in the bag in order to permanently mark thieves then exploded, creating a temperature of around 425°F (218°C)!

Granny's Jackpot

Just as she was about to run out of coins, grandmother Josephine Crawford won more than $10 million on a five-cent slot machine at Harrah's Atlantic City casino in New Jersey in 2006. Mrs Crawford, a widow, immediately received four marriage proposals while celebrating her good fortune.

Pillow Talk

An Indian man was ordered to leave his wife in 2006 after he said "talaq"—the Arabic equivalent of "I divorce you"— three times in his sleep.

Hounded Out

An elderly Polish man was chained up by his wife in a dog kennel for three weeks in 2006 because she was angry with him repeatedly arriving home drunk on vodka. The 75-year-old man had to survive in freezing temperatures wrapped in an old blanket and existing on dog food and water. He was freed only after his drinking friends, concerned by his absence, informed the police.

Python Package

Staff at a post office in Mechernich, Germany, were horrified to see a 5-ft (1.5-m) albino python escape from a parcel. The package, labeled "Attention—Glass," had been accepted by the staff and put in the back of the office. But then it started to move and the large snake slithered out of the wrapping.

Fake Fur

In 2004, a high-tech X-ray machine at Chicago's Field Museum revealed that a mummified cat on display was actually a 2,500-year-old fraud made of cotton and twigs.

Serial Offender

By 2003, Alison Graham of Halifax, Nova Scotia, Canada, had collected 229 parking fines totaling $10,000 in just a couple of years.

Father's Folly

Troy Stewart's plan to cure his 10-year-old daughter's fear of heights backfired when he broke his leg as the pair jumped into water from a 15-ft (4.5-m) bridge in Lantana, Florida, in September 2006. While Stewart writhed in pain, the uninjured Meagan cycled home to fetch help.

Winning Bet

When England national soccer team goalkeeper Chris Kirkland made his international soccer debut against Greece in August 2006, he earned his father Eddie $20,000. Eddie had bet $200 at 100–1 in 1997 that his son, then aged 15, would one day play for England's national team.

Food Haul

An escaped prisoner was caught trying to get back into Roane County Jail, Tennessee, in 2005 with four McDonald's hamburgers. The man, who had escaped for only a short time, was found carrying a package containing liquor, prescription pills, clothes, and the burgers.

Poisoned Pigeons

The 2006 city festival at Texarkana, Texas, was marred when more than 25 sick or dead pigeons nose-dived onto downtown sidewalks. They had apparently eaten poisoned corn from the roof of a nearby bank.

Pork Talk

Karim Tiro of Xavier University in Cincinnati, Ohio, teaches a college-level class on the history of pigs in America.

Many Tongues

Although it has a population of only 5.5 million, Papua New Guinea has more than 700 spoken languages, most of which are entirely unrelated.

Cozy Coffin

Kay Groom keeps a coffin in the spare bedroom of her home in Swaffham, Norfolk, England, and likes to take the mystery out of death by lying in it. Kay, who also has a collection of more than 300 ornamental skulls and admits to being fascinated by death, was measured for the $400 satin-lined pine box a few years ago. "It's the coffin I'm going to buried in," she says. "It's very comfy, although I don't like it with the lid down because I'm a bit claustrophobic. People think I'm mad, macabre, and some think I'm a witch. But I'm not."

FANTASTIC FEATS!

SET IN CONCRETE

In memory of his hero, Harry Houdini, Canadian escape artist Dean Gunnarson freed himself from a locked Plexiglas box filled with two tons of wet cement. He was the first person in the world to attempt such a great escape. Not even Houdini himself had tried it.

The sensational stunt was timed to take place in Winnipeg at 1.26 p.m. on Halloween 2006 (the exact 80th anniversary of Houdini's death). Gunnarson was bound with several pairs of police handcuffs that were chained and padlocked around his waist and entire body, and tightly around his neck. He was then lowered into the box, the cement was poured in, and the lid of the box was locked tight with six maximum-security padlocks. Gunnarson was totally encased in a concrete prison.

To the amazement of the crowd, who could see his every move, Gunnarson escaped from his would-be tomb in 2 minutes 43 seconds. He had to get out before being crushed and suffocated by the sheer weight of the cement. "It felt like being crushed by a boa constrictor," said Gunnarson, who had trained for the death-defying ordeal by wriggling in fast-setting cement. "I could feel it pushing against my ribs and lungs every time I struggled." But he emerged with nothing worse than cement burns.

His inspiration for the stunt came when he escaped while dangling by his toes from a trapeze bar while locked in a straightjacket, 726 ft (221 m) above the Hoover Dam just outside Las Vegas. He learned that some workers had been killed while working on the dam, having been buried alive after falling into wet cement. "I thought to myself, 'What a horrible way to go.'"

Gunnarson bends down before becoming totally immersed in wet concrete.

He starts to work on the locks.

After just 2 minutes 43 seconds, Gunnarson makes good his escape.

Human Flag

In May 2006, more than 18,000 people gathered in Lisbon's soccer stadium to create a human depiction of the Portuguese national flag.

Kazoo Parade

In 2006, more than 500 people turned out on the streets of Nazareth, New Jersey, to celebrate the Fourth of July by playing the kazoo.

Old Prices

Michael "Mickey" Di Fater of Greenburgh, New York, celebrated his 75th year selling hot dogs by rolling back his prices to 10 cents for a hot dog and a nickel for a soda!

Melon Grower

Ivan Bright of Hope, Arkansas, devoted the last 30 years of his life to growing huge watermelons, notably a 268-lb (122-kg) Carolina Cross. He died at the age of 92 on August 12, 2006—the 30th anniversary of the Hope Watermelon Festival.

Water-ski Challenge

Dirk Gion went water-skiing behind a huge German cruise liner in 2006 to disprove a claim made on TV that the feat was impossible. The 40-year-old stayed upright for more than five minutes.

Truck Drink

Rather than drink Milo (a milk beverage with chocolate) from a glass, 620 staff and students at the National University of Singapore decided to drink it from the back of a truck! They drank 92 gal (350 l) of Milo from the truck in 30 minutes.

Baby Marathon

The city of Cali in Colombia hosted a crawling marathon for babies in 2006—and more than 1,100 babies took part. Infants aged between 8 and 18 months were eligible and they crawled along a 16-ft (5-m) covered track. The winner's prize was a bag full of baby goodies.

Elvis Parade

In a variety of sequined jumpsuits, bright pink jackets, and blue suede shoes, 94 sideburned, hip-swivelling Elvises took to the stage at Collingwood, Ontario, Canada, in July 2006 to perform the King's classic hit "All Shook Up."

Massive Mural

In 2006, Boeing completed a mural on its factory building in Everett, Washington, that comprises more than 100,000 sq ft (9,290 sq m) of pressure-sensitive graphic film. It consists of some 475 sheets, each 60 x 4 ft (18 x 1.2 m) and took over five months to install.

Bowling Mission

Larry Woydziak from Lawrence, Kansas, made it his mission to bowl in every county in Kansas that had a bowling alley. He bowled his 79th and final game in the town of Sterling.

Bra Chain

Hundreds of volunteers linked together more than 114,700 bras around Paphos harbor in west Cyprus in April 2006 to form a 70-mi (113-km) long chain to raise breast-cancer awareness. Bras were flown to Cyprus from all over the world, including Canada, the U.S.A., Thailand, Brazil, Russia, Iran, and all 25 European Union member states.

Penguin Airlift

After more than 100 penguins were left stranded on beaches in Rio de Janeiro, Brazil, in 2006, the Brazilian air force and navy transported them safely back to Antarctica. Penguins arrive from the Antarctic on ice floes that melt near Brazil's coast every winter and the flightless birds then find themselves washed up on Rio's beaches. Usually they are sent to local zoos, but this time the military intervened.

A Real Mouthful

In 2006, the city of Nanjing, in eastern China, played host to a TV show that featured people with highly unusual skills. Zhang Dong, shown here inserting a huge spoon into his mouth, was one of the show's participants.

SNAKE KISSER

Malaysian snake charmer Shahimi Abdul Hamid kissed a wild, venomous king cobra 51 times in three minutes outside Kuala Lumpur in March 2006.

He used agility, skill, and quick reflexes to dodge bites from the 15-ft (4.6-m) snake with only his bare hands to protect him. He was also an hour's drive from the nearest hospital—a daunting prospect considering that a person can be killed with just one drop of cobra venom, and each bite can produce up to 12 drops of poison.

Newspaper Models

Zhu Zhonghe from Shanghai, China, at the age of 70, discovered the art of making models created entirely from newspaper. He has made the Eiffel Tower, a Dutch windmill, bridges, boats, and the former residence of the late Chairman Mao Zedong.

Hoop Enthusiast

Ohio-born mother-of-three Lori Lynn Lomeli is never happier than when surrounded by hula hoops. Introduced to hula hooping at the age of eight, she once made headlines for spinning 82 hoops simultaneously for three complete revolutions in Reno, Nevada.

Milk Machine

Joey Chestnut of San José, California, drank a gallon of milk in 41 seconds to qualify for the 2006 Philadelphia Wing Bowl eating contest, and then ate 173 chicken wings to win the competition!

Temporary Park

In November 2005, the arts group Rebar transformed a downtown San Francisco parking space into a temporary park. They put coins in the meter and proceeded to position turf, a bench, and a tree to create a green space for two hours. In a previous venture, they spent five days digging a filing cabinet into the New Mexico desert to serve as a library.

Insect Feast

To mark Montréal Insectarium's 15th birthday in 2005, the attraction staged an insect-tasting celebration—a six-legged lunch prepared by chef Nicole-Anne Gagnon. The menu included atta ants in a tortilla, roasted crickets served on a cucumber canapé, barbecued locusts, and bruschetta with olive tapenade and bamboo worms.

Radio Rev

Jay and Jason Plugge of Sunnyvale, California, have invented a car radio that plays the engine sounds of classic cars and motorbikes, including Ferraris, Corvettes, and Harley-Davidsons from the 1950s, 1960s, and 1970s.

Stretch Sari

Weavers in India created a silk sari that is 1,585 ft (483 m) long and more than 4 ft (1.2 m) wide. Up to 120 weavers worked 24 hours a day on it for more than 80 days, and the finished article weighed over 125 lb (57 kg).

Doggie Surfing

The world's first canine surfing championships took place in California in 2006 at, naturally enough, the Coronado Dog Beach. Riding the waves on custom-made dog surfboards, each surf-loving hound had three chances to impress a panel of professional surfing instructors. The animals were scored on confidence level, length of ride, and overall surfing abilities.

Watery Conference

Wearing full diving gear, a group of 21 Austrian journalists swam 16 ft (5 m) below the surface of the Traun Lake to stage an underwater press conference in June 2006! An underwater flipchart was set up for the presentation and the reporters were given special waterproof paper and pens to enable them to take notes.

Jones Gathering

A small town in North Wales united 1,224 people with the same surname in November 2006. Blaenau Ffestiniog out-performed Sweden, which had previously held an assembly of 583 Norbergs, by inviting anyone around the world with the surname Jones to a 1,600-seater venue. The town was chosen for the gathering because the area boasts the highest concentration of Joneses in Britain.

Reverse Speller

Eight-year-old Raghav Srivathsav from Hyderabad, India, has made a name for himself by spelling words backward. He first started doing this aged three and can now spell 50 words in reverse in under three minutes, and can reverse spell any word or line given to him in just a few seconds.

Skydiving Dog

Wearing a specially made harness and a diaper—in case of mid-air accidents—Mindy, a three-year-old Jack Russell terrier, went skydiving in 2006 with the Jonoke Skydive Team in Alberta, Canada. Diving under a canopy strapped to a tandem skydiving master, Mindy made a successful free fall of 9,000 ft (2,743 m) in 40 seconds. Her owner, Al Christou, said: "She kept looking at us on the way down. When she landed the first time, she was spinning around in circles."

Polished Pictures

Mary Scott from Horn Lake, Mississippi, is an artist with a difference, for she paints using bottles of nail polish. Mary has a collection of more than 1,000 colors, and uses as many as 30 bottles of polish to create one painting. She paints with the small brushes that come with the bottles, and has to work rapidly, because the polish dries very quickly.

A Skip and a Jump

Kyle Nolte from Fort Smith, Arkansas, is a pogo-stick fanatic. Not only can he jump rope while hopping up and down on his pogo stick, he can also play baseball and hula hoop while pogoing.

Numerical Genius

If you give Nishant Kasibhatia a number, he's unlikely to forget it—for 10 years! The 29-year-old Indian man has a phenomenal memory for numbers, having started at the age of 17 by memorizing 100-digit numbers before graduating to 1,000 digits. He can now recite 1,000-digit numbers in reverse order and in 2005 he memorized 200 binary numbers in just over three minutes and recalled them in five minutes without a single mistake.

Pizza Order

Papa John's delivered an order of 13,500 pizzas to San Diego's NASSCO Shipyard on June 8, 2006. To meet the 11 a.m. delivery time, Papa John's used the resources of 15 San Diego restaurants, beginning at 6 a.m., with each making around 56 pizzas per minute throughout the morning—that's nearly one pizza per second! The 2,725 lb (1,236 kg) of cheese needed for the feat was the weight of an average family car.

SWORD SWALLOWER

Roderick Russell makes a living by inserting blades 24 in (61 cm) long into his esophagus. The average adult esophagus ranges in length from 12 to 15 in (30 to 38 cm), so the Burlington, Vermont, sword swallower gambles with death every time he performs his routine.

Russell learned the art of sword swallowing in Italy and practiced three times a day for a year before he was ready to perform in front of an audience. The first thing he had to master was the gag reflex. Some swallowers perfect this with an unfurled wire coat hanger or a peacock feather, but Russell used a sword from the outset. He also learned that the esophagus isn't as straight as a sword.

"The stomach is much shallower than it appears," he says, "and it curves to the left. The epiglottis and trachea were surprisingly difficult obstacles for me to push past. I learned to push the epiglottis closed with my hand before learning to control it with the tip of a sword. Then I hold my breath for a split second as the sword glides past the closed epiglottis. Getting past the heart is always a touchy moment. I need to turn the sword a little to the left to get into my stomach."

Russell took up sword swallowing to help audiences realize they could achieve anything they wanted.

This X ray shows just how far down Russell has actually swallowed a sword.

He describes the art as the Holy Grail of mind over body techniques. So far, the mind is definitely winning, although he does take one precaution. "Before I swallow a sword, I always lick the blade. A dry sword is even more difficult to swallow."

SHOW OF
TO-NITE
CHEVROLET
ROWE CHEVR
6 MILK ST
Champion of

Giant's Strength

Eddie Polo, known to all as "Little Giant," drew quite a crowd when he managed to pull this car 100 yd (91 m) along the road in Dover, New Hampshire, in 1937—using only his hair.

Alcatraz Swim

Fueled by pizza, seven-year-old Braxton Bilbrey of Glendale, Arizona, swam the notoriously difficult 1.4 mi (2 km) from Alcatraz Island to San Francisco in just 47 minutes in 2006.

Combine Speed

In August 2006, 105 combines harvested a quarter section of winter wheat (160 acres/65 ha) near Winkler, Manitoba, Canada, in just 11 minutes 8 seconds.

Big Buffet

Diners had an overwhelming choice of food at the Las Vegas Hilton, Nevada, in March 2006 when a buffet was laid out featuring no fewer than 510 different dishes. They ranged from Mongolian chicken and salmon Wellington to crème brûlée and homemade apple pie.

Hugging Saint

Mata Amritanandamayi, an Indian humanitarian known as "The Hugging Saint," travels around the world giving hugs—she has given an estimated 26 million hugs during the past 35 years!

Silver Ball

Stanley Jollymore of Brule Point, Nova Scotia, has spent the last 20 years creating a 77-lb (35-kg) silver ball made from more than 139,000 tinfoil cigarette wrappers.

Spoon Ensemble

A street-theater group rounded up 345 spoon players to bash out pub favorite "Knees Up Mother Brown" in Trowbridge, Wiltshire, England, in 2006. The spoons are played by holding two spoons between the fingers of one hand with the bowls facing each other and tapping them against a leg.

Backward Runner

A Brazilian pensioner claimed he owes his health to his unusual fitness regime of running 19 mi (31 km) every day—backward. Ary Brasil, 69, from Joacaba, has been running since he was 16, but started going backward only six years ago. "I used to feel a lot of pain in my back and legs," he said, "but I found that by running backward I felt less out of breath and my muscles got stronger. It's been nine years since I had a cold and I don't even remember the last time I went to the doctor."

Groucho Gathering

The town of Gorham, Maine, achieved an unusual claim to fame in July 2006 when nearly 1,500 people gathered together wearing Groucho Marx disguises! A total of 1,489 residents turned out wearing the familiar glasses, oversized nose, bushy eyebrows, and mustache.

Model Rebuilt

A detailed plastic model of Australia's Sydney Opera House, which had taken seven years to make but had vanished after appearing at the Washington World Expo in 1974, was painstakingly reassembled in 2006 after being found inside 24 storage crates at a Sydney warehouse. With no drawings or plans for guidance, it took 2,000 hours to rebuild the model, the exercise being described as "like a giant jigsaw."

Balloon Expert

As a boy, Nate Mikulich was fascinated by magic and when, at the age of 13, he met balloon artist Crazy Richard, he became hooked on making animals from balloons. These days, Mikulich of Eastern Michigan is so skilled at the art that he can tie a balloon poodle behind his back in less than eight seconds.

Giant Croquette

Cooks in Assabu, Japan, made a croquette nearly 7 ft (2.1 m) in diameter. It contained 397 lb (180 kg) of potatoes mixed with meat and onions and, at 705 lb (320 kg), was so heavy that a crane had to lower it into a vat containing 67 gal (252 l) of salad oil. The giant croquette was then cut into 1,300 pieces for visitors to taste.

Happy Shopper

In 2005, Edd China from Maidenhead, Berkshire, England, built a motorized shopping cart that can hit speeds of 60 mph (97 km/h). China, who has previously built a motorized sofa and shed, spent six months designing the cart, which is over 11 ft (3.3 m) tall, nearly 10 ft (3 m) long and 6 ft (2 m) wide. It is powered by a 600cc motorbike engine hidden in a huge shopping bag, while the driver sits in an oversized child seat.

Prize Peach

Paul Friday of Coloma, Michigan, has grown a peach that weighs an incredible 30½ oz (864 g).

Light Display

October 2005 saw 24,581 jack-o-lanterns lit up on Boston Common, Massachusetts, in a mass gathering of more than 45,000 people.

Extreme Croquet

Bob Warseck of West Hartford, Connecticut, enjoys a game of croquet—but not on a conventional lawn. For Warseck is a pioneer of the sport of extreme croquet, which is played through woods, over rocks, up and down hills, and across streams. He and his fellow players have had to design special heavy-duty mallets to cope with the rough terrain.

Paper Folders

In 2006, a total of 545 nimble-fingered staff and students from the National University of Singapore folded 9,300 origami paper cranes in just one hour.

Corny Proposal

When Brian Rueckl proposed to Stacy Martin in the summer of 2006, he did it in style—in the form of a message measuring 4,000 sq ft (372 sq m) tilled in his boss's cornfield near Luxemburg, Wisconsin. The message read "Stacy will you marry me?" and included two intersecting hearts. The unusual proposal required a year of planning and 40 hours of work. Naturally, Stacy accepted.

Long Lunch

For one weekend a year husband-and-wife chefs Doug and Helen Turpin find themselves preparing a larger Sunday lunch than usual. They are responsible for "The Long Lunch," an annual barbecue at Warkworth, Ontario, Canada, that stretches on tables 500 ft (152 m) down the village's main street and draws as many as 1,000 people from as far afield as Europe. The Long Lunch is based on a similar event offered by its twin town of Warkworth, New Zealand.

Weighty Balls

In Germany in 2006, Milan Roskopf from Slovakia juggled three shot balls weighing a hefty 22 lb (10 kg) each for 15.8 seconds. He started to juggle balls at the age of nine, moving from small balls to cricket balls, to 2.2-lb (1-kg) balls cast in bronze.

BIG BAND BALL

This giant rubber-band ball was made from more than 175,000 rubber bands in November 2006.

Seen here being rolled toward a set of scales, it weighed in at an incredible 4,594 lb (2,084 kg). It was created by Steve Milton from Eugene, Oregon, who spent a few minutes a day, for just over a year, adding bands to his ball. The result reaches 5½ ft (1.7 m) in height, and has a circumference of 19 ft (5.8 m).

Jogglers Duel

The 2006 Boston Marathon provided a unique spectacle: the first time two jogglers—runners who juggle—had competed head-to-head in a marathon. The combatants were Zach Warren, from West Virginia, an expert juggler who can juggle blindfold and while riding a unicycle, and Michael Kapral, who once ran the marathon in his home city of Toronto in 2 hours 49 minutes—while pushing his baby daughter Annika in a stroller. In Boston Kapral juggled three bean-filled balls and Warren juggled three beanbags, never taking more than two steps without juggling. Warren (911th overall) emerged the winner of their personal duel in a time of just under three hours, with Kapral eight minutes behind in 1,761st place.

Clog Dance

Nearly 500 teenagers from 26 countries donned oversized wooden clogs to perform a modern ballet version of a traditional Dutch clog dance in The Hague in July 2006. The dancers learned the steps in their own countries, which included Canada, Jamaica, Israel, and Finland, before traveling to the Netherlands for the performance.

Grandad's Grumbles

An unlikely Internet hero emerged in 2006—a 79-year-old British grandfather, Peter Oakley. Peter hit the top of the most subscribed list on a popular free video sharing website with his ramblings and grumbles about the modern world. Equipped with headphones and a mike, he posted a series of videocasts, attracting some 30,000 subscribers. He also

Surfs Up

Brazilian surfing legend Rico de Souza rode a surfboard that measured an amazing 26 ft 5 in (8.05 m) in length at Macumba beach in Rio de Janeiro, Brazil, in November 2006. It had taken two months to develop a board strong enough to withstand the waves, and the result needed five people to lift it. De Souza managed to paddle the huge board into the sea and to stand up on it, alone, on the crest of a wave, for 11 seconds.

received more than 4,500 e-mails from fans in Japan, the U.S.A., Australia, Germany, and Ireland.

Word Perfect

Mahaveer Jain of Lucknow, India, has memorized the entire Oxford Advanced Learner's Dictionary, which includes 80,000 entries in all!

THE GREAT ESCAPE

World-renowned escape artist David Straitjacket, 32, from Manchester, England, can release himself from straitjackets, handcuffs, and ropes within minutes. Dubbed the "Modern Houdini," he claims the old master had it easy!

How did you discover your talent for escaping?
When I was about seven, my cousins and I played a game tying each other to chairs. I was by far the best at getting free!

When did you decide to pursue it?
When I was 13 I was a Sea Cadet and we spent a week with the older boys who were going into the Navy. Two 18-year-olds were bullying us, making us wash their dishes! I refused, so they tied me to the sink and left me there. Two minutes later I caught up with them and handed them the rope. They left me alone after that... that was probably when I thought: "I am going to do this for a job!"

So do you have to practice?
Yes! I have a strong working knowledge of locks and cuffs. I fiddle with handcuffs while I'm sitting watching the TV. On top of that, you have to have a natural talent—and a few personal trade secrets!

Is your body "different" from everyone else's?
I have very nimble fingers which are good for picking locks, but I'm not double-jointed and can't dislocate my joints.

What is the most dangerous escape you have attempted?
I was in China on a huge lake. It was murky and deep. The Chinese police took me out on a boat tied up with three pairs of handcuffs and about 10 kg of chain with two padlocks. I jumped off, hit the bottom about four meters down, and couldn't see more than six inches. I had no safety divers. It was touch and go.

When did you get your first straitjacket?
About ten years ago. I was a poor street performer and bought it cheap. It tore in half the first time I used it. I spent the next week rebuilding it to make it strong enough for me.

Do you do any mental training—and is it true you don't like enclosed spaces?

I'm actually really quite claustrophobic! I train myself to relax. If you panic, you fail. Underwater, you've got three minutes to escape, but if you panic, you run out of oxygen in just one minute.

How do you cope with injuries?

I carry on. I did a televized escape called "Barbed Wire" five days after I'd had surgery on my shoulder. I was bruised all over my chest and arm—the make-up department had a field day. I had barbed wire round my neck, attached to a chain between my legs, which led to more

barbed wire round my wrists. I was padlocked, handcuffed, and hung upside down by my feet.

Are you "the modern Houdini?"

I understand people say that as a compliment—but I'm just me. He used to do the straitjacket escape in about 80 or 90 minutes—he'd disappear behind a curtain for that long while the orchestra played, then appear again. If I'm still going at 90 seconds, people get bored! These days we have much shorter attention spans... and better locks.

What will you try next?

I'm preparing for some big high-risk stunts. One involves the Burj al-Arab building in Dubai, and me training in free-fall parachuting, to give you a clue!

79

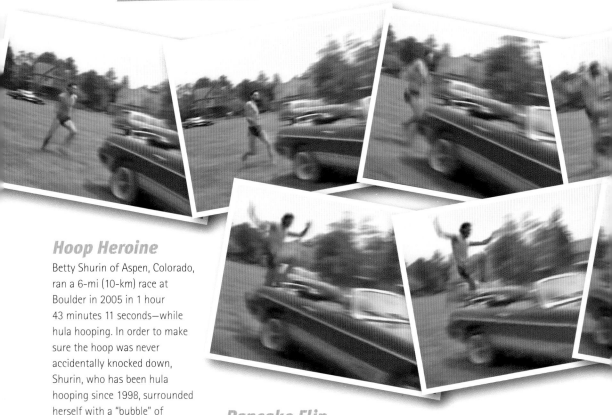

Hoop Heroine

Betty Shurin of Aspen, Colorado, ran a 6-mi (10-km) race at Boulder in 2005 in 1 hour 43 minutes 11 seconds—while hula hooping. In order to make sure the hoop was never accidentally knocked down, Shurin, who has been hula hooping since 1998, surrounded herself with a "bubble" of friends throughout the race. "I communicated with the bubble and it communicated with me," said Shurin. "For every water station, they would circle around me and hold hands. I had about three inches of mistake room."

Brush Off

As part of a special challenge, at exactly 1.45 p.m. on August 7, 2006, some 32,000 people—both young and old—across New Zealand brushed their teeth simultaneously.

Pancake Flip

Nobody tosses a pancake quite like Dean Gould of Felixstowe, Suffolk, England. Gould, renowned for his dexterity at flipping beer mats, can also toss a pancake 424 times in two minutes. He practiced his new skill with a plate and a Whoopee cushion!

Team Effort

Thirty students from the Ishii Higashi Elementary School in Japan ran a 31-legged race over 164 ft (50 m) in a time of 8.8 seconds in October 2005.

Skimming Champion

Dougie Isaacs of Scotland was crowned World Stone Skimming Champion in 2005 at a disused quarry in Argyll. Each of the 220 competitors was allowed five skims using special slate stones. The stone had to bounce on the water's surface at least three times and was then judged on the distance it traveled before sinking. Isaacs hit the flooded quarry's back wall, recording a distance of 207 ft (63 m).

Car Hurdler

This amazing montage of images shows Jeff Clay of Rossville, Georgia, performing the astonishing feat of hurdling lengthwise over a car. Clay, who hurdles in the correct style of track athletes, also hurdles cars widthwise, and once jumped 101 different cars that were lined up inside a track stadium in 38 minutes flat.

Balloon Mural

A mural of the Chicago skyline, 58 x 86 ft (18 x 26 m), made from 70,000 balloons was once displayed in Rosemont, Illinois.

Rocket Man

Thousands of people flocked to the 2006 U.K. Fireworks Championships in Plymouth, Devon, to see 55,000 rockets launched simultaneously. The idea was the brainchild of Roy Lowry who, by using 15 specially constructed frames that were laced with a pyrotechnic fuse and ignited electrically, managed to launch all the rockets in the space of five seconds.

Quick Shave

In April 2006, a team of five hairdressers shaved 662 heads in just four hours at Sudbury, Ontario, Canada.

Big Bowl

In 2004, Australian chefs cooked a 7.5-ton bowl of risotto—a rice dish—that was so big it took spoons the size of oars to stir it!

Busy Bubble

Canadian bubble artist Fan Yang linked 15 pairs of people in a "bubble cage" at the Discovery Science Center in Santa Ana, California, in April 2006. The following month he encapsulated 22 people inside a single soap bubble in Madrid, Spain.

Three-legged Race

Ben Scott and Jo Gittens from the Isle of Man competed in the London Marathon three-legged and dressed as fairies! Their legs tied together with a scarf, they got round in an impressive 5 hours 45 minutes.

Drum Beat

Col Hatchman, drummer with Sydney, Australia, rock band Dirty Skanks, drums so loudly it is the equivalent of listening to a jet plane taking off 100 ft (30 m) away! In 2006, he recorded a massive 137 decibels, compared to the 85 decibels of busy city-center traffic.

Tunnel Vision

Germany's Christian Adams specializes in cycling backward while playing the violin. Adams, who has been playing the instrument since 1970, once cycled over 37 mi (60 km) backward through a Swiss motorway tunnel while playing Bach on his violin.

150-Slice Pizza

Mama Lena's Pizza House in McKees Rocks, Pennsylvania, produces a commercially available 53½-in (136-cm) pizza that offers 150 slices, for $99.99. It contains 20 lb (9 kg) of dough, 15 lb (6.8 kg) of cheese, and 1 gal (4 l) of sauce.

Speedy Hairdresser

Even at the age of 71, Trevor Mitchell can give a decent haircut in less than a minute. To prove it, in August 2006 he clipped exactly 1 in (2.5 cm) of hair from all over the head of former England soccer manager Kevin Keegan in just 59 seconds.

Simultaneous Cartwheels

Almost 1,000 people, wearing an array of leotards, T-shirts, and shorts, converged on the Minnesota State Capitol lawn at St. Paul in 2006 to perform an amazing display of simultaneous cartwheels.

Milk Squirter

An Indian teenager has become a national celebrity for his ability to suck milk up through his nose and squirt it out of his eyes for distances of up to 12 ft (3.7 m). Praveen Kumar Sehrawat, a 16-year-old wrestler from the Delhi region, can also eat 170 chilies in just over five minutes and hammer a nail into his nose without suffering discomfort.

Quick Carver

Stephen Clarke of Haverton, Pennsylvania, can carve a face into a pumpkin in less than 25 seconds!

Car Crush

Twenty-one Malaysian students, all of whom were over the age of 18, somehow managed to cram themselves into a Mini Cooper in June 2006. And what's more they had to do it twice after the TV crew sent to cover the event turned up late!

Cream Dress

Ukrainian baker Valentyn Shtefano created an edible wedding dress for his bride. Made from 1,500 cream puffs, the dress weighed 20 lb (9 kg) and took him two months to complete.

83

BOARD SURFER

A French veterinary surgeon became the first person to cross the shark-infested Indian Ocean on a sailboard.

Raphaela Le Gouvello of Brittany, France, landed on the island of Réunion, off the eastern coast of Africa, in June 2006, having completed a solo 3,900-mi (6,300-km) voyage from Exmouth in Western Australia. Throughout much of the 60-day journey she battled seasickness, strong winds, and rough seas. She made the epic crossing on a simple board—26 ft (8 m) long and 4 ft (1.2 m) wide—

named Mahi Mahi. Her board capsized twice, and on one occasion cost her essential supplies of fresh water. Mme. Le Gouvello said that although the heavy winds had been a problem, the hardest times were when there was no wind at all. "I couldn't make any progress," she said. "I waited below deck, being tossed around in all directions. It wasn't very comfortable."

www.raphaela-legouvello.com

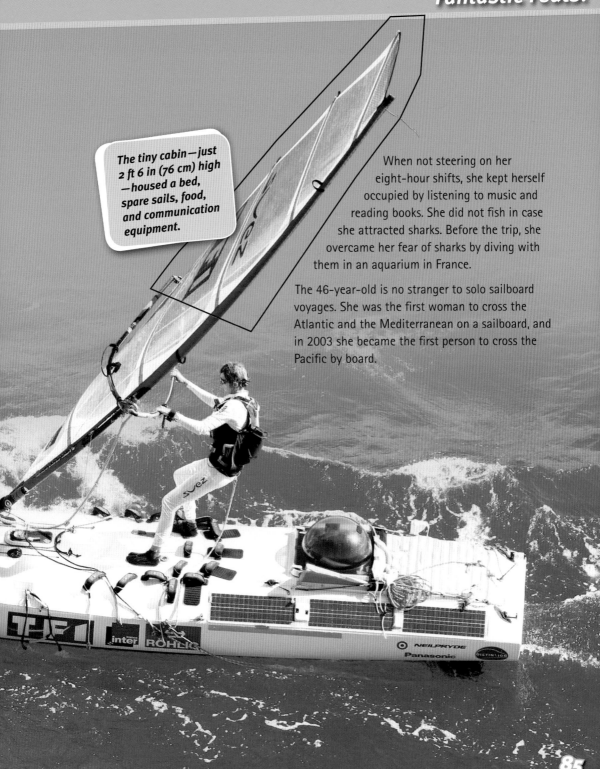

The tiny cabin—just 2 ft 6 in (76 cm) high —housed a bed, spare sails, food, and communication equipment.

When not steering on her eight-hour shifts, she kept herself occupied by listening to music and reading books. She did not fish in case she attracted sharks. Before the trip, she overcame her fear of sharks by diving with them in an aquarium in France.

The 46-year-old is no stranger to solo sailboard voyages. She was the first woman to cross the Atlantic and the Mediterranean on a sailboard, and in 2003 she became the first person to cross the Pacific by board.

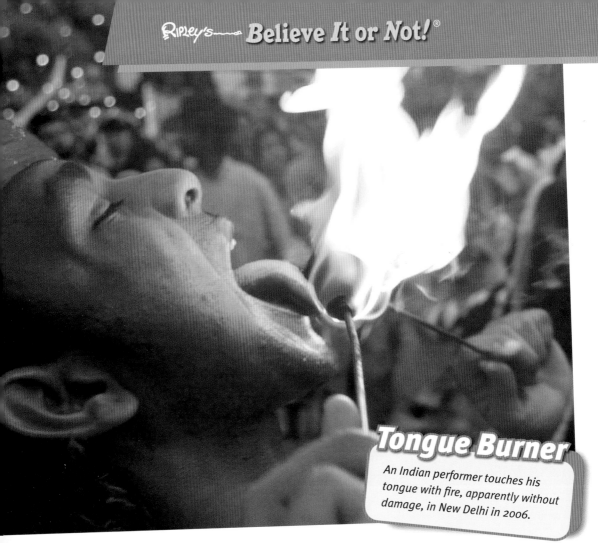

Tongue Burner

An Indian performer touches his tongue with fire, apparently without damage, in New Delhi in 2006.

Honey Trap

Denzil St. Clair of Spencer, Ohio, allowed himself to be covered from head to toe in more than half a million honey bees in June 2006. He wore a mask that covered his nose and mouth, goggles to protect his eyes, and stuck cotton in his ears, but he was still stung up to 30 times. He said afterward: "It was like being blind, covered with wet towels, and very hot."

Young Unicyclist

Whereas other youngsters are into skateboards, 15-year-old Jonny Peacock of Shalimar, Florida, is a budding extreme unicyclist. He can walk on his wheel and twist it 360 degrees, jump off picnic tables on a unicycle, and zigzag between wooden posts. He owns five different unicycles, including one called the "giraffe" with an elongated seat and another called the "impossible wheel" that has no seat at all.

Lizard Boy

Mukesh Thakore, a 25-year-old Indian man, has eaten more than 25,000 lizards over the past 20 years! He first became addicted to eating the reptiles as a five-year-old when, spotting a lizard in the wild, he popped it in his mouth out of curiosity. Now Thakore, known locally as the Lizard Boy, devours up to 25 live lizards every day for his breakfast, lunch, and dinner.

Huge Umbrella

In October 2005, Sun City Umbrella Industries of Jin Jiang city, China, made an umbrella that was 31½ ft (9.6 m) tall and over 53 ft (16 m) in diameter.

Body Painting

At Sherman, New York, in July 2006, body artists Scott Fray and Madelyn Greco of Reidsville, North Carolina, sponged 337 people in head-to-toe non-toxic washable paint. The volunteers then laid down in a colorful pattern to be photographed by a passing helicopter.

Apple Picker

George Adrian of Indianapolis, Indiana, once picked 30,000 apples in one eight-hour day—that's about 1,000 lb (454 kg) every hour!

Harpists' Huddle

A total of 45 harpists (ranging in age from 5 to 55) gathered in the town of Harlech's 13th-century castle in north Wales, to play a concert in 2006. It was the first time so many harpists had played simultaneously in a Welsh castle.

Balloon Hats

At Hillsboro, Oregon, in 2006, 20 volunteers used air pumps to blow up 7,000 balloons—so that they could be used as hats! Over 1,800 people then gathered for a group photo in the Civic Center Plaza, wearing the inflatable headgear.

Noodle Tree

Workers at a hotel in Bangkok, Thailand, spent 16 hours creating a Christmas tree 17 ft 4 in (5.3 m) tall made entirely from noodles and decorated with colored sugar.

Eye Blower

In 2005, Yu Hongqua from China blew out candles with his eyes using a specially crafted pair of glasses with air tubes attached.

Coin-covered Car

In February 2006, Scott Hampton from Davenport, Iowa, finished covering his Ford car, inside and out, with 30,500 penny coins. Every single penny was glued on, head side up, and covered with two coats of varnish. The car is still fully operable, and catches the sun beautifully as Scott drives around town.

Hair Coloring

In a period of less than 24 hours in August 2006, hair stylist Amjad Habib of New Delhi, India, colored the hair of 113 women. The marathon exercise included shampooing, coloring, washing, and blow-drying.

Egg Hunt

Over 10,000 children and adults searched for more than 300,000 Easter eggs, weighing a total of more than 12,000 lb (5,443 kg), that were hidden around Stone Mountain Park, Georgia, in April 2006.

Texan Fruitcake

Gladys Farek, a baker from Cistern, Texas, made a specialty fruitcake that was in the shape of her home state that measured 5 x 6 ft (1.5 x 1.8 m) and weighed 150 lb (68 kg).

Chicken Dance

In an event organized by Texas-based Konrad Bouffard, more than 200,000 people took part in a nationwide chicken dance on July 4, 2006, at 57 minor-league baseball stadiums in the U.S.A.

Birthday Cake

To celebrate the 230th birthday of the U.S.A., caterers in Fayetteville, Arkansas, baked a 230-layer cake for the Fourth of July, 2006. The cake, which was 2 ft (60 cm) high and weighed more than 100 lb (45 kg), took 21 hours to bake.

Basketball Star

Riley McLincha of Clio, Michigan, is a "drubbler"—he can juggle and dribble three basketballs at the same time!

Picture Mosaic

Over eight months, more than 29,000 people of all ages snapped with their digital cameras and cell phones the funniest close-up pictures of themselves and their friends and sent them to a website. The result was unveiled in Milan, Italy, in June 2006—a huge photo collage of 20,400 pictures covering an area of 1,518 sq ft (141 sq m).

Fish Feast

An Irish pub in Boston, Massachusetts, served a portion of fish and chips weighing a colossal 77 lb (35 kg)—34 lb (15 kg) for the cod fillet and 43 lb (20 kg) for the fries.

Penny Pyramid

This pyramid is made from 298,318 U.S. pennies and weighs a hefty 1,969 lb (893 kg). Its creator, Marcelo Bezos from Miramar, Florida, has been building the pyramid since 1971, and he plans to continue adding to it until he reaches one million pennies. Each penny is placed individually, and Marcelo uses no adhesives of any kind.

FAST FEATS

David Gonzales performed an astonishing 21 different strongman acts in a single afternoon in Fort Meyers, Florida, in November 2006.

Ten of these were completed in less than a minute, including tearing a 1,000-page telephone book in half, bending a steel bar 4 in (10 cm) thick over his head, and standing on his head while holding himself steady with hands resting on glass.

Tall Story

Canadian stilt walker Doug Hunt has taken 29 independent steps on a pair of stilts 50 ft 9 in (15.5 m) tall and weighing a combined 137 lb (62 kg).

Pregnant Robot

At Kaiser Permanente Hospital in Vallejo, California, doctors teach students by using a full-size "pregnant" robot patient, Noelle, to simulate giving birth!

Tricky Texter

Tell Ben Cook he's all thumbs and he'll probably take it as a compliment. The 18-year-old from Orem, Utah, proved himself an expert texter in July 2006, by sending a 160-character message in just over 42 seconds at a contest in Denver, Colorado.

Foil Art

Pete Schwickrath from Piscataway, New Jersey, makes sculptures from household aluminum foil, which he then paints. Here, a newly transformed werewolf threatens a young maiden.

Outsize Painting

Working for two and a half years and using 100 tons of paint, artist David Aberg produced a painting that measured a staggering 86,000 sq ft (7,990 sq m). The picture, titled "Mother Earth," is a symbol for peace and is so big it had to be created inside an aircraft hangar in Angelholm, southern Sweden.

Balloon Feat

John Cassidy of Philadelphia, Pennsylvania, inflated and tied more than 700 balloons in an hour at New York City in May 2006. Cassidy has also completed 654 balloon sculptures in an hour.

A.T.V. Parade

Members of Harlan County, Kentucky, A.T.V. club paraded over 1,100 all-terrain vehicles one Saturday in 2006. The parade began in Verda and ended 2 mi (3.2 km) away in Evarts.

Pillow Fight

Nearly 1,000 people lured by Internet postings and word-of-mouth took part in a half-hour outdoor pillow fight in San Francisco on Valentine's Day 2006. Participants arrived with pillows concealed in shopping bags, backsacks, and the like, and within minutes the area around the city's Ferry Building was covered in white down.

Dual Talent

Drew Tretick, a graduate of the prestigious Juilliard School of Music in New York City, who now lives in southern California, plays beautiful tunes on the violin— while riding a unicycle!

Bumper Beach Towel

A gigantic terry-cloth beach towel was unveiled at Hermosa Beach, California, in June 2006. It measured 131 x 78 ft (40 x 24 m) and weighed nearly 1,000 lb (454 kg).

Quick Cleaner

If you want your windows cleaned quickly, ask Terry Burrows. In Birmingham, England, in 2005, Burrows cleaned three windows, each measuring 45 in (114 cm) square, and wiped the sill—all in under 10 seconds!

Guitar Solo

Apart from a short break every eight hours, Chicago musician Jef Sarver played the guitar uninterrupted for 48 hours in 2006. Sarver, who prepared for the challenge by doing push-ups and sit-ups, played a set of more than 600 songs.

Snowball Fight

More than 3,700 people took part in a mass snowball fight at Houghton, Michigan, in February 2006!

Mutton Bustin'

At just eight years old, Ryan Murphy is already a retired champion. Ryan's chosen sport is riding sheep rodeo-style, or "mutton bustin'" as it is popularly known. At the 2006 Truckee Rodeo at Sierra, Nevada, Ryan won the title for the second successive year, but must now retire because he will soon exceed the riding weight limit of 60 lb (27 kg). The secret of his success is to sit on the sheep backward so as to get a better grip. Whereas other riders quickly bit the dust, Ryan's individual style helped him to stay on for an unbeatable 22 seconds.

Nine-hour Rap

In 2006, rapper Supernatural performed a freestyle rap in San Bernardino, California, that went on for an incredible 9 hours 10 minutes! Afterward, he said the hardest parts were keeping his breath and pacing himself.

Footprint Trail

National Geographic Kids magazine spent 1½ days taping together 10,932 paper footprints that zigzagged 1.8 mi (2.9 km) heel-to-toe along the walls and hallways of its headquarters in Washington, D.C. The footprints had been submitted by children from as far away as Australia, Japan, and Mongolia. One was from a child with six toes!

Air Guitarist

After years of mocking air guitarists, Craig Billmeier of Alameda, California, finally realized that they struck a chord with him. And four months and two victories after entering a regional competition, Billmeier (whose stage name is "Hot Lixx Hulahan") was crowned U.S. Air Guitar Champion of 2006. Contestants at air guitar competitions play for 60 seconds while judges mark them on their technical ability and stage presence.

Roller Riders

Marriage is definitely a roller-coaster ride for Don Tuttle and Carol Deeble. The couple from Manchester, Connecticut, were married on their favorite roller coaster, the Comet at Lake George, New York, in 2001, and in 2006 they renewed their vows on it. In all they have ridden nearly 750 roller coasters in 15 countries. They visited Japan in 2005 and South Africa in 2006 to add to their list.

Rooftop Music

In 2006, three "extreme cellists"— Clare Wallace, Jeremy Dawson and James Rees—set out to play on the roof of every cathedral in England! They visited all 42 Anglican cathedrals in England over 12 days, and were allowed to play on the roofs of 31 of them. Their repertoire included "Up on the Roof" and "Climb Every Mountain."

Vending Fun

On October 21, 2006, Robert Moore, aged three, unhappy at his unsuccessful attempts at scooping out a stuffed toy with the machine's plastic crane, decided to go in and get one. He climbed into the stuffed animal vending machine at a small store in Antigo, Wisconsin. Robert was later rescued by the Antigo Fire Department, who broke the lock and passed a screwdriver to Robert, who managed to undo the necessary screws to effect his release!

Two-handed Bowler

Edward Soloff from Atlantic City, New Jersey, was able to bowl two games in two different bowling lanes simultaneously in 1930. What's more, he averaged an impressive score of 270 points for each of the games.

Band of Outlaws

A total of 307 children, dressed as legendary British outlaw Robin Hood, gathered at Ravenshead Church of England Primary School in Sherwood Forest, Nottinghamshire, England, in March 2006. The children provided their own outfits, including bows and arrows, and made their green hats in school.

Lengthy Lecture

Botany lecturer Anniah Ramesh of Mysore, India, delivered a talk on "Molecular Logic of Life" in March 2006 that lasted for over 98 hours! He spoke continuously for three days and three nights until aching legs and sleepless nights finally took their toll. He was so tired that he could be seen dozing while writing on the blackboard.

Super Smoothie

After 3½ hours of blending, using seven blenders, a store in Kitchener, Ontario, Canada, produced a 25,000-oz (740-l) smoothie in August 2006. The monster drink was sold afterward in 24-oz cups.

Sketch Skill

A group of around 3,000 people collaborated in making a drawing of a giant teapot on a huge Etch A Sketch™ that measured 20 x 35 ft (6 x 11 m) at Boston, Massachusetts, in 2006.

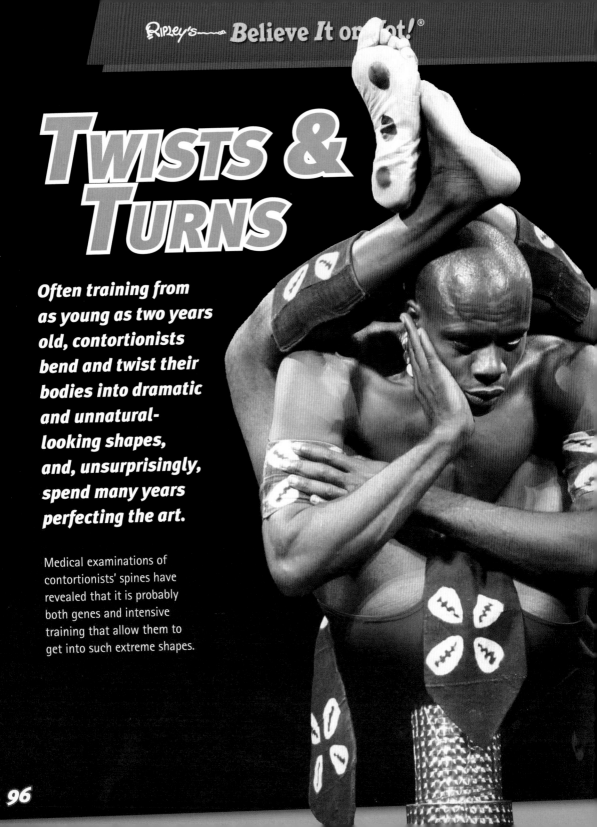

TWISTS & TURNS

Often training from as young as two years old, contortionists bend and twist their bodies into dramatic and unnatural-looking shapes, and, unsurprisingly, spend many years perfecting the art.

Medical examinations of contortionists' spines have revealed that it is probably both genes and intensive training that allow them to get into such extreme shapes.

Hendrix Tribute

In May 2006, 1,581 guitarists simultaneously played Jimi Hendrix's "Hey Joe" at the Old Town Square in Wrocław, Poland. The guitarists traveled from Germany, Hungary, the Netherlands, Sweden, and even the U.S.A. to take part.

Bicycle Bells

Conducted by Jörg Kärger, 500 people played six pieces of music on bicycle bells at the University of Leipzig, Germany, in 2003.

Fairway to Heaven

Don't tell Tiger Woods, but a Russian man has driven a golf ball over a billion miles! In 2006, cosmonaut Mikhail Tyurin launched the ball into orbit using a gold-plated six iron from a special tee attached to a platform on the International Space Station 220 mi (355 km) above Earth. Scientists say the ball is likely to circle the Earth for up to four years at a speed of five miles per second before falling from orbit and burning up in the atmosphere.

Furman's Feats

Ashrita Furman, a 52-year-old healthfood store manager from New York City, shows no sign of easing up. The man who has climbed Mount Fuji on a pogo stick, somersaulted the entire length of Paul Revere's ride, and ran 7 mi (11 km) in Egypt while balancing a pool cue on his finger didn't stop there. Among other achievements he balanced on a ball at Stonehenge, England, for more than two hours, did 9,628 sit-ups in an hour, and ran 6 mi (10 km) in 1 hour 25 minutes while hula hooping!

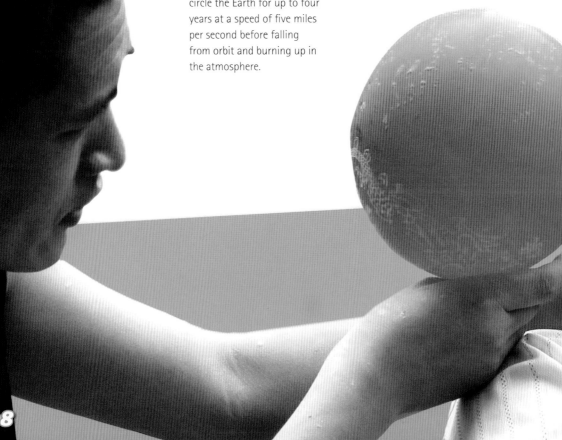

Hogwarts Model

Pat Acton of Gladbrook, Iowa, has created detailed and realistic models of ships, airplanes, space shuttles, and buildings—all from matchsticks. His first project 30 years ago was a country church that took 500 matchsticks and a couple of days to complete. His latest, a model of the Hogwarts School immortalized in J.K. Rowling's *Harry Potter* books, took more than two years and 600,000 matchsticks!

Vast Verse

In 2006, a Frenchman produced a poem of epic proportions—nearly 7,600 verses written on a half-mile roll of fabric. Patrick Huet spent a month and a half composing "Pieces of Hope to the Echo of the World" and then a further month copying it on to the material, which was unrolled with the help of a tractor and put on display around a racetrack in southeast France.

Barking Bikers

At the 2006 Hogs for Dogs charity run at Amherst, New York, Harley-Davidson bikers brought their dogs along for the ride. Some pets sat on the passenger seat, but Beau, Don Wereski's Maltese Yorkshire, rode in a carrier across his chest. "He goes everywhere with me," said Wereski. "He loves the ride."

Eyes and Ears

Zhang Yingmin from China's Shandong Province, seen here in 2006, has an unusual method of inflating balloons—he blows them up by expelling air from his eyes and ears!

WEIRD WORLD!

Copyrighted by Chas. Thompson 1912.   Length 48 FT.

BATTLE OF THE TOMATOES

At Buñol in Spain every August, 30,000 people take part in a huge tomato fight—a two-hour battle during which more than 150,000 lb (68,000 kg) of overripe tomatoes are thrown.

Many truckloads of tomatoes are driven into the center of Buñol, and then the fun begins.

The La Tomatina festival, which draws visitors from all over the world, dates back to 1944 when the local carnival in Buñol was marred by hooligans hurling tomatoes at the procession. But the fruity frolics proved so popular that they were re-created the following year and now the carnival is little more than a sideshow to the huge tomato fight.

The tons of tomatoes are brought in each year on large trucks from the Extremadura region of Spain, where the fruit is cheaper. Participants are encouraged to wear protective goggles and gloves and must squash the tomatoes before throwing them, to reduce the risk of injury.

Although it is a free-for-all, there are vague rules, and anyone caught tearing another person's clothing is likely to be ejected. Meanwhile, storekeepers take steps to cover their storefronts to guard against the widespread carnage.

The action starts around 11 a.m. A ham is placed on the top of a greased pole and as soon as someone is able to climb the pole and bring down the ham, the tomato fight begins. A cannon is fired to signal the end of the battle, after which fire truck hoses spray the town's streets and the combatants with welcome water, and Buñol returns to normality for another year—until the next battle.

The small town of Buñol turns red with squashed tomatoes before being hosed down for another year.

Shapely Sundial

At Roselawn, Indiana, there is a huge sundial in the shape of a lady's leg. The leg, which is properly positioned to tell the time, is 63 ft (19 m) long and was built at the request of the owner of the adjoining nudist resort.

No Garbage

Hugh and Jo-Ann Robertson of Ottawa, Ontario, Canada, recycle so much that they had only two bags of actual garbage over a four-year period.

Ice Dip

Masamitsu Nakagawa (left), a Japanese Shinto priest in his nineties, winces as he bathes in iced water as part of an annual New Year's purification ceremony for good health and happiness at the Teppozo Shrine in Tokyo.

Spoilt for Choice

Heladeria Coromoto, an ice-cream parlor in the Andean hills of Venezuela, boasts more than 800 different flavors. They include smoked trout, pumpkin, black beans and rice, tuna, avocado, rose petal, bubblegum and honey, chili pepper, corn, beetroot and cream, and fried pork rind.

Oldest Caves

In 2006, geologists concluded that the Jenolan caves, west of Sydney, Australia, date back to around 340 million years ago, making them the oldest known open caves in the world. They had previously been estimated to be around 90 million years old.

River Lottery

In the town of Nenana, Alaska, residents take part in an annual lottery that offers a jackpot of $300,000—to predict the exact moment that the onset of spring will cause the ice on the nearby frozen Tanana River to break.

Toy Story

Over a period of three months, 40 stuffed animals were removed from power lines and telephone wires in Canmore, Alberta, Canada. The toys were stuffed with metal railway spikes and large stones, and some were mysteriously marked with the number 26.

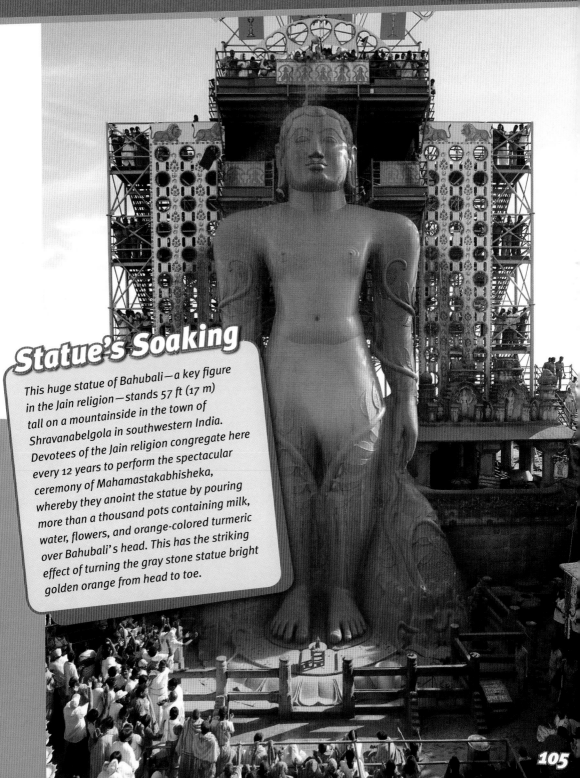

Statue's Soaking

This huge statue of Bahubali—a key figure in the Jain religion—stands 57 ft (17 m) tall on a mountainside in the town of Shravanabelgola in southwestern India. Devotees of the Jain religion congregate here every 12 years to perform the spectacular ceremony of Mahamastakabhisheka, whereby they anoint the statue by pouring more than a thousand pots containing milk, water, flowers, and orange-colored turmeric over Bahubali's head. This has the striking effect of turning the gray stone statue bright golden orange from head to toe.

Sleeping in the Trees

Germany's first tree-house hotel opened in the village of Zentendorf in the eastern state of Saxony in July 2005. The hotel offers five wooden rooms that are suspended in the branches of black locust trees, 30 ft (9 m) above the ground. The rooms all come with electric lights, small balconies, and shared bathrooms, and are connected by narrow walkways.

Double Time

Churches in Malta have two clocks showing different times. This is to confuse the Devil about the time of the next service.

Weather Delay

The international golf tournament in Castle Rock, Colorado, has been delayed by weather every year for the past 20 years.

Wheelbarrow Race

The Black Rock Stakes lays claim to being one of the world's premier wheelbarrow races. It takes place at Pilbara, Western Australia, and is run over a distance of more than 75 mi (120 km). The wheelbarrows can be modified, but must have headlights and red taillights.

Potato Race

In the Millthorpe Murphy Marathon at Millthorpe, New South Wales, Australia, contestants carry a bag of potatoes weighing 110 lb (50 kg) over a course measuring 5,282 ft (1,610 m).

Fish Festival

In Prairie du Chien, Wisconsin, there is an annual "Droppin' of the Carp" celebration whereby a carp is dropped from a tall crane into the Mississippi River at midnight on New Year's Eve to welcome the New Year.

Bamboo-Choo-Choo

Cambodia has a railroad with trains built mostly from bamboo and scavenged parts.

Tough Marathon

The annual Barkley Marathon in Wartburg, Tennessee—a run of 100 mi (160 km) through rugged woodland that takes 60 hours to complete—is so grueling that only six people have completed it in the past 20 years.

Dog Permit

According to Oklahoma law, dogs must have a permit signed by the mayor in order to congregate on private property in groups of three or more.

Mountain Cathedral

In Zipaquira, Colombia, there is a cathedral built into the walls of a salt mine, 600 ft (180 m) deep inside a mountain.

ROLL OUT THE BARREL

The streets of Ottery St. Mary in Devon, England, are lit up each November 5 by flaming tar barrels, which are carried by the town's strongest men as part of a custom dating back more than 300 years.

Women and boys also compete in the festival, earlier in the evening, carrying barrels that are lighter than the men's.

Seventeen heavy barrels are pre-coated with tar and primed with paraffin. They are lit in turn and carried through the streets on the shoulders of muscular men whose arms are swathed in protective sacking, soaked in water. When each man can stand the heat no longer, the barrel is passed to another. The last barrel is rolled into the main square around midnight, after which the tar-barrelers triumphantly tear off their protective cladding and toss it into the flames. The tradition of tar-barrel rolling is believed to cleanse the streets of evil spirits.

Ripley's ——∽ **Believe It or Not!**®

A Pain in the Neck

"*Antzar Eguna*" (Day of the Goose) is the highlight of a centuries-old fiesta that takes place each year in the Basque village of Lekeitio in northern Spain. It features an unusual competition whereby contestants hang on to a dead goose's neck while the bird is raised and lowered into a river. The aim of the contest is to decapitate the bird while withstanding the vigorous dunking.

Vast Building

The Boeing Commercial Airplane factory in Everett, Washington, is such a huge building that the entire Disneyland amusement park, including its parking lots, could fit inside.

No Menus

In Salt Lake City, Utah, there is a restaurant called the One World Café in which there are no menus and patrons pay what they feel their meal is worth.

Bridge Layout

Because of the layout of the Boston University Bridge in Boston, Massachusetts, it is possible for a boat going under it to float beneath a train, passing under a car, driving under an airplane!

Designer Kennels

Dog owners in Olmsted Falls, Ohio, are required by law to have waterproof doghouses that are equipped with self-closing doors!

Grit Roll

In St. George, South Carolina, there is an annual Roll in the Grits contest, where contestants wallow in a swimming pool filled with grits in order to see how much they can collect on their body.

Variable Rainfall

At its peak, enough water flows along the Iguaçu River and over the Iguaçu Falls, located on the border between Brazil and Argentina, to fill six Olympic swimming pools every second. Yet in some years rainfall in the region is so low that the river dries up completely.

Whale Shark

This extraordinary whale shark, 45 ft (13.7 m) long, 23 ft 9 in (7 m) in circumference, and weighing 30,000 lb (13,600 kg), was captured after a fight lasting 39 hours on Knights Key, Florida, on June 1, 1912. It was loaded onto a flatbed truck and driven to Miami—a very smelly load!

COPYRIGHTED BY CHAS. THOMPSON 1912.   LENGTH 48 FT.

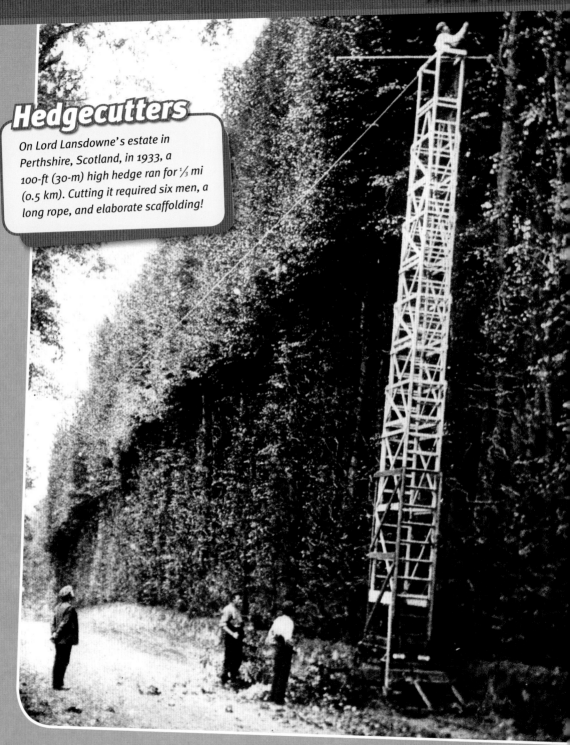

Hedgecutters

On Lord Lansdowne's estate in Perthshire, Scotland, in 1933, a 100-ft (30-m) high hedge ran for ⅓ mi (0.5 km). Cutting it required six men, a long rope, and elaborate scaffolding!

BUSH TUCKER
ZEBRA
CAMEL
RATTLESNAKE
IMPALER
OSTRICH
KANGAROO

What's for Dinner?

Steve Ritchie is a butcher from London, England, with a difference. Proprietor of Theobald's Specialist Butcher shop in the Clerkenwell district of the city, he sells a range of highly exotic meats, including zebra, camel, rattlesnake, ostrich, and kangaroo.

Beer 'n' Bacon

The Pub in the Paddock at Pyengana, Tasmania, is home to a pair of pigs that drink along with the patrons.

Tall Dutch

The Netherlands may be one of the Low Countries, but its people are officially the tallest in the world. A 2006 survey revealed that the average Dutchman stands just over 6 ft (1.83 m) while Dutch women average nearly 5 ft 7 in (1.69 m).

Goat Couture

It's not only the people who wear fancy dress at the famous Lake County Fair in the city of Crown Point, Indiana—they dress their goats up, too! The dairy goat costume contest is for the best-dressed owner and animal combination, and in 2006 it featured one goat that was dressed as a chicken and another who was sporting a clown costume.

Huge Hydrant

An operational fire hydrant that is 30 ft (9 m) high has been built in Elm Creek, Manitoba, Canada, complete with a 12 ft (3.6 m) chain. It took volunteer firefighters seven months to build.

Robot Kitchen

A new restaurant in a Hong Kong shopping mall is causing something of a stir with diners because of its unusual waiting staff. The owners of Robot Kitchen claim that it's the first restaurant in the world to have robots as waiters. Seen here is Robot No. 2, who can recognize voice patterns and take meal orders, which are sent by infrared technology to the kitchen. It also helps to serve the meals to customers.

Hark at Barkers

Every year, West Salem, Wisconsin, stages a Bark in the Park, where local dogs compete to produce the loudest bark. Levels have been known to exceed 110 decibels.

Concrete Commandments

In Murphy, North Carolina, there is a huge set of the Ten Commandments written in concrete letters 4 x 5 ft (1.2 x 1.5 m) in size.

Sky High

A new cocktail from Croatia can be mixed only by a bartender free-falling from 10,000 ft (3,000 m). The Wings of Zadar cocktail is poured upside down so that the drink flies upward into the mixer and is then shaken as the skydiving barman performs a series of somersaults. Chilled by the freezing air rushing over the shaker, it is served on landing. Naturally the price of the cocktail is sky high.

POTTER'S MUSEUM OF CURIOSITY

For over 100 years, Potter's Museum of Curiosity was one of Britain's most bizarre attractions. It showed rabbits at school, kittens enjoying a tea party, and a marching band of mice.

Squirrels often feature in Potter's tableaux, such as these pipe-smoking friends, seen here enjoying a game of cards.

A group of mice in one of Potter's tableaux enjoys a game of dominoes around a table.

"The Rabbits' School" features a group of young rabbits at lessons in their classroom.

However, what made it so weird was that the 6,000 animals on display weren't mere models—they were real stuffed creatures, the work of master taxidermist Walter Potter.

Potter developed a taste for taxidermy in his teens and began by stuffing his own pet canary after it had died. The hobby was popular in Victorian England and in 1861 Potter opened his museum at Bramber, West Sussex, charging two pennies' admission. All of the animals were supplied to Potter by local breeders and farmers—he was at pains to point out that no animal had been deliberately killed for his personal use.

He then arranged them into charming tableaux. "The Rabbits' School" showed 20 rabbits sitting on benches, reading books, and doing their sums. "The Kittens' Tea and Croquet Party" featured 37 ginger-and-white kittens—the ladies decked with jewels, the men wearing cravats—all sitting at a long table eating baked mouse tart. There were also guinea pigs playing cricket.

His collection moved to several different homes before ending up at the famous Jamaica Inn in Cornwall. But, in 2003, Potter's Museum was split up and sold at auction, the scenes raising around $1,000,000.

Jumbo Home

Architect David Hertz is planning to build a home made out of a scrapped jumbo jet. He paid $110,000 for the Boeing 747-200 and says he will incorporate all 4.5 million parts of the plane in the building in Victorville, California. The jet's wings will be used in the roof and the top deck of the plane will convert into a guesthouse.

Short Ride

Even if you don't have sea legs, you should be able to cope with the Kemah Boardwalk Shuttle, a Texas passenger ferry where the ride is just 65 ft (20 m), or .01 nautical miles, and the boat itself is 26 ft (8 m) long! The ferry connects parking lots under a bridge at Highway 146 with the Kemah Boardwalk attractions, and perhaps the biggest surprise is that the ride takes as long as two minutes.

Cash Bash

Some 200 treasure hunters from 15 American states arrived in Woodbury, Connecticut, in 2006 for the Cash Bash, the National Metal Detector Championships. Competitors have half an hour to find and dig up as many pre-planted tokens as possible from a field the size of a football field.

Tall Skis

The pair of cross-country skis that stand vertically outside the town of 100 Mile House, British Columbia, Canada, are definitely not for beginners. The 39-ft (12-m) aluminum skis and their 30-ft (9-m) poles weigh a combined 1,200 lb (545 kg).

Grays Only

A horse race run at Newmarket, England, every August is for gray horses only!

Fast Food

The Karne Garibaldi restaurant in Guadalajara, Mexico, claims to serve a customer's food within just 13 seconds of the order being made.

Plane Vane

In Whitehorse, Yukon, Canada, there is a giant weather vane—an actual DC-3 airplane mounted on a swivel—that always points its nose to the wind.

Long Fence

A continuous fence—known as the "dingo fence"—runs through central Queensland, Australia, for 3,436 mi (5,530 km). It is 5.9 ft (1.8 m) high and is designed to keep sheep safe from Australia's native wild dog.

Holy Haul

Every July, 120 men carry a 65-ft (20-m) seven-story tower that weighs four tons and honors St. Paulinus, through the streets of Williamsburg, New York.

Cement Potato

Wearing a top hat and a smile, a 19-ft (5.8-m) cement potato greets visitors to Maugerville, New Brunswick, Canada. It was built in 1969 to promote a roadside vegetable stand.

Tiny Gallery

A tiny art gallery in Buenos Aires, Argentina, has a ceiling that is just 1 ft (30 cm) high. Patrons must put their heads through a hole to see the 27 miniature paintings and sculptures on exhibition.

Restroom Art

The public restrooms inside a replica of an 1880 train station in Yellow Springs, Ohio, show work by local artists. Dubbed the Chamber Pot Gallery, they display 19 bathroom-themed exhibits, including a dress made of pink, blue, and yellow tissues, and a painting where a person's face screams: "Got paper?"

Bee-sting Therapy

A Chinese man receives a stinging treatment for rhinitis, when two bees are held against his nose until they sting him, at a clinic in the town of Xian in China's Shaanxi Province. The bee venom is also said to help cure diseases such as multiple sclerosis, arthritis, and rheumatism.

Grab the Grapes

Steve "The Grape Guy" Spalding successfully caught an astonishing 1,203 grapes in his mouth in the space of 30 minutes in Sydney, Australia, in November 2005. The grapes were thrown from a distance of 15 ft (4.6 m). Steve has also caught a grape that was dropped from a height of 900 ft (274 m), and once managed to catch 116 grapes in his mouth in three minutes.

Spray-on Sistine

The famous Sistine Chapel has been re-created in a rundown building in Iowa. Graffiti artist Paco Rosic studied the real Sistine Chapel in Rome before practicing painting sections of it upside down in his garage at home. He then spent four months—and $10,000 on spray-paint cans— lying on his back on scaffolding painting a half-scale replica of Michelangelo's fresco on the ceiling of the former Waterloo antique store.

Passport Mountain

Every day, more than three million passports are checked at airports and border crossings throughout the world. If all these passports were stacked on top of each other, they would form a column higher than Mount Everest.

Himalayan Railway

At its highest point, the Himalayan railway from Beijing, China, to Lhasa, Tibet, reaches an altitude of 16,640 ft (5,072 m)— that's higher than any mountain peak in Europe and more than 656 ft (200 m) higher than the Peruvian railway in the Andes.

Giant Yo-Yo

A working yo-yo at a museum in Chico, California, weighs 250 lb (113 kg), is 50 in (127 cm) high, 31½ in (80 cm) wide, has a diameter of 5½ ft (1.7 m), and a 75-ft (23-m) string. An 80-ft (24-m) crane is needed to operate it!

Scary Monkey

There are so many wild monkeys causing problems on India's Delhi Metro rail line that officials now use a trained black-faced langur monkey to scare the others away.

Magic Museum

Among the exhibits at the American Museum of Magic at Marshall, Michigan, is the custom-made milk can into which a handcuffed Harry Houdini crawled before being thrown into the Detroit River. The museum was started by Bob Lund, who went without a car and ate peanut butter sandwiches for years just so that he could collect more magicians' artifacts.

Underwear Protest

Every year, villagers from Veracruz, Mexico, hold farmers' rights protests in Mexico City—dressed only in their underwear!

Plane Landmark

Visitors to Milwaukie, Oregon, have grown accustomed to seeing a grounded World War II B-17G airplane by the roadside. Between 1947 and 1991 it served as the state's most unusual gas station and it is now linked with an adjacent restaurant where visitors can buy souvenir Bomber placemats.

Dung Islands

Peru's Guano Islands had accumulated piles of dung hundreds of feet high by the time people began harvesting it for use in gunpowder and fertilizer in the 19th century.

Spit the Pit

Franz-Wolfgang Coersten is the German cherry-pit spitting champion, and can spit a pit an impressive 63 ft 4 in (19.3 m). He is seen here training for the Cherry Pit Spitting World Championship, which featured 80 participants and was held in Dueren, Germany, in 2006.

BIZARRE BUILDINGS

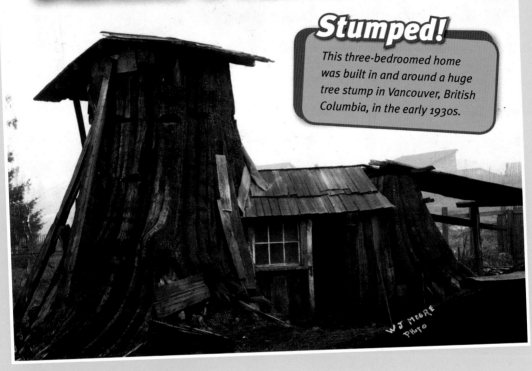

Stumped!

This three-bedroomed home was built in and around a huge tree stump in Vancouver, British Columbia, in the early 1930s.

Holy Trees!

Known as The Hymn House, this home in Herstmonceux in Sussex, England, featured a tree that was trained to grow across the front of the building to form the words "Praise the Lord."

In Dry Dock

An old river steamer that ran aground on Sauries Island in Portland, Oregon, in 1936 got a new lease of life when it became a houseboat. The dwelling, which was also used as a dairy farm, sat on the Willameth River in the state.

Log House

This unique house on Redwood Highway in Garberville, California, was built in the 1930s by Arthur Johnson, who ran a business building log cabins.

HOUSE OF THE FIGURINES

In the French town of Dieulefit, self-taught artist Roland Dutel has designed his "House of the Figurines," decorating the walls and the garden with curious creations made from 150 tons of recycled materials.

Dutel started work on his collection of sculptures, paintings, and mosaics in 1989. He used off-cuts, broken tiles, and rejects from the town's pottery workshops, teaming them with flotsam washed up by the stream that runs past his house together with metal, wood, concrete, and paper, which formed the bizarre faces and figures.

Stair Lift

Scotland's Ferniehirst Castle has staircases that spiral counterclockwise, giving advantage in sword combat to the left-handed defenders of the property.

Chicken Festival

At the 17th World Chicken Festival in London, Kentucky, in 2006, chicken-related events included impersonating a chicken, a wings-eating contest, and dropping eggs without breaking them.

Road Bowls

Competitors in Northern Ireland take part in the sport of road bowls, where they toss an iron ball along a winding country road to see who can cover a distance of 2.5 mi (4 km) in as few throws as possible. Bowls of half a mile are not uncommon.

Comfy Cats

A bungalow in San Diego, California, has been transformed into a cat's dream playground by owner Bob Walker. Cat-themed mementoes adorn the walls, and his feline friends enjoy more than 100 ft (30 m) of specially built runways that snake around the house.

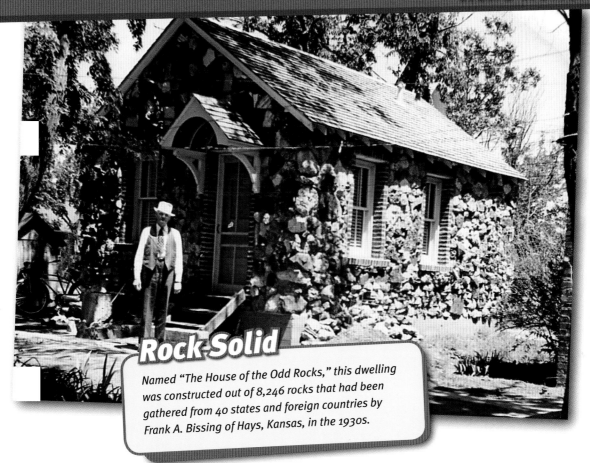

Rock Solid

Named "The House of the Odd Rocks," this dwelling was constructed out of 8,246 rocks that had been gathered from 40 states and foreign countries by Frank A. Bissing of Hays, Kansas, in the 1930s.

Pickle Flinging

In Berrien Springs, Michigan, there is an annual Pickle Flinging contest. The record throw is nearly 300 ft (90 m).

Stiletto Sprint

A total of 150 women wearing stiletto heels at least three inches high ran 80 yd (75 m) along a cobbled street in Amsterdam, the Netherlands, in March 2006. The winner of the race was 20-year-old Nancy Karels who had never worn high heels before.

Urban Housework

Mark Tilbrook and James Doherty from the U.K. invented the sport of Urban Housework, which includes mop-jousting and riding a vacuum cleaner outdoors downhill in as fast a time as possible.

Cold Planet

The average temperature of the coldest place on Earth, Antarctica, is about four times warmer than the daytime temperature on Pluto.

Volcanic Inn

The Lava-Side Inn, a bed-and-breakfast located near Kilauea, Hawaii, is built on an active volcano. Guests at the $100-a-night establishment, who have included actor William Shatner, must cross a treacherous crust of freshly formed volcanic rock that runs over bubbling lava that has a temperature of 2,000°F (1,090°C). The fumes are toxic and even the cracks in the path are hot enough to cook a potato or melt your shoe.

Aerial Beds

Paying guests sleep in tree-supported hammocks 30 ft (9 m) in the air at a bed-and-breakfast in Cornwall, England.

Toilet Contest

The Montgomery County Agricultural Fair in Gaithersburg, Maryland, stages an annual toilet-decorating contest. The 2006 winners of the $25 grand prize were two Boy Scouts with their Camp Stinkalot Scouthouse. They painted their toilet brown and built an outhouse around it, complete with a plastic vine and fake snake.

Tall Sunflowers

At Goodland, Kansas, stands a huge easel, 80 ft (24 m) tall, and bearing a 32 x 24 ft (9.7 x 7.3 m) copy of Van Gogh's "Three Sunflowers in a Vase." The outsized tribute was painted by Canadian artist Cameron Cross and is particularly appropriate, as Goodland is the center of the local sunflower industry.

Shallow Roots

Although redwood trees can reach the height of a 40-story building, their root systems are only 10 ft (3 m) deep. Instead of growing down, the shallow roots grow out and spread sidewise up to 250 ft (76 m) from the trunk.

Cow Remembered

A cow that died in 1932 still has its own marble tombstone near the historic barns of the former North Michigan Asylum at Traverse City. Traverse Colantha Walker was a grand champion milk cow, producing 200,114 lb (90,770 kg) of milk and 7,525 lb (3,415 kg) of butterfat in her life. When she died, hospital staff and patients held a banquet in her honor and gave her a ceremonial burial.

Coconut Delivery

More than 10,000 coconuts are delivered daily to the Maa Tarini Temple in Ghatagaon in India's Orissa State by devotees from around the country for rituals and sacrifices to the gods.

Sea Dogs

At the annual LobsterDog Parade in Los Angeles, pet owners dress up their dogs as a variety of sea creatures and seafood, including lobsters, seals, whales, starfish, sushi, and fish cakes.

Dirty Players

A player comes up for breath in the U.K.'s first ever Swamp Soccer tournament, held in Dunoon, Scotland, in July 2006. Swamp soccer originates in Finland and is fast becoming an alternative sport, with tournaments taking place worldwide.

BURNING AMBITION

Scrap metal worker Eddie Heath of Staffordshire, England, has become a local legend in his home county on account of setting fire to several famous buildings including the White House!

Eddie's scaled-down version of the White House burns against the night sky.

Happily the White House that went up in smoke in November 2006 was only a model that Eddie had built from 2,000 donated wooden pallets and 60 pt (30 l) of white paint. Measuring 60 ft (18 m) wide and 15 ft (4.5 m) high, the impressive structure had no less than 28 windows. It took him eight weeks to create but just minutes to destroy. He said he chose the White House because it is square and simple and everyone recognizes it.

This was the latest of Eddie's annual extravaganzas. In recent years he has built and burned models of Captain Hook's galleon, Dracula's castle, and the clocktower of Big Ben.

Catwalk Crustacean

Hermit crabs disguised as the Green Goblin and Spiderman walk through a display during the annual Miss Crustacean Beauty Pageant held in Ocean City, New Jersey. Each entry features a theme and a set for its crab or crabs, and children from across the U.S.A. come to compete in the contest, which is billed as the world's only beauty pageant for hermit crabs.

Ice Ride

Competitors from across North America are invited to pedal through ice and snow in Montréal to compete in the Ice Cup, an annual contest exclusively for bicycle couriers.

Small Office

There's not much room for a queue at the Post Office in Ochopee, Florida. The former tool-shed building measures just 62 sq ft (5.75 sq m)—about the size of a child's playhouse.

Web Art

Will Knight harvests spiderwebs at his farm in Williamstown, Vermont, and sells them as art. He originally got the idea from a Girl Scout manual. He sprays a mist of white paint to identify his chosen web and then sticks it to a board that has been sanded smooth or painted black. Finally, he seals the web in place by lacquering both it and the board. "Spiderwebman," as he is known, even has spiderwebs tattooed on his elbows.

Wrestle of the Titans

Since 1357, the city of Edirne in northwestern Turkey has been home to the annual Kirkpinar Wrestling and Culture Festival. This popular traditional event is believed to be the oldest wrestling festival in the world, and features titanic bouts of oil wrestling between hundreds of pairs of men. Olive oil is applied to the body before the wrestling bouts begin. Until 1975, the wrestling bouts had no upper time limit, and were sometimes known to continue for up to two days—now, they last for a more comfortable 30 to 40 minutes.

Candy Counter

A candy store in Littleton, New Hampshire, has a counter that is 111 ft (34 m) long. Run by Jim Alden, Chutter General Store displays 700 jars of sweet treats on its three-tiered counter, including eight different kinds of black licorice.

Converted Carrier

In 2006, the Minsk—a Russian aircraft carrier that had been converted into a floating entertainment center complete with a movie theater and restaurants—was put up for sale in Shenzhou, China.

Sock Burning

Every year on the first day of spring, boaters in Annapolis, Maryland, gather for a sock-burning ceremony to celebrate the return of warm weather.

Undersea River

An undersea river known as the Cromwell Current flows eastward beneath the Pacific for 3,500 mi (5,633 km) along the Equator. It is 190 mi (305 km) wide and reaches a depth of 1,300 ft (400 m) in places. Its volume is 1,000 times that of the Mississippi River.

Pet Beds

A leading British hotel chain announced in 2006 that it was offering pets their own beds. The special pet beds, which measure 2½ ft x 2 ft (76 x 60 cm), were introduced by Travelodge to cater for customers who hate being parted from their cats and dogs.

Cover-up

Kira, Japan, famous for its recuperative hot spring baths, had its springs dry up in 1980. Townsfolk used boiling tap water to hide the fact for over a decade.

Worm Gruntin'

The town of Sopchoppy, Florida, has an annual Worm Gruntin' Festival, where locals use vibrations of all kinds to lure earthworms out of the ground.

DARING DIVERS

Each year as part of a local festival, Japanese women dive 30 ft (9 m) beneath the sea without oxygen tanks to find shellfish such as clams, oysters, and lobsters.

The Amas, as they are known, have as long as their breath holds—about 1 minute 20 seconds—to prise the mollusks from the rocks. Here, the women are shown making their procession into the sea.

Fun Burial

Dutch entertainer Eddy Daams has launched a new extreme sport—fun burials—in which competitors are buried 5 ft (1.5 m) down in a coffin for an hour under a concrete block weighing 3½ tons. The coffin has an oxygen supply and a panic button and is linked by webcam to a computer so that friends and family can watch.

Deer Drop

The deer pellet drop is the highlight of the Friends of Black Moshannon Summer Festival near Philipsburg, Pennsylvania. Competitors must hold a piece of deer excrement near the tip of their nose and drop it into a milk bottle at their feet. Winners of the women's section earn a pair of deer-pellet earrings.

Rubber Residence

Pat and Chuck Potter of Bancroft, Ontario, Canada, built a home that is 100 ft (30 m) long on the side of a hill using 1,200 old car tires, and solar panels for heat.

Ice Angel

This photo of an angel in ice was taken by Vicki Whitehill of Alachua, Florida, in Great Smokey Mountain National Park in Tennessee in 2003.

Cold Comfort

A warmly dressed chambermaid plumps up the pillows in a room in Eastern Europe's first ice hotel in February 2006. The Balea Lac Ice Hotel is located at the end of a remote valley in the Fagaras Mountains, which are the highest in Romania and lie 186 mi (300 km) northwest of the capital Bucharest.

In the Dark

A new restaurant opened in London, England, in 2006 where diners eat in total darkness. Customers do not know what they are eating, the idea being that not being able to see what is on your plate heightens the senses and liberates the taste buds. The food is served by partly sighted or blind waiters and anything that might shatter the blackness, such as a cell-phone display or a burning cigarette, is banned.

Rainmakers

A Chinese government agency aims to control the country's weather! The Beijing Weather Modification Office mobilizes cloud-seeding aircraft, artillery, and rockets to induce rainfall and prevent drought in agricultural areas. It also tried to guarantee blue skies for the opening ceremony of the 2008 Beijing Olympics by studying the effects of firing certain chemicals into clouds with anti-aircraft guns.

Solid Cobs

A former cornfield in Dublin, Ohio, has 109 concrete corncobs, each standing more than 6 ft (1.8 m) tall—a tribute to Sam Frantz, a developer of hybrid corn plants.

Miniscule Particles

Protons, the positively charged particles in the center of an atom, are so small that 500,000,000,000 could fit into the period at the end of this sentence.

Pizza City

To celebrate the 859th anniversary of the founding of their city, pizza lovers in the Russian capital Moscow created a map of the city made from pizza. Almost 20 ft (6 m) in diameter, the prodigious pizza featured sculptures of the Kremlin and other Moscow landmarks made from gooey cheese on the top.

Peace Symbol

A wooden tomahawk with a 54-ft (16-m) handle and weighing 2,750 lb (1,250 kg) is displayed with a concrete teepee that is 30 ft (9 m) high in Cut Knife, Saskatchewan, Canada, as a symbol of peace and unity between white people and the neighboring Indian reserves.

Sulfur Blast

Mount St. Helens in the state of Washington spews out twice as much sulfur dioxide as all of the state's industries added together.

Best Baggers

Store workers from across the U.S.A. compete in the National Grocers Association's Best Bagger Contest. Competitors fill two bags with a selection of grocery items and are judged on appearance, attitude, time, weight distribution, and technique. There are separate categories for paper and plastic bags.

Handy Sculpture

The brainchild of evangelist Oral Roberts, a huge pair of praying hands guards the Oral Roberts University at Tulsa, Oklahoma. Made of bronze, the massive sculpture is 60 ft (18 m) high and weighs 30 tons.

Partly Submerged

Measured from its base—on the floor of the Pacific Ocean—to its peak, the tallest mountain in the world is not Everest, but Hawaii's Mauna Kea. This volcanic peak rises to a height of 33,474 ft (10,203 m) from the seabed, but only 13,794 ft (4,205 m) of this is above sea level.

Cube House

Designed by Ben Kutner, a bizarre house in Toronto, Ontario, Canada, consists of three green cubes perched at angles above the ground on a single column. A traditional house sits on the ground and the cubes—each 24 sq ft (2.2 sq m) and with around 1,130 sq ft (105 sq m) of floor space—stick out as limbs like the branches of a tree.

High Finance

An Indian bank set up an ATM machine along a trade route that leads from Lhasa, Tibet, to the State of Sikkim—at an altitude of 13,200 ft (4,025 m)!

Motor City

Nearly one quarter of the land area of Los Angeles is taken up by cars, and there are at least half a million more cars in L.A. than there are people—the population of Los Angeles County is 10 million, and there are 10.5 million registered vehicles. And in the city of L.A.—the most car-populated metropolis in the world—there are 1.8 registered cars per licenced driver.

Sputnik Relic

The most unusual exhibit at the Rahr-West Art Museum in Manitowoc, Wisconsin, is a lump of metal weighing 20 lb (9 kg), which is an exact replica of a piece that crashed into the street outside when the Soviet Union's Sputnik IV spacecraft fell to Earth in September 1962. The rest of the seven-ton craft burned up in the atmosphere.

Royal Waves

The Queen of England is the legal owner of all of the sturgeons, dolphins, porpoises, and whales in the waters within 3 mi (4.8 km) of U.K. shores.

I Love Snakes

This Thai man is an inhabitant of one of the world's strangest villages—Kok Sa Nga, which means "King Cobra Village," in northeast Thailand. Many of Kok Sa Nga's villagers keep venomous king cobra snakes in wooden boxes under their homes, and every year the village stages a three-day festival celebrating this deadly snake. The entertainment on offer includes men who fight the snakes barehanded and women who dance with the cobra's heads in their mouths.

INCREDIBLE ANIMALS!

REALITY SHOW

The fur definitely flew during a U.S. TV reality show in 2006, because all the contestants were cats!

Ten cats—all taken from animal shelters or rescue groups—spent ten days in a New York shop window inside a specially constructed house complete with mini sofas, beds, and even a fish tank... with fake fish. There, they completed tasks and were graded on such activities as purring and catching toy mice.

Each day one of the ten was eliminated by public vote. The show was created by a pet-food company eager to promote cat adoption. All of the cats were found homes after their eviction.

The ten lucky cats lived in the lap of luxury and provided much amusement to passing shoppers.

Sheep Snack

A python was discovered stuck in the middle of a road in the village of Kampung Jabor, Malaysia, in 2006 after swallowing a pregnant ewe. Unable to move, the greedy snake, which measured 20 ft (6 m) in length, was easily captured by local firefighters. It weighed 200 lb (90 kg) when found —but much of that was its dinner!

Eagle Swoop

Freddie, a Pekingese dog belonging to the Slevin family of Bozeman, Montana, was snatched by an eagle and spent a week in the freezing wilds before he managed to find his way home.

Athletic Bear

Jennifer Ehrlichman of Hayward, Wisconsin, found a bear hibernating in an eagle's nest at the top of a 45-ft-high (14-m) aspen tree!

Turkey Terror

An aggressive 20-lb (9-kg) wild turkey terrorized the residents of Woburn, Massachusetts, in 2005. Many people were afraid to leave their homes, and when the police tried to move it on it kept returning.

Therapy Dog

Hans, the disabled dog, lost the use of both of his hind legs in an accident. Now with wheels attached to the back of his legs, he does his rounds twice a week at Florida Hospital. Complete with personalized license plate, he visits patients who are confined to wheelchairs.

Battered By Fish

While Blake Fessenden was riding a personal watercraft on Florida's Suwannee River in 2006, a 4-ft (1.2-m) sturgeon jumped out of the water and hit him with such force that it knocked him unconscious.

Trapped Chipmunk

In 2003, a chipmunk got trapped in Dixie Goldsby's car while she was camping in Utah and rode with her all the way to California!

Plan Backfired

A woman in Jacksonville, Florida, set her apartment on fire in 2006 while trying to kill a snake. Finding the snake on her porch, she doused it with petrol and torched it, but in doing so caused $1,000 of damage. The snake got away!

Lucky Chance

A man jumped on the back of a 10-ft (3-m) alligator to save his girlfriend's pet dog as it was being dragged into a lake. Brent Carey was at the park in Charleston, South Carolina, when the alligator leaped from the water and began to drag the dog, Chance, into the lake. But Carey jumped on the reptile's back, grabbed it near its back legs, and persuaded it to free the dog.

Jumbo Operation

Dr. William Baldwin, a surgeon at Scarborough General Hospital in Ontario, Canada, performed a nine-hour operation to remove a kidney stone from an elephant.

Elephant Art

An exhibition of paintings by elephants went on display at an art gallery in Edinburgh, Scotland, in 2006. By holding the brushes in their trunks, the elephants—all from Thailand—produced a series of pretty pictures, the best of which was painted by six-ton Paya and was claimed to be a self-portrait.

Talented Terrier

Tillie, a Jack Russell terrier from Brooklyn, New York, creates abstract paintings that have been shown in 16 exhibitions. Tillie has sold more than 100 paintings, with the sale proceeds reaching five figures!

Roadkill Art

Nate Hill of Brooklyn, New York, doesn't believe in letting roadkill go to waste—instead he turns it into works of art. Inspired by a friend who stapled a guinea pig's head to a snake, he sews together paws, tails, and heads of dead animals to create his own crazy creatures.

Hopping Canine

In 1932, Nellie, a dog with no front legs who belonged to Dr. P.W. Horner from Elkhart, Indiana, used to move around by "hopping" along, balanced on her hind legs and tail.

Identity Crisis

J.R. the pot-bellied pig seemed to have suffered an identity crisis in August 2006. The stray was taken to an animal shelter in Shelbyville, Kentucky, after scaring local dogs, but during his two-week stay in a dog kennel he developed canine tendencies, including a sudden taste for dog biscuits!

Canal Hazard

In January 2005, an alligator measuring 12 ft (3.6 m) in length and weighing 400 lb (180 kg) was found living in a downtown Miami canal. It was believed to have grown that big by eating the animals cast into the water following religious voodoo sacrifices.

Kangaroo Horse

This young foal was born in the early 20th century, without any front legs.

Dogs Reunited

In four years British dog lover Jayne Hayes has reunited over 2,500 dogs with their owners via the Internet. Her website receives four million hits a month and has 100 lost or stolen dogs added to its database every week.

Great Escape

In April 2006, Rosco, an American bulldog, had had enough of being locked up, so he chewed open the lock on his cage and climbed a 7-ft (2-m) wall topped with barbed wire to escape from the Animal Control Center in Virginia Beach, Virginia.

Canine Wedding

As Bethel Park, Pennsylvania, staged its most eagerly awaited wedding of 2006, there was hardly a dry eye—or nose—to be seen. The bride wore fur, and so did the groom. This was hardly surprising because the groom, Buck, was a Bernese mountain dog and the bride, Peaches, was a collie-beagle-basset mix! Buck was resplendent in a bow tie and Peaches wore a tasteful veil. The ceremony was staged by a local dog club for residents of a retirement home, and had a full supporting cast. The best man was a Shetland sheepdog, the flower girl was a Yorkshire terrier, and the beautiful bridesmaids included a toy poodle and an Irish setter.

Dog Jockey

A Jack Russell terrier who lives in Gloucestershire, England, likes to ride on the back of a Shetland pony who is just 37 in (94 cm) tall! Freddie the dog often leaps on the back of his neighbor's pony, Daisy, for a trot around the farm. His owner Patricia Swinley said: "Freddie is a natural jockey. When he first saw Daisy, he rushed across the yard and just jumped straight on her back."

Rat Catchers

In 2006, a Chinese village treated more than 200 cats to a fish dinner to thank them for their hard work. Residents of Sanjiang, in Guangdong Province, wanted to thank the cats for eradicating rats from their farms.

Fish Fire

Kipper the catfish was blamed for starting a fire that destroyed a house in Poole, England, in 2006. During a fight in his tank, water splashed out onto an electric plug, sending a power surge up the tank cable. This burned the tank's plastic lid, which then melted onto a sofa, setting it, and the house, alight.

Penguin Pullovers

Chilly penguins are being kept warm and snug thanks to these brightly colored pullovers, which have been knitted by a group of seniors from New South Wales, Australia. The small, 18-in (46-cm) tall fairy penguins had been hit by oil slicks off the coasts of New South Wales and Tasmania. When they had the spilt oil scrubbed off their coats by rescue workers they lost the natural oils that help them to keep out the cold. The little pullovers are designed to keep them warm while they recuperate.

Rat Lover

Roger Dier of Petaluma, California, kept 1,300 rats in his one-bedroom home!

Flood Damage

A goldfish carried from a garden pond by floodwaters in New Zealand was found alive in a roadside ditch more than a mile away. The fish had been swept from Craig and Julie Struthers' pond by a flash flood in the town of Mosgiel on South Island five days earlier.

Color Code

Con Slobodchikoff, an Arizona professor, found that prairie dogs have very specific verbal calls, including calls that identify a person's height or shirt color.

Patched Up

A snapping turtle hit by a car in Traverse City, Michigan, survived after its cracked shell was fitted with a fiberglass patch at an auto body shop!

CHOLLA THE HORSE ARTIST

When Cholla stands at his easel and paints, passers-by do a double take—because Cholla is a horse!

Cholla—a 24-year-old quarter horse-mustang owned by Renee Chambers of Reno, Nevada—has been painting for two years and has made quite a splash in the art world. His work has been displayed in several galleries and magazines and he even has his own website. "He loves to do it," says Chambers. "He can be in the back pasture and he sees me bring his easel and he's just right there. He doesn't even have to be called."

"Purple Heron"

"Birds in Flight"

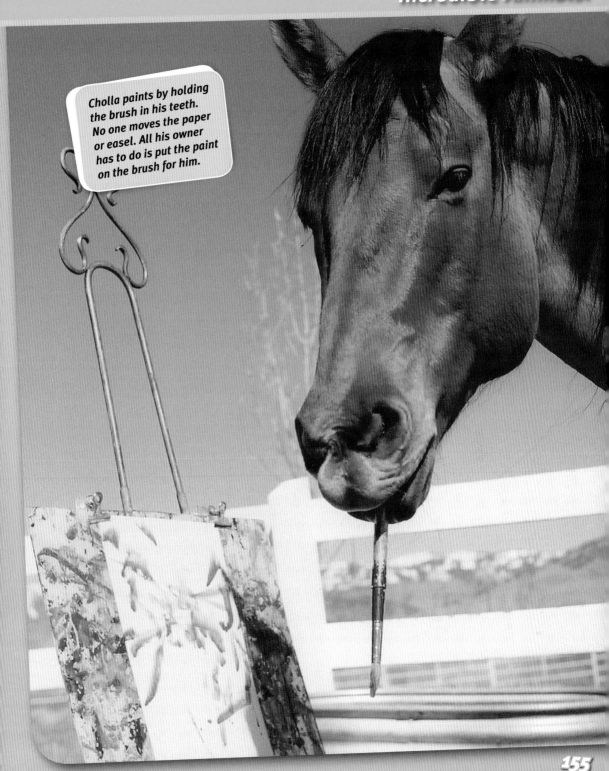

Cholla paints by holding the brush in his teeth. No one moves the paper or easel. All his owner has to do is put the paint on the brush for him.

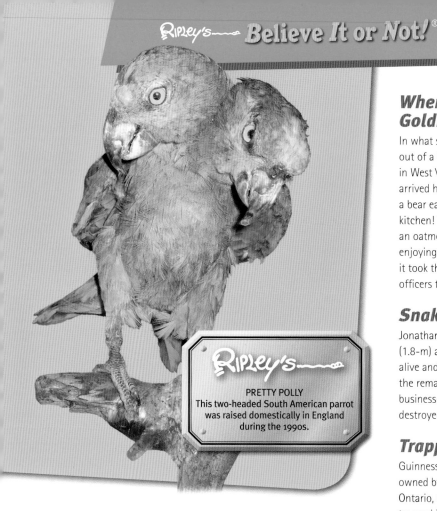

Where's Goldilocks?

In what sounds like something out of a bedtime story, a woman in West Vancouver, Canada, arrived home in 2006 to find a bear eating porridge in her kitchen! The bear had broken into an oatmeal container and was enjoying the feast so much that it took the efforts of three police officers to persuade it to leave.

Snake's Alive

Jonathan Kent's pet, a 6-ft (1.8-m) anaconda, was found alive and well, crawling through the remains of Kent's California business—that was totally destroyed by fire!

Trapped in Snow

Guinness, a golden retriever owned by Terry Coward of Barrie, Ontario, Canada, survived being trapped in a snowbank for 11 days after being hit by a car.

Mistaken Identity

When a woman in Koblenz, Germany, heard what sounded like a child next door constantly screaming "Mama, Mama," she called the police. But instead of finding a youngster left home alone, they found the cries were coming from the family's talking parrot!

All Shook Up

Barney the Doberman pinscher was supposed to be guarding the valuable exhibits at a teddy bear museum at Wookey Hole, Somerset, England. But, during a 15-minute rampage in 2006, he inexplicably went berserk, tearing more than 100 of the toys limb from limb and causing $40,000 damage. Among his victims was Mabel, a valuable Steiff bear that had once belonged to rock star Elvis Presley.

Wild Ride

A cat that hitchhiked a ride on the underbelly of a sport utility vehicle in 2005 survived a 70-mi (113-km) journey on the New Jersey Turnpike. The cat—nicknamed Miracle—was finally freed when another motorist spotted it through the S.U.V.'s wheel well and flagged down the driver. The cat emerged with burned paws, singed fur, and one claw missing.

Crazed Croc

Aggravated by a chainsaw's noise, Brutus, a 14½-ft-long (4.4-m) crocodile living at the Corroboree Park Tavern in Australia's Northern Territory, ran 20 ft (6 m) to snatch the tool from the hands of a terrified worker and smashed it beyond repair.

Snake Find

A Chinese woman from the city of Xi'an returned to her locked sixth-floor apartment after two months away to find a 5-ft (1.5-m) snake in her bed! The snake was caught and released in hills nearby.

Magpie Decoy

To protect their eyes from highly aggressive magpies, Australian pedestrians wear sunglasses or put photos of eyes on the back of their heads to fool the birds!

Jet Healed

When a California gunman took aim at Patricia Maupin, her dog Jet, a five-year-old Australian Shepherd mix, instinctively defended his owner and, leaping in front of Maupin, took three bullets meant for her. While Maupin hailed her dog a hero, Jet was making a steady recovery from his injuries.

Thugs Bunny

At just one year old, Rudi the rabbit, owned by Erwin Teichmann of Berlin, Germany, weighed 22 lb (10 kg), was 3 ft 1 in (94 cm) in length, had 8-in (20-cm) ears—and was still growing.

Head Stuck

In 2006, a dog spent two hours with its head stuck in a 4-in (10-cm) aluminum pipe before Animal Control in Fort Worth, Texas, freed it by using mineral oil as a lubricant. It is thought the dog had been chasing a squirrel or a rabbit.

Donut Dog

A donut-loving dog was blamed for starting a house fire in Vancouver, British Columbia, Canada. Investigators believe the dog caused the blaze by jumping up to reach a box of donuts and then accidentally switching on the stove.

Sheep Boots

Sheep in Germany have been given miniature P.V.C. gumboots to prevent foot infection. Businessman Wilhelm Fennen started by making the footwear for dogs until a farmer from Hamburg requested some for his flock.

Angry Swarm

A teenage driver in Indiana crashed into a hollow tree and stirred up tens of thousands of angry honey bees, creating a swarm that landed her and nine others in hospital. By the time rescuers arrived, a black cloud of insects had engulfed Jacqueline Cossairt's vehicle, forcing firefighters to wear full safety gear during the rescue.

Skin Feeder

A Kenyan worm-like amphibian, *Bolengerula taitanus*, has a unique way of feeding her offspring—she allows them to peel off her own skin and eat it!

Glove Thief

Other cats bring home dead birds or mice, but Willy, owned by Jennifer and Dan Pifer of Pelham, New York, collects gardening gloves! His haul from neighborhood gardens was so great that the Pifers took to pinning the stolen gloves on their clothesline with the message: "Our cat is a glove snatcher. Please take these if yours." In the first four months of the 2006 summer, Willy seized at least 25 gloves. In winter, when gardening gloves are thin on the ground, he switches to his off-season prey, dirty socks, which he removes from the family laundry room.

Feline Forecaster

Fanny Shields of Baltimore, Maryland, owned a cat named Napoleon that could predict the weather with such accuracy that its predictions were regularly published in daily newspapers.

Pig Ban

A Russian farmer was barred from taking his pig into a soccer stadium in 2006 for fear that it could spark a riot. After exhibiting the animal at a Moscow pig show, Vladimir Kisilev was prevented from taking it to the match between Spartak Moscow and St. Petersburg Zenit on the grounds that the home team's fans are referred to as "pigs" by their St. Petersburg rivals.

Hungry Houdini

The latest trick by Houdini, a pet Burmese python measuring 12 ft (3.6 m) long, was very nearly his last. The snake had such a voracious appetite that when, in July 2006, his regular food, a rabbit, became tangled up with the queen-size electric blanket used to keep him warm, he ate the blanket too! He underwent an operation at a pet clinic in Ketchum, Idaho, where X rays revealed that he had not only eaten the blanket's wires but the heating control unit as well. In fact, the blanket's wiring extended through 8 ft (2.4 m) of the 60-lb (27-kg) reptile's digestive tract.

What a Catch!

In 1934, J.J. Holcomb from Panama got more than he bargained for when he hooked a large sailfish. As he was reeling in his catch, his fishing line snagged around a second large sailfish and Holcombe landed both fish at the same time. His catch had a combined weight of 208½ lb (95 kg).

Woolly Wonder

George, a merino wether sheep, died at his home in Warren, New South Wales, Australia, in 2006 at the grand old age of 21 years, 5 months and 3 days. He was such a popular character that his owners, Phil and Myra Tolhurst, invited local schoolchildren to attend his 21st birthday party—which featured a poem written in his honor and a cake.

Lucky Leap

A dog survived with only cuts and bruises in 2006 after accidentally running off the edge of a 450-ft (140-m) cliff while chasing rabbits. Russett the Jack Russell terrier was out with his owner Martin Coombes on the Isle of Wight, England, when he suddenly disappeared over the edge of the cliff and landed on rocks down by the sea.

Bird Toll

In 2006, the Royal Ontario Museum, Canada, staged a gruesome display of around 2,000 birds that had been lured to their deaths by the bright lights of the Canadian city of Toronto. The exhibition was part of a campaign to persuade Toronto office and apartment-building owners to dim their lights at night in order to reduce the number of bird deaths owing to collisions with lit skyscrapers. No fewer than 89 different species were scraped off downtown Toronto sidewalks during the 2005 migratory season.

Glowing Fish!

A Taiwanese company has created a new species of genetically engineered fish that glows fluorescent gold in the dark. Glow-in-the-dark fish are created by injecting a fluorescent protein, which is extracted from jellyfish, directly into the fish embryo. The new rice fish is even more spectacular than previous neon fish because, while it glows with gold fluorescence under white light, it is also able to change color under other kinds of aquarium lights.

SWINGING PARTY

Cheeta the chimp—veteran of a dozen Tarzan movies—celebrated his 74th birthday in April 2006, making him the world's oldest living primate.

Cheeta enjoys playing the piano at the Cheeta Primate Foundation in California. It is rare for chimps to live beyond the age of 50 in captivity.

Metro-Goldwyn

Cheeta, who is 4 ft (1.2 m) tall and weighs 150 lb (68 kg), was discovered on an animal scouting trip to Liberia, Africa, by a Hollywood animal trainer named Tony Gentry in 1932. Long since retired from acting—his last role was opposite Rex Harrison in *Doctor Doolittle* (U.S. 1967)—Cheeta spends his days at the Cheeta Primate Foundation, playing the piano or painting. His masterpieces have been exhibited in art galleries and sell for more than $100 apiece.

Cheeta in his younger days with co-stars Maureen O'Sullivan and Johnny Weissmuller in the Tarzan movies of the 1930s.

163

Kitten Chariot

When a kitten suffered a broken back after being attacked by a raccoon, Dr. Alice Davis of Ashland, Oregon, gave it a new lease of life by fitting it with a wheeled chariot made from a K'NEX™ set.

Hook Horror

Karen and Phillip Vavro of Butler, Pennsylvania, have a cat named Nippy that swallowed a metal hook, 2½-in (6.4-cm) long, from a Christmas tree ornament. The cat survived and the hook simply passed through its digestive system 20 days later!

Cat Snatch

Bamboo, a cat weighing 6 lb 8 oz (2.9 kg) that was owned by Colleen Hamilton of Esquimalt, British Columbia, Canada, survived after being snatched from the back porch by a great horned owl. Bamboo limped home 22 hours later with three broken legs and puncture wounds from the owl's talons. From the injuries, veterinarians concluded that the cat had fallen from a significant height.

Iguana Walk

Robert Garnett from Essex, England, takes his pet iguana for a walk every day.

HOWLER MONKEY
Five-limbed South American howler monkey, acquired by Ripley's in 2004.

The Best of Friends

Gohan the 3½-in (9-cm) dwarf hamster and Aochan the 3-ft (1-m) ratsnake live happily side by side in a Tokyo zoo. What's all the more surprising is that Gohan—whose name means "meal" in Japanese—was presented to Aochan in October 2005, as his dinner! The ratsnake decided not to eat the hamster, preferring to make friends with him, and the pair have shared a cage ever since.

Cliff Plunge

Pepe the Jack Russell terrier was so intent on chasing a squirrel in 2006 that he dived over a cliff. After tumbling down the cliff, he landed next to the busy Pacific Coast Highway near Los Angeles and narrowly missed getting run over by a big truck. While a passing motorist came to Pepe's aid, his owner, Brandon McMillan, was unaware of the rescue and, scrambling up the cliff in search of the dog, had to be saved by firefighters when the ground suddenly gave way beneath him.

Ant Colony

More than 307 million ants were once found in a single colony in Japan. There were 45,000 connecting nests built over one square mile (2.6 sq km).

Deputy Dog

In 2006, the sheriff's department of Geauga County, Ohio, unveiled its latest weapon in the war against crime—a 2-lb (900-g) Chihuahua named Midge. Sheriff Dan McClelland plans to train Midge, who stands only 2 ft (60 cm) tall even on tiptoes, as the smallest drug dog in the state.

Pet Yoga

Heather Stevens of West Hollywood, California, teaches 30-minute yoga classes that dogs and their owners take together. Stevens, whose clients include poodles, dachshunds, and pointers, says that the classes helped her own aging female dog regain mobility in her hips.

Stealing Starlings

Bill Dougherty, a car-wash manager from Fredericksburg, Virginia, was surprised to discover that starlings had been raiding his washing machine, crawling up the change chute to steal quarters!

Keeping Mum

A 14½-ft (4.4-m) hammerhead shark caught near Boca Grande, Florida, in May 2006, was found to be pregnant with a record 55 babies!

Naughty Polly

Polly the parrot stopped a plane from taking off in 2006 when she escaped from a box on her owner's lap and started pecking passengers. As the aircraft prepared for take-off, Polly proceeded to circle passengers' heads and nibble their shoulders. She was recaptured ten minutes later and the flight—from Alderney in the Channel Islands, U.K., to Southampton, England— went ahead.

Drunken Pelicans

Four pelicans were rounded up on suspicion of being drunk in the Los Angeles area in June 2006. Three of the California brown pelicans were found wandering dazed in the streets of Laguna Beach after another pelican struck a vehicle's windshield on a nearby coast road. Experts believed the birds had been eating poisonous algae in the ocean.

White Mischief

Albino animals are rare and extremely eye-catching creatures, (squirrel below, kangaroo right), whose unusual appearance is caused by a genetic condition. In some cultures, they are considered sacred; in many others, they have appeared in many myths and legends.

High Horse

Radar, a Belgian draft horse, owned by Bill Priefert of Texas, stands a colossal 6 ft 7 ½ in (2 m) from foot to shoulder, weighs 2,400 lb (1,088 kg), and wears a size 9½ shoe. Every day he eats 18 lb (8 kg) of grain and 40 lb (18 kg) of hay and drinks 20 gallons (75 l) of water.

HIGH-FLAT DIET

There's nothing Arthur Boyt enjoys more than sitting down to a nice weasel casserole, perhaps with a side plate of bat wings. The former taxidermist from Davidstow, Cornwall, England, gets his meat for free by regularly tucking into roadkill.

His freezer is stacked with the carcasses of animals he has found squashed on the road: hedgehogs, cats, otters, even a Labrador. He once brought a porcupine back from Canada! He says: "People are happy to eat an apple that has fallen out of the tree and is lying on the floor, so what's the difference?" Arthur, who has been eating roadkill since he was 13 and has never been ill once, strongly recommends badger sandwiches, but was disappointed with giant horseshoe bat ("a bit like gray squirrel, not a lot of flavor") and

fox ("a pungent taste that went on and on repeating"). However, his wife Su doesn't share his unusual tastes and refuses to cook them—because she's a vegetarian.

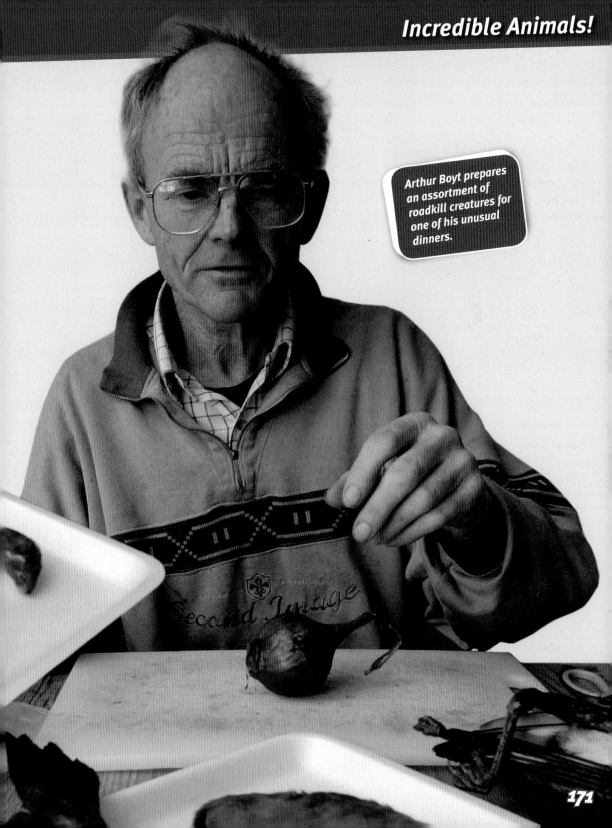

Arthur Boyt prepares an assortment of roadkill creatures for one of his unusual dinners.

Grizzly Hybrid

While hunting in northern Canada in April 2006, 65-year-old Jim Martell from Idaho shot a grizzly-polar bear hybrid, the first ever found in the wild. Wildlife officials took an interest after noticing that the bear's white fur was interspersed with brown patches. It also had long claws, a concave facial profile, and a humped back—all characteristics of a grizzly. Genetic tests confirmed that the animal's father was a grizzly and its mother was a polar bear. Previously, the two species had interbred only in zoos.

Wandering Cat

A cat who wandered away from his Seattle home in 1996 was finally reunited with his family ten years later, thanks to animal care workers in California. Sneakers, a long-haired black tabby, was dropped off at the Sacramento animal shelter in April 2006 by owners who could no longer care for the cat, but an electronic tag revealed that he had actually gone missing a decade earlier—in Seattle, Washington. His original owner, Alison MacEwan, was delighted to have her pet back, but remains puzzled as to how Sneakers came to make the 600-mi (965-km) journey south.

Bear Wrestler

In February 2006, Lydia Angyiou of Ivujivik, Quebec, Canada, who weighed 90 lb (41 kg), wrestled a 700-lb (320-kg) polar bear that appeared on the street where her seven-year-old son and his friends were playing. Seeing the bear begin to size up her son, Angyiou started kicking and punching the animal while a fellow villager fetched a rifle.

Suffered in Silence

A dog with no bark survived after being stuck down a 10-ft (3-m) ditch for a month. Holly, a 12-year-old collie, fell into the ditch in Cornwall, England, after being scared by a thunderstorm and was rescued only when a passerby heard her whimpering.

Cool Cat

An American dentist has given his one-year-old Persian cat gold teeth. David Steele of Alexandria, Indiana, fixed $1,900 gold crowns on Sebastian's two protruding bottom canines to stop them breaking off.

House Arrest

After repeatedly attacking people in the neighborhood, Lewis, a cat living in Fairfield, Connecticut, was put under house arrest by police—and was banned from ever leaving the house.

Extra Shipment

When a business owner from Tampa, Florida, opened a shipment of 400 parrot cages sent from China, he found an additional order that he wasn't expecting—a severely undernourished cat. The female cat tipped the scales at just over 3 lb (1.4 kg) after spending nearly a month trapped in the container.

Territorial Tabby

A territorial cat defended his yard in spectacular fashion in 2006 by chasing a wandering black bear up a tree—twice. While Jack, a ten-year-old tabby owned by Donna Dickey of West Milford, New Jersey, stood guard under the tree, the petrified bear clung to the branches. It stayed there for about 15 minutes, frequently looking down at Jack. When it eventually slid down the tree and tried to escape, a hissing Jack immediately gave chase, forcing the bear to take refuge up a second tree until Dickey called the cat home. As the bear ran off into the woods, Dickey summed up Jack's philosophy. "He doesn't want anybody in his yard," she said.

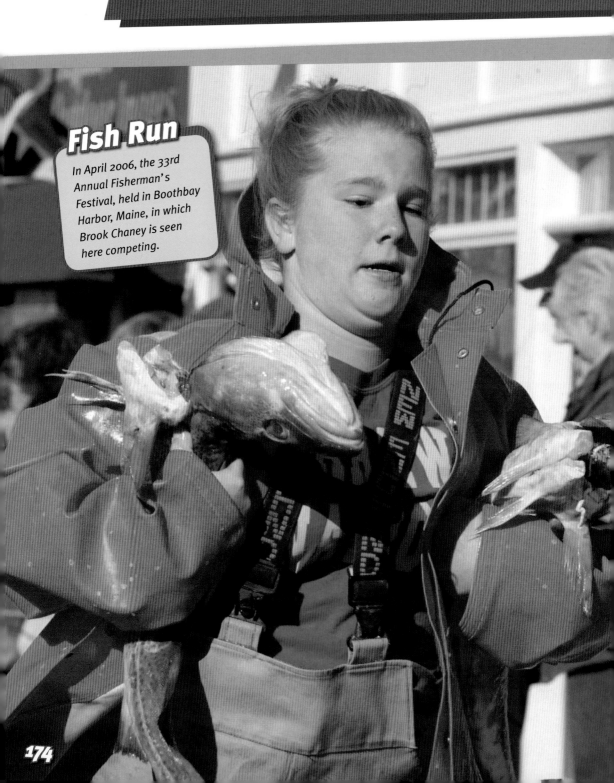

Fish Run

In April 2006, the 33rd Annual Fisherman's Festival, held in Boothbay Harbor, Maine, in which Brook Chaney is seen here competing.

Cold Cat

A cat in Oklahoma City, Oklahoma, amazingly survived being shut in a refrigerator for four weeks without food or water. His four-year-old owner had put Louis in the fridge in the family barn for safekeeping, but the cat's plight was discovered only a month later when the boy's father decided to clean it out and the cat fell out. Louis had lost 7 lb (3.2 kg) in weight, but experts agreed that he was lucky to be alive at all.

Night Bird

The oilbird spends its entire life in darkness. It lives in the caves of South America, venturing out only at night to feed on fruit, and finds its way around by using echolocation, in the same way as a bat.

Footballing Crocs

Erroberto Piza Rios of Ixtapa, Mexico, enjoys nothing more than kicking a soccer ball around. But the guys he plays with can certainly put in crunching tackles—because they are all crocodiles! He has tamed 47 crocodiles in all, and every one is named after a famous footballer. Their skills include heading the ball and raising their heads to allow the balls to roll down their backs to their tails.

Shrinking Frog

The paradoxical frog of South America is smaller as an adult than as a tadpole. Whereas the tadpole can reach a length of 10 in (25.4 cm), the adult never exceeds 3 in (7.6 cm).

Savior Cat

In December 2005, Tommy the cat called 911 when his owner, Gary Rosheisen of Columbus, Ohio, fell from his wheelchair! Nobody knows how the cat managed to hit the right buttons, but when the emergency call went through to the police, there was no one on the phone. When they called the number back and there was no answer, they decided to investigate. Rosheisen had previously tried to teach Tommy to call 911, but hadn't known if the training had worked.

Mighty Crocs

The Bhitarkanika sanctuary on India's Orissa coast is home to the world's largest saltwater crocodiles. A 2006 census showed that several saltwater crocodiles there have grown to 16 to18 ft (4.9 to 5.5 m), five are up to 20 ft (6 m) long, and three are over 20 ft, including one 23-ft-long (7-m) monster. Saltwater crocodiles can live to 100 years and devour a human in minutes.

Pigs in Water

Pinky and Perky are two Tamworth pigs that love nothing more than a morning swim in their owner's swimming pool. The pigs live in Worcestershire, England, with farmers Craig and Marjorie Walsh, who first let them swim to stop them getting bored. Now the nautical porkers eagerly look forward to their daily dip.

Greatest Dane

In 2006, a three-year-old Great Dane called Gibson, owned by Sandy Hall of Sacramento, California, stood an amazing 7 ft 2 in (2.2 m) tall on his hind legs! And his best pal Zoie is a Chihuahua measuring only 7 in (18 cm) tall!

Dogs' Dinner

A restaurant in Denver, Colorado, organizes an annual "Three Dogs Night Out" where dog owners can enjoy a gourmet meal with their four-legged friends.

Owl Vision

Dr. Chris Murphy, a veterinary ophthalmologist in Madison, Wisconsin, performed eye surgery on a blind great horned owl, and then fitted the bird with contact lenses.

Doggie Dating

Dog lovers who are looking for mates for their pets may find a match on a website. Believed to be the U.K.'s first lonely hearts website for dogs, it also offers canine welfare advice.

Restless Daisy

A female tortoise who decided she wanted a change after 55 years with the same partner made a break for freedom in 2006. Daisy was discovered 12 days later, having ventured nearly one mile (1.6 km) from her home in Devon, England—a journey that took her up a steep hill and across a road and tractor trails. It was the first time Daisy had been away from pal Bert since the early 1950s.

Mixed Dining

A new restaurant in China encourages human customers to eat at the same table as their pets! Although the menu is primarily for animals, it also offers drinks and snacks for their owners. The Paradise Pet Club in Shanghai disinfects its dishes three times a day.

Unwelcome Visitor

When Lori Pachelli heard a knock at the door of her Florida home, she looked out to see an 8-ft-long (2.4-m) alligator on her front porch. While a hysterical Mrs Pachelli phoned her husband, the alligator, which was aggressive and had a bloody lip from banging its head against the door, remained there for about an hour before returning to the lake behind the house.

Sinister Storker

In 2006, an elderly couple from Potsdam, Germany, revealed that they were being stalked by a stork. Gerhard Schneider told how for weeks a large stork followed him and his wife whenever they left their farmhouse. The bird's campaign of intimidation extended to standing on their car waiting for them and tapping on the windows of their house day and night if they stayed in.

Not Choosy

Common toads unable to find a female in the breeding season will try to mate with just about anything—including sticks, water lilies, and goldfish!

Roof Home

In 2006, a raccoon made its home on the roof of a 43-story building in downtown Chicago. The raccoon, which was spotted climbing scaffolding on the 36th floor of the Kluczynski Federal Building, was released after being captured with tuna bait.

Dribbling Crows

Four carrion crows at Tokuyama Zoo, Japan, use their beaks to dribble a miniature ball toward a soccer goal, sometimes tackling each other for possession before scoring. The zoo is hoping to teach them to pass and take free kicks.

Sheep-dog

A sheep belonging to Emlyn Roberts in north Wales, U.K., has started to behave like a sheepdog. The sheep, which was raised with sheepdogs, joins them in herding ducks and likes to be taken for a walk on a leash. She also likes to watch TV and can jump through hoops and slide down a ramp—just like the dogs!

Star Chicken

Arguably the most famous chicken in the U.S.A. died in February 2006 at the grand old age of 16. Matilda, who lived to twice the age of most chickens, had appeared on *The Tonight Show* as feathered assistant to magician Keith Barton of Birmingham, Alabama. She appeared magically from beneath the lid of a closed pan where only an egg yolk had been before.

Dog Wedged

After being hit by a passing Peugeot, a small dog traveled nearly 60 mi (97 km) through Northern Ireland one night in November 2005 wedged in the grille of the car. He emerged unscathed, only to be run over again—this time fatally—three weeks later.

Locust Swarm

An estimated 12.5 trillion locusts swept across about 198,600 sq mi (514,370 sq km) of Nebraska in 1874.

Extra Passenger

A muntjac deer survived a 25-mi (40-km) ride through England in 2004 while stuck in the air-intake slot above the bumper of a Rover car. The driver didn't know the animal was there, thinking he had hit a stone instead.

Pet Academy

Viviane Theby of Wittlich, Germany, has set up a talent academy with a difference—all her pupils are pets! Theby has already taught a dog to dance, a chicken to play the xylophone, and a cat to play the piano! The cat, Fuchs, has been so successful that he has sold CDs and given concerts.

Shell Shock

In 2006, a pet tortoise accidentally thrown out with the trash survived a nightmare trip through a recycling plant. After taking a ride in a garbage truck and narrowly avoiding being scooped up by a bulldozer, the tortoise was saved as he was about to be thrown into a crusher in Kent, England.

Emergency Landing

A snake forced a pilot to make an emergency landing in 2006. Monty Coles of West Virginia was 3,000 ft (915 m) up in his single-engine plane when he saw a 4½-ft (1.4-m) snake looking at him from the instrument panel. As the snake fell at his feet, he grabbed it with one hand while controlling the plane with the other. When the snake then coiled around his arm and started pulling a floor lever with its tail, Coles decided to make an emergency landing in Ohio.

Black (Bear) Jack

A bear wandered into a Nevada casino in 2006! The Montbleu Resort Casino and Spa promotes itself as a "habitat for everything wild," but hadn't reckoned on the 150-lb (68-kg) bear, who was eventually scared off by the casino's employees.

Holy Cow

Some 20,000 people from all over southern Egypt came to Mohammed Abu Dif's house in February 2006 to seek blessings from a calf that they believed held religious significance. According to reports, when the calf was born, folds in its skin formed the words: "There is no God, but Allah."

Vampire Finch

During times of drought, the sharp-beaked ground finch of the Galapagos Islands (which is also known as the vampire finch), drinks the blood of larger birds.

Undercover Kitten

Joining the lineup of police and fire officers being recognized for heroism by Brooklyn District Attorney Charles Hynes in 2006 was a cat named Fred! The crime-fighting kitten was given a special award for undercover work that helped trap a bogus veterinarian.

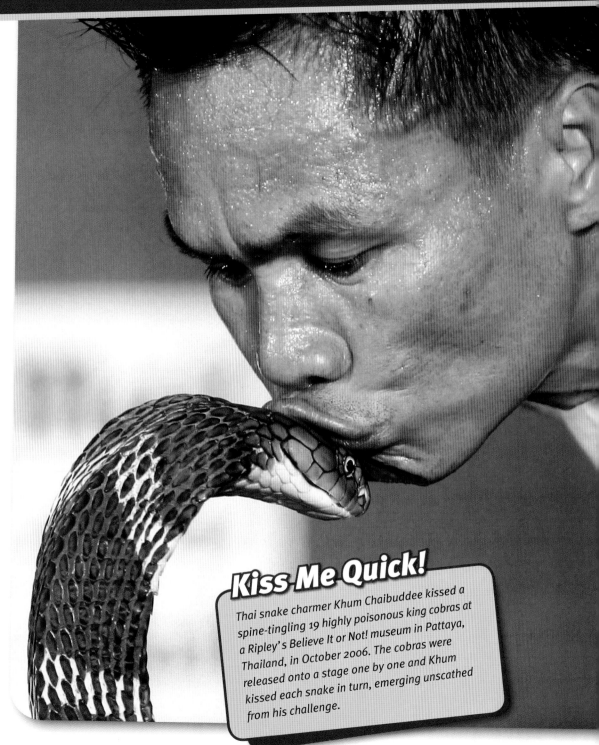

Kiss Me Quick!

Thai snake charmer Khum Chaibuddee kissed a spine-tingling 19 highly poisonous king cobras at a Ripley's Believe It or Not! museum in Pattaya, Thailand, in October 2006. The cobras were released onto a stage one by one and Khum kissed each snake in turn, emerging unscathed from his challenge.

A FEW TOO MANY

Conjoined Crocs

Two baby crocodiles at a farm in Bangkok, Thailand, look like they have been accidentally stuck together. In fact, they are conjoined—they both have all their own limbs but are joined at the bottom.

Two Snouts

A piglet with two distinct mouths was born on a farm in the suburbs of the city of Liaocheng in eastern China in 2006.

Two-nosed Pup

Duo is a Staffordshire bull terrier with two noses who lives in an animal shelter in Newcastle, England. Given to the shelter by police after apparently being lost or abandoned, Duo has the canine equivalent of a cleft lip. Veterinarians said that they had never before seen a cleft lip to such an extent in a dog.

181

Clever Corgi

Tim Pennings, an associate professor of math at Hope College in Holland, Michigan, has a Welsh corgi that "understands" calculus!

Artificial Legs

Footsie, a Shepherd-mix dog adopted by Helen DePinto of Ann Arbor, Michigan, was fitted with a pair of artificial hind legs by prosthetic limb specialists Steve Hoover and Kenneth Woodard in 2004. Missing the lower halves of his hind paws, before the fitting Footsie used to have to tuck his two back legs under his backside and scoot along with his front paws.

Survived Avalanche

A Burmese mountain dog named Tiga escaped a Colorado avalanche that killed her owner, and then survived for six days in freezing temperatures before being found alive and well.

Smallest Cat

Heed is a tiny cat from the unusual short-legged munchkin breed. His owner, Tiffani Kjeldergaard from San Diego, California, has measured him at just 3 in (7.6 cm) in height and a mere 2.3 lb (1 kg) in weight.

Lap of Luxury

A firm in Essex, England, is manufacturing a temperature-controlled waterbed for dogs. The bed comes with an extra-tough cover to withstand canine claws.

Snappy Pets

Neighbors rarely play with James "Bugs" Brown's pets. For Brown of Tualatin, Oregon, keeps three alligators: Hisser, Chomper, and Snapper.

Gold Tooth

Bosnian dentist Milan Vujnovic gave his pet dog, an eight-month-old Russian terrier called Atos, a gold tooth as a reward for his loyalty.

Brave Squirrels

Aaron Rundus, a scientist at the University of California, has discovered that Californian ground squirrels bravely stand their ground when confronted by a rattlesnake. Moreover, the squirrels wave their tales at the rattlesnakes in a taunting gesture that is picked up by the snake's sensitive heat sensors.

Cat Art

An art gallery in Woodstock, Ontario, Canada, raised money for a local animal shelter by selling paintings made by cats. The collection, entitled Paws and Prints, was achieved by putting paint on the cats' paws and letting the feline artists run around on canvases.

Baby Chameleons

In August 2006, Charles and Camilla—a pair of veiled chameleons—became the proud parents of no less than 56 healthy babies! It is very rare for such a large number of baby chameleons from one clutch of eggs to survive, and owner Vicky Fox from Dorset, England, had to quickly find homes for the inch-long offspring before instinct kicked in and they became violently territorial at around the age of three months.

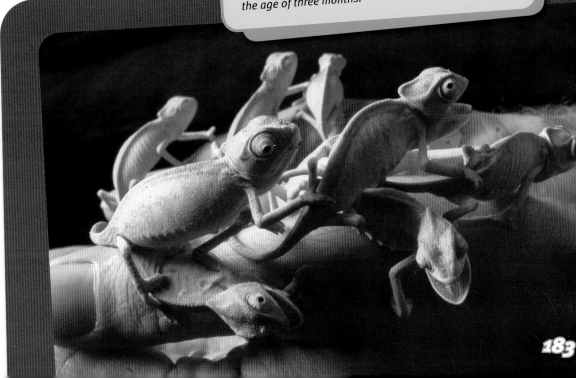

Flying Cow

One windy day in Oklahoma in the 1930s, this unfortunate cow was astonishingly whisked up into a tree by a tornado!

Surfing Moose

In January 2006, a fully grown moose was spotted surfing down Norway's rain-swollen Namsen River on a large chunk of ice!

Metal Mickey

One of just 12 southern ground hornbills in Britain, this lucky bird was given a new lease of life when keepers at Birdland in Gloucestershire, England, fitted him with a 6-in (15-cm) stainless steel beak in 2006. Metal Mickey, as he soon became known, had broken his beak, and would have starved had it not been for this inventive solution. He is now the proud owner of what is believed to be the first avian steel jaw in Britain.

Surprise Package

Dutch customs officials detected a live poisonous snake that was sent by airmail from Hong Kong to the Netherlands in 2006. When they first scanned the package, which was labeled "toy goods," they thought the snake was a rubber novelty, but then they saw it move! It turned out to be a Fea's viper, found in the forests of Southeast Asia.

River Ordeal

A dog that was presumed drowned after falling into an icy river channel that feeds Lake Michigan was found alive 13 hours later. Robert Chavez was walking his German Shepherd beside the Grand River in March 2006 when the dog fell into the channel and through the ice. It saved itself from certain death by swimming into a tunnel.

Lucky Kangaroo

A female kangaroo in Hangzhou, China, was the fortunate recipient of an artificial limb in August 2006. After the juvenile animal was involved in an accident, zoo officials contacted a local artificial limb factory, and commissioned a specially designed new back leg for her. She was back happily hopping about in no time.

Moose Suspended

Power crews near Fairbanks, Alaska, found a bull moose weighing nearly 1,200 lb (545 kg) suspended from an electrical pole 50 ft (15 m) in the air!

Fish Attack

Marcy Poplett of Peoria, Illinois, was injured and knocked off a personal watercraft on the Illinois River after a silver carp leaped out of the water and smacked her in the face!

Chameleon Snake

Scientists in Borneo have discovered a species of snake that has the ability to change color. The venomous water snake's chameleon-like behavior was discovered accidentally by researchers from Germany and Chicago when they put it into a dark bucket and saw it change from a reddish-brown color to almost entirely white.

Bear Bard

The 2006 Lake Tahoe Shakespeare Festival at Sand Harbor, Nevada, proved a big attraction—to local bears. Raiding the deserted food court, one bear helped itself to a feast of salmon, beef steaks, and cherry ice cream. Another appeared during an actual performance, forcing organizers to tell the audience to stay seated until the animal was chased away.

Flying Dog

A Saint Bernard dog survived being thrown from a second-floor window of an apartment in the Polish city of Sosnowiec when it landed on a passerby walking in the street below. The 110-lb (50-kg) dog was apparently pushed out of the window by its drunken owner, but escaped with just a few scratches while the man it landed on was more shocked than physically hurt.

Mystery Guest

Members of the Leroy family of Washington discovered that a stray dog was opening their car door and climbing inside every night to sleep!

Died at 176!

Harriet the Galapagos tortoise, claimed by Queensland's Australia Zoo to be the oldest living animal in the world, died of a heart attack in 2006 at the probable age of 176. Harriet, who spent seven years of her early life in England until the country's lack of sunshine sent her into hibernation, was a sprightly 84 when World War I broke out and 139 when Neil Armstrong set foot on the Moon. Also, for more than a century she was thought to be a male tortoise and was known as Harry.

Horn of Plenty

Lurch, an African Watusi steer has horns that are 7½ ft (2.3 m) across and 38 in (97 cm) around—and still growing! Lurch, who lives with his owner, Janice Wolf, in Arkansas, is something of a freak, as his parents had normal-sized horns. But his popularity is such that he has attracted visitors from as far afield as Sweden, South Africa, and Ecuador.

Cunning Cat

In 2006, a cat in Porto Alegre, Brazil, adopted a small bird that hurt itself when it fell out of its nest. The pair ate meat from the same plate and the cat even used the bird to help catch other birds!

Quick Thinking

Malcolm Locke, aged 12, of Orlando, Florida, survived being dragged into the water by an alligator by punching it on the nose and then swimming away.

LIFE'S CURIOSITIES!

LONG-ARMED RESCUE

When two dolphins at an aquarium in Fushun, China, became sick after chewing plastic, the only man who could save them was Mongolian herdsman Bao Xishun, who is 7 ft 9 in (2.4 m) tall.

He was able to use his 41¾-in (106-cm) long arms to pull the dangerous shards of plastic from the animals' stomachs.

Bao reaches in his arm...

...and removes the plastic.

The offending articles.

The dolphins suffered depression and loss of appetite after nibbling plastic from the edge of their pool. Veterinarians failed to remove the debris with surgical instruments, because the dolphins' stomachs contracted in response to the tools. The arms of ordinary people were unable to reach the plastic, so the Royal Jidi Ocean World aquarium sought the help of Xishun. With the dolphins' jaws held back by towels so that he could stretch in without being bitten, Xishun successfully removed the biggest pieces of plastic. The dolphins were able to digest the few remaining smaller pieces and were expected to make a full recovery.

Toe Transplant

Gaeton Foos from Rochester, New York, lost two fingers and a thumb on his left hand in an accident when he was just three years old. When Gaeton reached the age of six, surgeons from the University of Pittsburgh Medical Center transplanted one of his big toes onto the hand to act as a thumb.

Charmed Life

Mark Cook really does lead a charmed life. The 35-year-old electrician from Oban, Scotland, has cheated death time and time again. He has been involved in two motorbike accidents, has plunged into the sea from a pier, and emerged from a car wreck in which he and his wife were nearly crushed when a truck fell onto their vehicle. Then, in January 2006, he fell 25 ft (7.6 m) down an elevator shaft and came within inches of being impaled on a spike. His family calls him a cat with nine lives.

Favorite Track

Jesse Maggrah was listening through earphones to heavy metal music while walking on Canadian Pacific Railway tracks near Red Deer, Alberta, in April 2006, when he was hit from behind by a train traveling at 30 mph (48 km/h). Believe it or not, he survived!

11-story Fall

In July 2006, four-year-old Hasim Townsend of Albany, New York, survived falling 110 ft (33.5 m) from an 11-story window, bouncing off a metal awning before hitting the ground.

Twins Reunited

Twin Chinese sisters, separated and abandoned in their homeland, were reunited in America after their adoptive parents met by chance on an Internet site. When Diana Ramirez of Miami, Florida, wrote about her daughter Mia Hanying's forthcoming birthday on an Internet site for parents who had adopted from the Chinese orphanage, the message was seen by Holly Funk of Chicago, Illinois. Mrs. Funk wondered whether there was a connection with her own three-year-old daughter Mia, and sure enough it turned out that the two Mias were sisters.

Holy Tooth

A Phoenix, Arizona, dentist claimed that an X ray of one of his patients taken in December 2004 revealed an image that looked like Jesus. The patient described himself as a devout Christian, but said he had never before seen Jesus in a dental X ray.

In Luck

In the 2004 Spanish Christmas lottery, which had prizes totaling $648 million, the jackpot was shared by 195 winning tickets that were sold in the Catalan town of Sort, which means "luck" in the northeastern region's language.

Real Corpse

Florida criminology course tutor Sue Messenger planted cardboard skeletons riddled with fake bullet holes at mock crime scenes. But in 2006, her students from a Fort Lauderdale high school got a shock while combing Holiday Park for clues. They found a real corpse of a homeless man in his fifties.

Dogged Devotion

Michael Monkeymeat from New York City has had his body tattooed at locations all across the globe since the age of 13. The tattoo of a paw print on his left hand was actually applied using ink that included the ashes of Michael's dead dog.

193

Long Tongue

Annika Irmler from Hamburg, Germany, has a tongue that measured an incredible 2¾ in (7 cm) in length when she was just 12 years old, in 2001.

The Future's Orange

Since the age of three, Gemma Williams from Rochdale, England, has suffered from a rare form of dyslexia that meant she could only read and write upside down and back to front. She would astonish friends and family by reading a book or magazine upside down and she even turned her computer screen upside down so that she could read the words. But when she was 17, experts found that, whereas her brain was confused by the glare from plain white paper, the information became clear when viewed through an orange filter. She can write normally on orange paper and read anything using an orange filter. She even hopes to take her driving test—provided she can wear orange glasses.

Head Drill

In 2003, Dr. Keith Sivertson of Shoshone, Idaho, saved Ben King's life by using a $300 power drill to bore a hole in his head. King sustained a head injury after falling down a flight of stairs and, with no neurosurgeon available at his local hospital, Dr. Sivertson made the decision to relieve the growing pressure on King's brain by using the best tools at his disposal.

Sleep-cooking

A former chef who cooks meals in his sleep is receiving medical help amid fears he could burn down his house. Robert Wood of Fife, Scotland, gets up four or five times a week and heads to the kitchen where he has made omelets, stir fries, and chips without waking up.

In a Twist

Matt Suter was picked up and carried nearly a quarter of a mile by a tornado—yet he survived with nothing worse than a scalp wound. He was in his family's trailer home near Fordland, Missouri, in 2006 when it was hit by the twister. Propelled by 150-mph (240-km/h) winds, he was hurled up into the air and thrown over a barbed wire fence before landing in a field.

Fire Reunion

Allen O'Neil, a firefighter from Long Beach, California, treated a woman for smoke inhalation and, upon hearing her name, realized he had helped deliver her as a baby 20 years earlier!

Bladder Growth

Scientists at Wake Forest University, North Carolina, have grown human bladders in a laboratory and have successfully implanted them into patients who require new bladders.

Suicide Attempt

In 2006, a man in Portland, Oregon, survived a suicide attempt in which he shot 12 nails into his head with a nail gun.

Double Tragedy

In August 2006, two brothers were killed in separate motorcycle accidents on the same stretch of road in Butler, Pennsylvania, within two hours of each other. The second was heading to the scene of his brother's accident.

Up to Scratch

In 2006, Harold Gray of Beaufort, South Carolina, won $100,000 on a lottery scratchcard—just 20 days after winning $250,000 on another. And what's more, he used to live on Lottery Lane!

Mammoth Mustache

Ram Singh Chauhan from the Indian state of Rajasthan proudly displays his impressive mustache. At 6 ft 5 in (1.96 m), it is longer than Ram is tall. It's not surprising that his favorite saying is "a man is incomplete without a mustache."

Lucky Escape

In May 2006, a 79-year-old Indiana woman lost control of her car and drove straight through a house and out the other side before striking a tree. She survived, but with serious injuries.

First Births

In both 2004 and 2005, Terri and Mike Gavel had the first baby of the year at Sturdy Memorial Hospital in Attleboro, Massachusetts. Rory Ann was born at 12.16 a.m. on January 2, 2004, and her sister Kelsey arrived at 9.37 p.m. on New Year's Day in 2005.

Bullet Slowed

Near Tampa, Florida, in May 2006, Robin Key survived a .38-caliber gunshot through the windshield of her minivan when the bullet came to rest in her lap after being slowed by hitting her seat belt and bra strap.

Hangover Cure

After having too much to drink, a man from Rogers, Arkansas, fell asleep in his driveway and was run over by his wife! Kristine Bolson was returning home after midnight when she heard a loud cracking sound as she turned the car into the driveway. Her husband, Richard Gonzalez, was taken to hospital, but luckily sustained only minor injuries.

Remarkable Recovery

Brian Paolo of Cheshire, England, woke from a coma after his life support was switched off on February 4, 2006—and ten days later gave his daughter away at her wedding. Doctors had given up on him, but were astounded when, after the machine was switched off, he began to breathe on his own.

Pop-eye

Avelino Perez Matos, of Baracoa, Cuba, had the ability to dislocate each of his eyes out of their sockets whenever he chose.

Eye-mazing

Jalisa Mae Thompson is a high-school student from Atlantic City, New Jersey, with an unusual talent. Since the age of nine, she has been able to roll her tongue and "pop" her eyeballs almost out of their sockets! Jalisa won the Funny Face Contest at the Ripley's Museum in Atlantic City in 2006, and now has her photo displayed there. She says she enjoys popping her eyes because of the surprised and shocked reaction she gets from most people.

New Tongue

A Polish man has a new tongue—amazingly made using tissue taken from his buttocks. After 23-year-old Jarislav Ernst from Gliwice had his old cancerous tongue removed, doctors collected skin, fat, and nerve tissue from his buttocks, and modeled that into a new tongue, which they then sewed into his mouth.

Bottle Voyage

A bottle dropped into the sea by a four-year-old girl in England was washed ashore six months later in Australia—9,000 mi (14,500 km) away. Alesha Johnson launched the bottle, which contained her name and the address of her nursery school in Lancashire, in July 2005 and, in January 2006, it was found by a boy in a boatyard near Perth.

Musical Urn

When Winona, Minnesota, musician Roger Busdicker died in 2006, his ashes were put in his clarinet! His family decided that the ebony and silver clarinet that he had played for the last 50 years was the ideal resting place for his cremated remains, and what didn't fit in the instrument itself went into the lining of the case.

Bear Attack

Bill Murphy of Alaska survived being attacked by a grizzly bear in September 2003, then bound his wounds with duct tape, rode his all-terrain vehicle 15 mi (24 km) to his truck, and drove himself another half-hour to the hospital.

Ice Bite

When Hungarian skater Ani Zoltany fell through ice and into a freezing lake in February 2006, she survived by holding on to the broken ice with her teeth for ten minutes. She had been practicing on Lake Velence when the ice cracked and, as frostbite set in her hands, the only way she could keep her head above water until help arrived was to grip the ice with her teeth.

Three Aces

Playing at a course in Edinburgh, Scotland, golfer Stewart Sneddon hit a hole in one at the same hole on three consecutive Saturdays in 2006. Each time, he aced the 147-yd (134-m) 13th hole with an eight-iron, beating odds of two trillion to one!

Slept On

John Betteridge of Quispamsis, New Brunswick, Canada, fell victim to an electrical fault that sent 7,200 volts surging through his home, exploding lamps and appliances. His son, John Jr., slept through the ordeal unharmed—in a metal bed.

Big Baby

A 14-lb (6.3-kg) girl born at a Brazilian hospital in 2006 was so large that her feet reached over the edge of the crib. Isabel Vitoria Ribeiro measured nearly 2 ft (60 cm) long at birth.

Multiple Births

Angela Magdaleno of Los Angeles, California, gave birth to seven children in just three years. In 2003, she gave birth to triplets and in July 2006, she had quadruplets, bringing her total number of children to nine. The odds of conceiving quads without fertility drugs, as Mrs. Magdaleno did, are one in 800,000.

Lightning Lady

They say that lightning never strikes twice—this is certainly true in the case of 84-year-old Christine Moody from Somerset, England, who has actually been struck no less than four times! Christine suffered her first shock in 1980 while she was having a cup of tea in a hotel; the second strike happened 22 years later when she was at a friend's funeral; the third when she was walking down a street near her home six months later; and the fourth while she was lying in bed in December 2004. Luckily, Christine was not seriously injured by any of the strikes, but they have left her "allergic" to electricity and she experiences pain if she gets too close to electrical appliances.

Jeanie in her performing days in 1933 with the Barnum and Bailey and Ringling Brothers Combined Circus Sideshow.

Savior Saved

In 2006, a teenager who saved the life of an apparent stranger in a restaurant in Buffalo, New York, was amazed to discover that it was a woman who had done the same for him in 1999. Volunteer firefighter and boy scout Kevin Stephan, 17, rushed to perform the Heimlich maneuver when he saw Penny Brown choking on her lunch, and only learned afterwards that she was the nurse who had got his heart beating again following a baseball accident seven years earlier.

Happy Ending

A pregnant woman who fell 10,000 ft (3,050 m) in a 2005 skydiving accident gave birth to a healthy baby boy eight months later. When both her parachute and the reserve failed to open on her first solo skydive, Shayna West of Joplin, Missouri, spiraled out of control and landed face first in a parking lot at 50 mph (80 km/h), breaking her pelvis, five teeth, and shattering several facial bones. She had to have 15 metal plates inserted in her face. She hadn't known she was pregnant at the time.

Foreign Accent

Waking up following a stroke in 2006, an English woman found that her usual Newcastle accent had been transformed into a mixture of Jamaican, Canadian, Italian, and Slovakian. Linda Walker, 60, from Newcastle upon Tyne, was thought to be suffering from Foreign Accent Syndrome, an illness recognized since World War II whereby patients speak differently after a brain injury. Researchers have discovered that patients with the syndrome have suffered damage to tiny areas of the brain that affect speech. The resultant elongated or clipped vowels make it sound as if they are speaking in a foreign accent.

Milk Diet

An 88-year-old Indian farmer from the state of Rajasthan fathered a child in 2006—by drinking up to 3/4 gal (3 l) camel's milk a day. Virmaram Jat claimed the milk was an aphrodisiac, and as a result the price of camel's milk in India doubled overnight.

A Woman with Half a Body

Jeanie Tomaini was born without any legs and twisted arms on August 23, 1916 in Indiana. Jeanie began performing at the age of three with U.S. sideshows as "The Half Girl" where she would perform acrobatic stunts, including handstands and cartwheels. Despite her deformed hands, Jeanie was able to function fully and independently, even managing to walk on them. At the age of 15 Jeanie was adopted, after her mother died two years previously. She was forced to perform continually at circus sideshows until she fell in love with fellow sideshow worker, Aurelio "Al" Tomaini, who was 8 ft (2.4 m) tall! As a full adult Jeanie only ever reached a height of 2 ft 6 in (76 cm) and retired with her husband in the 1940s, until she passed away in 1999 at the impressive age of 82!

Personality Change

A Croatian lumberjack complained that a kidney transplant from a 50-year-old woman had left him addicted to housework. Stjepan Lizacic said he had not been warned about the possible side effects of the transplant, which, in his case, were a newfound passion for ironing, sewing, and knitting.

BEAR CRAWL

Five members of a family in southern Turkey get around by walking on all fours in a "bear crawl." Some scientists believe they could be evidence of backward evolution.

Three sisters and one brother from the large 19-member Ulas family have only ever walked on two palms and two feet, while another sibling only occasionally manages a form of normal human walking. Although all five can stand up, it is only for a short time and with both knees and head flexed.

Unlike gorillas and chimpanzees, who walk on their knuckles, the affected Turkish siblings, who are all aged between 18 and 34, use their heavily callused palms as heels, keeping their fingers angled up from the ground. Their quadrupedal gait has never before been reported in anatomically intact adult humans. Their language is also primitive. They cannot count from one to ten and do not know in which country they live. However, the four sisters can do needlework.

Their mother said they started walking at ten months, but began using their hands and never walked normally after that time.

The Ulas family show attributes of our apelike ancestors, before the switch to upright walking.

Butter River

A fire at a dairy plant in New Ulm, Minnesota, in December 2005 released a million-dollar wave of melted butter that covered streets, ruined firefighters' equipment, and clogged storm drains.

Ring Returned

Linda Blardo of Zephyrhills, Florida, lost her high-school class ring at a local swimming spot. Thirty-four years later, the ring was found in a Georgia state park 470 mi (756 km) away from the place where she lost it.

Swallowed Nails

Doctors in Vietnam removed 119 rusty 3-in (75-mm) nails from a woman's stomach in 2006! The 43-year-old woman had gone to the hospital with severe stomach pains, and X rays revealed the nails and other strange objects.

Three of a Kind

English comedian Vic Reeves shares the same real name, Jim Moir, and the same birthday—January 24—as both his father and his grandfather.

A Fine Mess

Matthew Buer of Essex, England, was fined by two different borough councils for littering in February 2006. The French fries that he had been tossing from his car as he drove along landed in two different boroughs.

Twincredible

Less than 18 months after identical twin Joanne Johnson married identical twin Richard McGee, she gave birth—to identical twin sons. Experts say the odds of such a thing happening are infinite. And what's more, the doctor at Royal Preston Hospital, Lancashire, England, who told the couple that they were expecting twins, was also an identical twin!

Car Found

Alan Poster was reunited with his beloved car—37 years after it had been stolen. The brand-new Corvette vanished from his New York garage in 1969, but was spotted in November 2005 on a ship bound for Sweden. Although the car was silver instead of blue and lacked a gas tank and radiator, it was worth about $20,000—three times what he had paid for it.

Unlucky Strikes

Mrs. G. Patterson of Baltimore, Maryland, and her two daughters all had their homes hit by lightning on the exact same day—March 17, 1996.

Double Injury

Twins Cassidy and Marissa Wiese of Laurel, Nebraska, both had roller skating accidents on the same day that resulted in each breaking their left arm.

Macabre Coincidence

Two women, both named April and with the middle name Dawn, lived in different parts of Fairfax County, Virginia, and dated 22-year-old men. In December 2005, in another amazing coincidence, both women were charged in separate murder-for-hire plots with trying to have those boyfriends killed.

Iron Lung

When he died in February 2006, polio patient John Prestwich of Chipperfield, England, had spent more than 50 years breathing with the help of a machine. He contracted polio in 1955 when he was 17 and was left totally paralyzed below his chin. Without the iron lung, which was then fitted to his chest, he would have died in minutes as he was unable to breathe for himself. Despite his incapacity, he went to the top of the Eiffel Tower in Paris, flew in a helicopter, and took a spin on the "London Eye" big wheel in London.

Age Gap

In northern Malaysia in 2006, a 33-year-old man, Muhamad Noor Che Musa, married a 104-year-old woman, Wook Kundor, saying their friendship had turned to love. It was his first marriage, and her 21st.

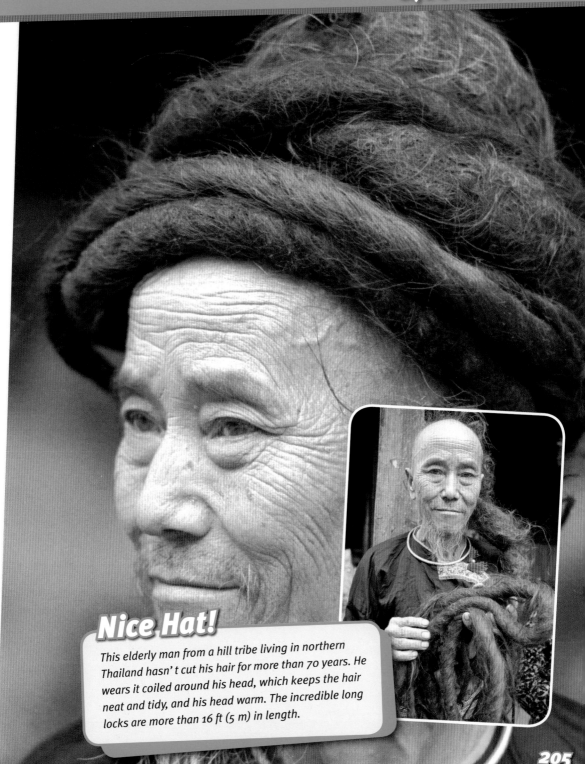

Nice Hat!

This elderly man from a hill tribe living in northern Thailand hasn't cut his hair for more than 70 years. He wears it coiled around his head, which keeps the hair neat and tidy, and his head warm. The incredible long locks are more than 16 ft (5 m) in length.

An Ill Wind...

After repeated hurricanes pounded the Florida coast in 2004, Joel Ruth examined the beach and found 180 Spanish silver coins that dated back about 300 years and were worth $40,000.

Lucky Ball

Playing at a course in Cleveland, Ohio, in July 2006, eight-year-old Harrison Vonderau hit two holes in one with the same golf ball in the space of 20 minutes!

Dog Driver

A woman in Hohhot, China, crashed her car in 2006—while giving her dog a driving lesson. The woman, Li, said her dog liked to crouch on the steering wheel and watch her drive, so she thought she would let it "have a try" while she operated the accelerator and brake.

Cotton-picking Delight

Double-thumbed cotton picker R.L. Stubblefield from Italy, Texas, had two thumbs on his right hand, which enabled him to pick an amazing 300 lb (136 kg) of cotton a day during the 1930s.

Horned Man

This photo was sent to Robert Ripley in the early 1940s, shortly after Ripley published a cartoon showing a man with a horn growing from his head. The sender said that it shows a man who lived in China in the late 1930s.

Stone Car

The mausoleum of the late Raymond Tse Jr. in Rosehill Cemetery, New Jersey, has a full-size stone Mercedes parked in the back of it.

Premature Diagnosis

While lying in a morgue in January 2005, hours after being pronounced dead at the scene of a car accident in North Carolina, Larry Green was seen breathing. His condition was upgraded to alive!

Bearded Lady

Grace Gilbert was the famous bearded lady with the Barnum and Bailey circus in the early years of the 20th century. Grace stood 5 ft 9 in (1.75 m) in height and her beard measured an impressive 10 in (25 cm).

Suitcase Returned

In 2004, Beverly Sherman of Lakewood, Washington, got back a suitcase containing her belongings that had been lost in a car accident in Lake Crescent—44 years earlier.

Acrobatic Tumble

Steven Jehu, a British junior gymnast, survived a 35-ft (10.6-m) fall from a fourth-floor hotel window. And he did a somersault on the way down so he could land on his feet.

Chest Impalement

While 8½ months pregnant, Jessie Wickham of Ann Arbor, Michigan, was accidentally impaled through her upper chest after falling onto a microphone stand in June 2003. She survived without serious injury and later gave birth to a healthy baby boy.

Fatal Funeral

Two people were killed at a funeral in the Dutch town of Vorden in 2006. The victims, who were musicians performing at the funeral of an elderly man, had been sheltering under a tree in the churchyard when the tree was struck by lightning.

Sheep Struck

Croatian shepherd Milan Prpic lost no fewer than 230 sheep during a single lightning strike in 2006. The dead animals represented half his flock.

Lofty Lady

Yao Defen, from Anhui Province in eastern China, stands an incredible 7 ft 8 in (2.36 m) tall. Seen here outside her home with a friend of average size in 2006 at 36-years-old, Defen suffers from agromegaly, a disease whereby a tumor on her pituitary gland caused excessive growth hormone to be produced in her body. She underwent surgery that partially removed the tumor when she was 28, but needs further operations to keep her condition in check.

Three-armed Baby

When a young Chinese mother, Xu, first set eyes on her new baby, she was amazed to see that the little boy had been born with three arms. Jie-jie was born in Anhui province in April 2006 with two left arms and one right arm. Although they were unusually complete, neither of the two left arms was fully functional and doctors decided to amputate the arm growing closer to his chest because it was thinner and always crooked. This arm was successfully removed in a three-hour operation. Jie-jie will need long-term physiotherapy to build up the strength in his remaining left arm.

Extra Heart

The body of a British tourist who died on holiday in Ireland in 2006 was flown back to the U.K. with an extra heart and pair of lungs. The extra organs were found in a plastic bag stitched inside the man's body.

Trapped Nut

Doctors feared that 67-year-old Derek Kirchen from Norfolk, England, had lung cancer as he had suffered from pneumonia eight times. But the cause was found to be a cashew nut that had been stuck in his lung for 18 months.

Late Graduate

Bob Brophy of Hillsboro, Missouri, is blind yet he graduated from college at the age of 72 with perfect grades.

Two Wombs

A woman with two wombs in Cariacica, Brazil, gave birth to healthy twin babies—one child from each womb, in May 2003.

Wallet Returned

In 2006, a lengthy 35 years after Gary Karafiat of Naperville, Illinois, lost his wallet in high school, it was returned to him—totally intact!

Same Fish

In July 2006, English angler Bob Watton from Poole, Dorset, caught the same fish twice within three days—two miles out at sea. The first time he hooked the 11-lb (5-kg) sea bass, his line snagged on a rock and the fish escaped. But three days later—at around the same spot off the Dorset coast—he reeled in a 2-ft (60-cm) bass that he recognized as being the same fish from the distinctive hook and broken line of the previous attempt.

Three-legged Man

Francisco Lentini was born in Sicily, Italy, in 1889 with three legs. He moved to the U.S.A. at the age of nine, and became a circus star. Lentini was highly successful, married with four children, and lived to the age of 77, but sometimes used to complain that even with three legs, he still didn't have a pair!

MERMAID GIRL

Little Milagros Cerrón certainly lives up to her name. For Milagros, which means "miracles" in Spanish, is truly a miracle baby—she is one of only three children in the world known to have survived the rare condition sirenomelia or "mermaid syndrome."

The condition—which occurs in approximately one in every 100,000 live births—causes the legs to be fused like the tail of a mermaid. Usually such babies die within days of birth but, in 2005, surgeons in Lima, Peru, carried out two successful operations on Milagros—first to separate her knees, then her thighs. Although she will need continued treatment for the next ten years, Milagros has already taken her first tentative steps.

Hitz Misses

At age 14, George Hitz sent a postcard with an incorrect address to California from his home in DeLand, Florida. That was in 1956—and it was returned by the Post Office 50 years later!

Snail Nail!

Bud Hart of Placerville, California, coughed up a rusty nail in February 2006—35 years after it had been embedded in his lung! The nail had pierced his body while he was mowing the grass and remained there until he coughed it up after brushing his teeth.

Amazing Tail

An Indian man is being worshiped because he has a tail 13 in (33 cm) long! Because of the tail—caused by a congenital defect—villagers believe that Chandre Oram, from Alipurduar in West Bengal, is an incarnation of Hindu monkey god Hanuman. Oram, who has refused all offers by doctors to have the tail removed and who also loves climbing trees and eating bananas, said: "People have a lot of faith in me. They are cured of severe ailments when they touch my tail. I believe I can do a lot of good to those who come to me with devotion."

Miniature Man

Although he was born in 1992, Khagendra Thapa Magar of Baglung, western Nepal, stands just 20 in (51 cm) tall and weighs less than 10 lb (4.5 kg). His mother said he didn't start moving around until he was eight and his physical growth stopped at the age of 11.

Flat Daddies

Although serving in Iraq or Afghanistan, members of the Maine National Guard are never far from their families. In fact, they ride with them in cars, sit at the dinner table, visit the dentist, watch soccer games, and even go to confession—all as life-size cutouts! As part of its family-support program, the National Guard has produced a series of Flat Daddies and Mummies. Photos of the service personnel in uniform from the waist up are enlarged and printed and the families then glue them to a $2 piece of foam board. Kay Judkins, whose husband Jim is a minesweeper mechanic in Afghanistan, says of her cutout, which she calls Slim Jim: "I prop him up in a chair, or sometimes put him on a couch and cover him with a blanket. The cat will curl up on the blanket, and it looks kind of weird. I've tricked several people by that. They think he's home again."

Whirlwind Toss

While four-year-old Grace Hove of Trenton, North Dakota, was hopping on a trampoline on May 7, 2006, a whirlwind picked her up and tossed her more than 25 ft (7.6 m) into the air! Grace survived with a broken arm and pelvis, and lots of bruises.

Tongue Swallower

Nicole Shaffer from Cocoa, Florida, has an extraordinarily long tongue, which she can also "swallow!" Because Nicole is missing a small skin flap at the back of her throat, when she points her tongue backwards, it travels along the roof of her mouth and goes down her throat, as if it has been swallowed. After accomplishing her feat, Nicole immediately retrieves her tongue without any difficulty.

Robot Clone

Hiroshi Ishiguro of Japan created a robot duplicate of himself so that he could teach his classes from a remote connection!

Grouper's Revenge

A 42-year-old diver shot a large grouper fish with a spear gun in 25 ft (7.6 m) of water off the Florida Keys in September 2006, but then drowned when the fish darted into a hole in a coral rock, entangling the man in the fishing line that was attached to the spear. The grouper had managed to wrap the spear line around the diver's waist and when it sped into the hole the man found himself effectively pinned to the bottom of the ocean.

Brown Snow

On February 16, 2006, brown snow fell across most of the state of Colorado. A wind storm in northern Arizona probably kicked up dust, which then fell to the ground with the snow.

Snake Bite

A man crashed his car in Naples, Florida, in 2006 after the pet snake he had wrapped around his neck suddenly bit him. The man was seen climbing out of the car and wrestling with the snake before driving off.

Police Lemmings

When a suspect ran straight off a 50-ft (15-m) cliff in Princeton, West Virginia, in July 2006, two police officers jumped over the edge to make an arrest. Only the suspect was seriously injured.

Big Baby

Born on January 28, 2007, Antonio Cruz is causing quite a stir in his home town of Cancún, Mexico, on account of his prodigious size. For baby Antonio, known as "Super Tonio," was born weighing a whopping 14 lb 1½ oz (6.4 kg) and measuring 21¾ in (55 cm) in length. Delivered by Cesarean section, he is a healthy baby brother to his seven-year-old sister, who weighed almost 11½ lb (5.2 kg) at birth herself. Antonio is seen here at three days old, next to an average sized baby, having already gained 7 oz (200 g)!

Skin Disorder

Despite being born with a rare and fatal skin disorder called Harlequin Ichthyosis, a disease that causes skin to develop into a hard shell, Ryan Gonzalez of San Diego, California, is now a successful young triathlete.

Nervous Robber

A 60-year-old man who robbed a bank in Troy, Michigan, in 2006 emerged from the bank with his haul of cash, spotted a passing police car, and promptly fainted.

On Time

There was a timely arrival for Samantha Noble of Florida who gave birth to her third child at 3.33 p.m. on March 3, 2003.

Soul Sale

A Chinese man from Jiaxing, near Shanghai, attracted bids from 58 would-be buyers in 2006 when he tried to sell his soul on-line. Taobao, a Chinese Internet auction site, eventually stopped the sale because it needed proof that the seller could actually provide the goods.

Funeral Service

Students from St. Ignatius High School in Cleveland, Ohio, have a volunteer pallbearer club that donates its services to nearby funeral homes.

Timely Arrivals

While driving alone on April 21, 2006, Carolyn Holt of St. Peters, Missouri, had a heart attack—and three of the first four people who stopped to help were two registered nurses and a defibrillator salesman.

Lobster Thief

A swimmer who lost his wallet on a late-night dip in the sea had it returned a few days later—after it was found in the claws of a lobster. Paul Westlake of Plymouth, Devon, England, thought he had seen the last of his wallet until a deep-sea diver discovered it in the clutches of a lobster on the ocean floor.

Fantastic Nails

On a whim back in 1979, Lee Redmond of Salt Lake City, Utah, decided to stop trimming her fingernails. She intended cutting them once they started twisting but somehow the idea of keeping them intact just grew and grew—and so did her nails. They measured an incredible 33 in (84 cm) long! And she says they would be even longer but for the fact that they broke once when she stepped on them. She concedes: "It's pretty bad when you're stepping on your own fingernails!" The great-grandmother admits that opening doors is not easy, nor is putting on a heavy winter coat. "By the time you thread the nails down through the coat, it's a tough job." Redmond is so attached to her nails that she even turned down $100,000 to part with them. "People always ask me, 'Don't they get in your way?' I say, 'No, they get in everybody else's way but mine. I'm used to them being in my way.'" Unfortunately, Lee's nails broke off in a car accident in February 2009.

Leg Stolen

Melissa Huff of Arcadia, California, had her prosthetic leg stolen and returned by a burglar twice in the space of five months. She lost her real leg in 2003 when a car hit her on the sidewalk.

Coughed Up

Chris Brown of Cheltenham, Gloucestershire, England, finally coughed up a twig 1 in (2.5 cm) long that had been stuck in his lung for 20 years!

Janitor's Legacy

When Genesio Morlacci retired, he took a part-time janitor's job at the University of Great Falls in Montana for a short while. And, wishing other people to have the education that he hadn't, when Genesio died at the age of 102, he left a gift of $2.3 million to the university.

Bit Off Tongue

In the course of a disturbance on May 13, 2006, Kaijuan Corbett of Brooklyn, New York, bit off his own tongue and spat it at police officers.

Chimney Tumble

Phil Harrison of Yorkshire, England, survived a 30-ft (9-m) fall from a mill chimney in 2006 because he landed in a pile of pigeon poop! Although he broke his neck as he plunged to the basement of the building, the impact was cushioned by a layer of bird droppings 6 in (15 cm) deep.

Believe It or Not!

Big Hair

Aaron Studham gives a whole new meaning to having "big hair." The high-school student from Massachusetts has a Mohawk that reaches a magnificent 21 in (53 cm) in height. Taking up to an hour and a lot of hairspray and blow-drying to create, the gravity-defying hairstyle is, according to Aaron, a "real icebreaker with the girls."

Debt Repaid

A man saved by a stranger from drowning in an icy Bosnian river 20 years earlier repaid the favor by donating a kidney to his rescuer. Remzo Pivic kept in touch with the brave rescuer, Ahmet Adulovic, even after the latter emigrated to Canada. And when he heard that Adulovic was suffering kidney problems, Pivic flew to Ottawa to donate the organ as a way to say thank you.

Mad Max

Runner Max Springer from Knoxville, Tennessee, competes in track-and-field meets and runs marathons even though he's 92!

Parallel Lives

When long-lost New York sisters Peggy Lill and Gladys Nohlquist found each other after 79 years in 2006, they discovered that they had led remarkably similar lives. Since being separated at an orphanage in 1927, both were raised on farms, both went back to school in middle age and became nurses, both were married twice, and both had five children—four girls and a boy!

Digger Hero

In July 2006, 45-year-old Colin O'Neill of Bury, England, lifted a three-ton backhoe digger off 14-year-old neighbor Jon Ashley Entwisle and held it for 20 minutes until he was rescued.

Unusual Reptiles

Fred Lally of West Fork, Arkansas, is an avid collector of mutant reptiles. He has been catching, selling, and exhibiting reptiles since he was a child and has provided a home for albino turtles and snakes, two-headed reptiles, and conjoined turtles, including one with two heads and six legs.

Final Struggle

In a desperate attempt to land a 150-lb (68-kg) catfish, a Hungarian fisherman drowned when he was dragged into the Szamos River in Hungary because he refused to let go of the line. It is thought he died after hitting his head on a rock. When the man's body was found, he was still clinging to his rod with the 4-ft (1.2-m) monster catfish hooked on the end.

Chocolate Dip

A man was trapped waist deep in a tank of thick chocolate for two hours in 2006. Darmin Garcia accidentally slid into the hopper at a chocolate factory in Kenosha, Wisconsin, and firefighters had to thin the chocolate with cocoa butter before they could free him.

Three Antlers

John Moore of Crestline, Ohio, bagged a three-antlered deer on the opening day of the state's 2004 hunting season.

Side Effect

A Scottish grandfather suffering from a rare disease found an unexpected side effect to his treatment—it made him look 20 years younger! When 62-year-old Reggie Myles of Clackmannanshire was struck down by the genetic disorder porphyria cutanea tarda, his mop of grey hair fell out and his weight plummeted from 230 lb (104 kg) to just 98 lb (44 kg). But after his treatment, his hair returned in a dark brown shade and most of his wrinkles vanished. And now he's often mistaken for his sons!

Speared by Fish

While fishing off Bermuda in 2006, Ian Card was impaled on the bill of a 14-ft (4.3-m) blue marlin that leaped over his boat. The 800-lb (363-kg) fish hit Card with such force that its 3-ft (90-cm) spear went through his chest and knocked him into the sea. As the fish dived, forcing Card underwater, he was able to push himself off the razor-sharp bill and swim to the surface with blood pouring from his chest wound. He was rushed to King Edward VII Memorial Hospital in Bermuda where he underwent emergency surgery. Doctors said that he would have died had the bill struck him a fraction of an inch to either side.

Family Business

When an adopted Iowa woman tracked down her biological mother, she was stunned to learn that they had once worked together. Michelle Wetzell, who was adopted when she was four days old, discovered that her real mother was a former colleague at a beauty salon in Davenport.

Ear Reattached

Doctors reattached a seven-year-old boy's ear after it was retrieved from the stomach of a Doberman Pinscher that had bitten it off. Brandon Olivas of Whittier, New Jersey, was attacked by two dogs in 1987, and his right ear was bitten off and then swallowed by the Doberman.

Tortoises Separated

A pair of conjoined tortoises born joined at the belly were successfully separated at an animal hospital in Tempe, Arizona, in 2004.

Severed Hand

When farmer Gerhard Frank accidentally sliced off his hand while splitting logs in Steeg, Austria, in 2006, he calmly packed it in his chilled lunchbox, and drove 3 mi (4.8 km) home. There, his wife put the severed hand in the refrigerator and it was later successfully reattached at Innsbruck Hospital.

Late Delivery

A postcard that a mother mailed to her son in 1948 was finally delivered 58 years later—after the town's postmaster bought it on eBay. Judy Dishman, from Spiceland, Indiana, bought the postcard because she liked the local view, but when she saw it was addressed to 82-year-old Charles Rose, she delivered it. The card turned out to be from Rose's late mother, Dollie.

Autistic Star

Jason McElwain overcame his autism to become probably the most famous basketball player in the U.S.A. for a few days in February 2006. McElwain, who didn't begin talking until he was five, was too small to make his high-school team in Rochester, New York, but because of his passion for the game he was appointed manager. Impressed by his dedication, coach Jim Johnson decided to put the 18-year-old on court for the last few minutes of the final home game of the season, and McElwain responded by scoring 20 points in four minutes to send the crowd wild. Within two months McElwain had agreed to allow Columbia Pictures to produce a film of his remarkable story.

Implanted Horns

Among a variety of unusual facial modifications, Louis Sanchez III's silicone implanted horns are probably the most extreme. So far, Sanchez, from Phoenix, Arizona, has had six procedures on his silicone horns, and he hopes to have more.

PIERCING MARATHON

Kam Ma, a hairdresser from Sunderland, England, had 1,015 metal rings pierced into his body in a marathon nonstop, unanesthetized piercing session in 2006.

Kam had been aiming for a massive 3,000 piercings, but his body went into shock after almost nine hours and more than a thousand rings. The rings were later removed. Kam fully recovered and is delighted with his achievement.

Stomach Churning

Matt "The Tube" Crowley, a pharmacist from Seattle, Washington, swallows 7 ft (2.1 m) of tubing through his nose, pours over a gallon of liquid into the tube, and then extracts it after it reaches his stomach. Even more shocking, fans drink the fluid after he's finished! Crowley can also use sheer lung power to blow up a hot water bottle until it bursts.

Weird Heirloom

The Peavy family of New Hampshire has passed down a mummified baby as a family heirloom since its discovery in a relative's home in 1947.

Ring Found

Diane Kurtz of Hartford, Connecticut, lost her engagement ring down a drain and had it returned to her 15 years later by a sewage treatment plant worker.

Methane Blaze

A fire started at a New Zealand hospital in 2006 after a patient broke wind. The fire was caused by methane in his flatulence igniting a spark from the electrical machine that was being used to remove his hemorrhoids.

Special Date

Dean Stephens and his daughter Brylee of Victoria, Australia, were both leap-year babies born on 29 February—that's odds of one in two million!

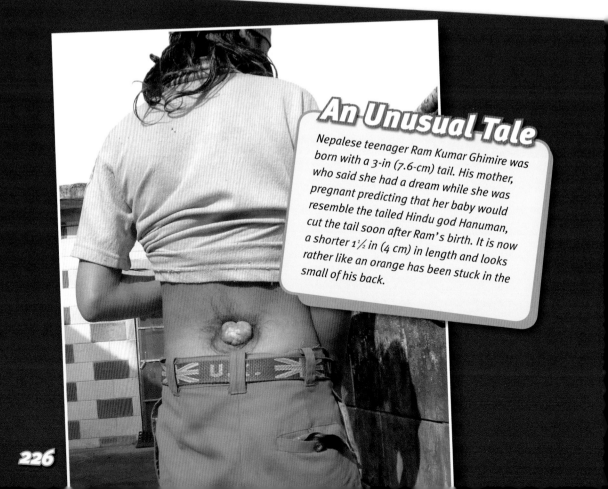

An Unusual Tale

Nepalese teenager Ram Kumar Ghimire was born with a 3-in (7.6-cm) tail. His mother, who said she had a dream while she was pregnant predicting that her baby would resemble the tailed Hindu god Hanuman, cut the tail soon after Ram's birth. It is now a shorter 1½ in (4 cm) in length and looks rather like an orange has been stuck in the small of his back.

Painless Pins

In the 1930s, B.A. Bryant was able to stick a hundred pins into his body without feeling any pain. He performed his feat at the Ripley's Believe It or Not! odditorium in Dallas, Texas.

Melted Cross

Russian teenager Marina Motygina survived a 2006 lightning strike that was so potent it melted a gold cross on her neck. The bolt hit her on the top of her head and seared through her body into the ground, destroying the necklace that she was wearing and leaving burns in the shape of a cross on her neck.

Struck Twice

Lightning has struck twice in the case of Florida construction worker Emory Johnson. In 1986, he was hit by a bolt as he sat in his truck, then, in 2005, he was working outside at Spring Hill when lightning hit him again. He said afterward: "There was a loud bang, and it felt like I was burning inside, and I passed out."

Accidental Meeting

Brothers Joe and George Ipser of Cleveland, Ohio, hadn't seen each other in 20 years until they were accidentally reunited at a local hospital on New Year's Eve.

Migration Clue

Scientists at the University of Massachusetts School of Medicine have determined that monarch butterflies use the angle and intensity of sunlight to set their internal clocks and migrate from eastern U.S.A. to Mexico.

Impressive Ear Hair

Seen here in February 2002, B.D. Tyagi from Bhopal, India, proudly displays long strands of hair growing from his ears that measured an incredible 4 in (10 cm) in length.

Heart-shaped Nostrils

Eleven-year-old Robin Boyce from Vancouver, Washington state, was born with heart-shaped nostrils!

Lotto Luck

In December 2002, husband and wife Angelo and Maria Gallina of Belmont, California, won two separate lottery jackpots of $17 million and $126,000 on the same day—that's odds of one in 24 trillion!

Speed Chase

A driver in La Porte, Indiana, led police on a high-speed, 70-mph (113-km/h) chase despite having sustained a broken collarbone, bleeding on the brain, and a fractured spine in an all-terrain vehicle accident.

Surrogate Gran

Tina Cade of Richmond, Virginia, gave birth to three of her own grandchildren on December 28, 2004! The 58-year-old was carrying the triplets as a surrogate for her daughter.

Secret Language

Identical four-year-old twins Luke and Jack Ryan from Cleckheaton, West Yorkshire, England, have developed their own language. The boys chat away to each other using made-up words that their parents struggle to understand.

Human Pincushion

Under his stage name "Happy the Human Pincushion," Dave Haskell of Chicago, Illinois, inserts spears, hooks, and other objects into his skin. He also lifts and pulls weights from his various body piercings.

Healed Heart

When Adrian Reid, aged two, of Akron, Ohio, suffered burns after accidentally spilling hot coffee on himself, the blister on his chest healed in the shape of a heart directly above his heart!

Natural Diet

Stranded in the Australian Outback in 2006, Ricky Megee of Brisbane, Queensland, said he survived for three months by eating leeches, frogs, grasshoppers, and lizards.

Smashing Time

Visiting the Fitzwilliam Museum, Cambridge, England, in January 2006, Nick Flynn tripped on a shoelace, tumbled down a flight of stairs, and smashed into three 17th-century porcelain Chinese vases, worth a total of $600,000. The vases, which had stood on an open windowsill for more than 40 years, shattered into hundreds of pieces and it took six months to repair just one of them.

Face Transplant

In November 2005, Isabelle Dinoire received the world's first partial face transplant in a 15-hour operation in Amiens, France. Isabelle had been severely disfigured after being bitten by her dog in May 2005, and agreed to the idea of a face transplant immediately. After waiting six months for a suitable donor, she had the ground-breaking surgery and is now doing well and able to smile again.

Pencil Piercing

Eleven-year-old Ben McKinley, of McComb, Mississippi, survived falling off a balance beam and landing on a pencil that pierced his chest and heart.

Three-way Tie

In 2002, in a general election in Comal County, Texas, County Judge Danny Scheel received 18,181 votes, State Senator Jeff Wentworth got 18,181 votes, and State representative Carter Casteel also got 18,181 votes!

Hearing Returned

A 72-year-old man who had been deaf for 15 years suddenly got his hearing back on a 2006 skiing trip. Derek Glover, from Lincolnshire, England, was descending from 7,000 ft (2,135 m) in a cable car when his ears suddenly popped and he was hit by an "incredible wave" of noise. It is thought that the miracle return of his hearing was the result of a sudden change in air pressure.

Extra Claws

A "mutant" crab with three pincers was caught off the coast of Cornwall, England, in 2006. Crabs can regrow lost or damaged limbs and claws, but experts believe this 8-in (20-cm) long edible crab's ability to regenerate lost limbs became confused and, rather than replacing a missing set of claws, it managed to grow an extra pair instead.

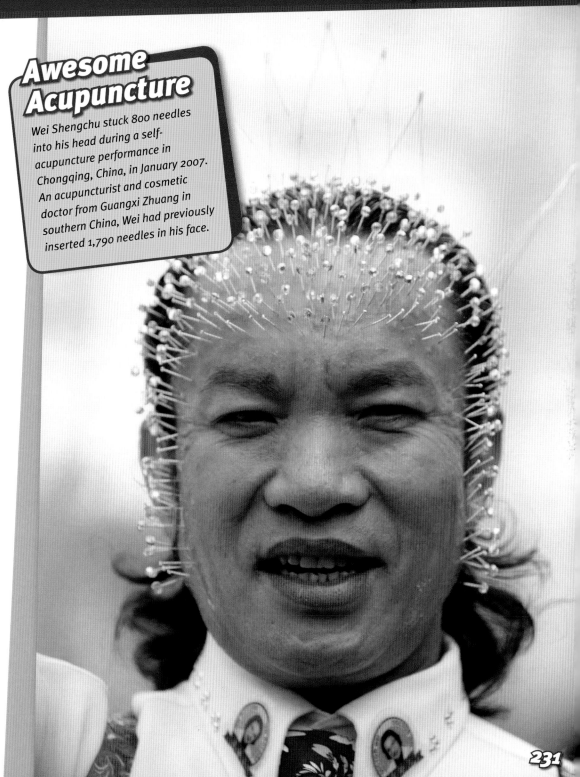

Awesome Acupuncture

Wei Shengchu stuck 800 needles into his head during a self-acupuncture performance in Chongqing, China, in January 2007. An acupuncturist and cosmetic doctor from Guangxi Zhuang in southern China, Wei had previously inserted 1,790 needles in his face.

CURIOUS CREATIONS!

DRIFTWOOD HORSES

Heather Jansch of Devon, England, makes incredible sculptures of horses... from old pieces of wood that are washed up on beaches.

She had the idea for creating driftwood artworks when her son, looking for wood to light a fire, chopped a piece of ivy that had grown round a fencing stake. He left behind a section that she thought would make a good horse's torso for the copper wire sculpture on which she was working. She makes both small and life-size equine sculptures. Her larger sculptures have a steel frame, which is coated with fiberglass to roughen it up and stop the wood from slipping, as it would do on bare metal. When Heather is happy with the position of the pieces of driftwood, they are tied with wire and then screwed together to hold them in place. The animals' hooves are made from old copper immersion heater tanks. As she usually places her finished works in natural, outdoor environments,

such as fields, they must be self-supporting and sturdy enough to cope with high winds without falling over. And for exhibitions, they need to be able to withstand being lifted by crane. Heather's biggest problem is a lack of driftwood. Her full-size sculptures require a number of pieces from which she selects the best. She often has to travel miles to find suitable specimens.

Heather finds the driftwood for her sculptures on beaches after high tides and storms.

Turkey Sounds

U.S. artist Jay Jones created "audio sculptures" by playing the sounds of gobbling turkeys to Christmas shoppers in West Yorkshire, England.

Shark Watch

The Pentagon is hoping to use remote-controlled sharks as possible spies. U.S. engineers have created a neural implant—a series of electrodes embedded into the brain—that is designed to enable the signals of a shark's brain to be manipulated remotely. They plan to test the device on blue sharks off the coast of Florida.

Wooden 'Gator

In 2005, Michael Smith of Baton Rouge, Louisiana, made a solid toothpick alligator from about three million toothpicks! He has also made a wearable hat, a saxophone, a fully functional briefcase, and delicate butterflies—all from common toothpicks.

Edible Exhibition

A show at an art gallery in Brighton, England, gave visitors a chance to eat the exhibits in 2005. "The Lost Apple Field" presented 700 varieties of apples to highlight how people have lost touch with traditional farming.

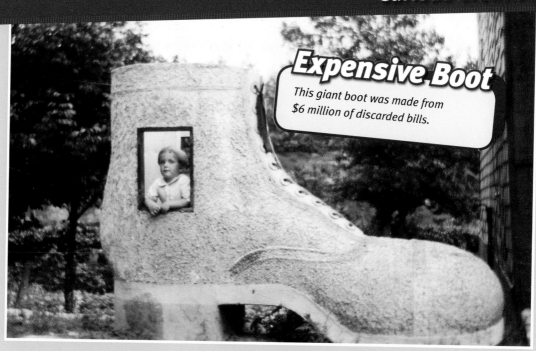

Expensive Boot

This giant boot was made from $6 million of discarded bills.

Brush Strokes

Calligrapher Zhang Kesi writes the Chinese character "Long" (dragon) on a banner measuring 190 ft (58 m) long and 92 ft (28 m) wide in China. Kesi used a brush 18 ft (5.5 m) long and 6 ft 9 in (2 m) in diameter. The total length of the character stroke is 469 ft (143 m).

Peter Pan
The cast of Peter
Pan on a fish hook.

Gold ship
A miniscule gold ship
on a tiny crystal.

Tiny Treasures

Under a microscope, Willard Wigan of Birmingham, England, can create tiny sculptures, some of which are many times smaller than the period at the end of this sentence. Cutting his materials with shards of glass and using his own eyelashes as a paintbrush, he has made majestic miniatures of the Titanic on the tip of a pin, Zeus on a grain of sand, and Elvis on a pinhead. All Willard's works have been purchased by a private collector and he now also undertakes private commissions.

Marilyn Monroe
The 50s icon on
a diamond-
topped pin.

Research Coup

A flock of 20 pigeons wearing cell phone backpacks were employed to monitor California air pollution in 2006. Each pigeon carried a cell phone with a satellite tracking chip and air pollution sensor, enabling data on air quality to be transmitted via text messages. The birds also had miniature cameras tied around their necks to record aerial pictures of environmental black spots.

Blinking Mouse

Dmitry Gorodnichy, an inventor from Ottawa, Canada, has developed a computer mouse controlled by nose movements and blinking. He calls the nose-steered mouse a "nouse" and blinking the left or right eye twice takes the place of left or right mouseclicks.

Tire Tree

British sculptor Douglas White has created a 16-ft (4.8-m) palm tree made from blown-out truck tires in the middle of a rainforest in northern Belize.

Outsize Cow

Harvey Jackson spent over 18 months and 220 gal (833 l) of paint creating a 220 x 56 ft (67 x 17 m) mural at Gillette, Wyoming. It depicted a tractor, a train, and a cow, representing the town's industries. The cow alone is larger than George Washington's face on Mount Rushmore.

Finger Painting

Elizabeth McLeod and Amanda Riley, both ten from Snelville, Georgia, created a giant finger painting that measured 3,100 sq ft (290 sq m).

Bathroom Play

A play in Sao Paulo, Brazil, in 2006 was staged in a theater bathroom! Only 30 audience members could fit inside the bathroom and they had to stand during the half-hour show.

Blind Devotion

For more than 30 years, John Cook has created masterpieces in wood. But the Tennessee man never gets to see the finished product—because he is blind. Although he lost his sight to glaucoma as a child, Cook uses a measuring stick and gauge blocks with brail marking to produce beautifully intricate furniture. Each cut he makes is steady, deliberate, and perfect. "My hands are my eyes," he explains.

Tall Topiary

In 1983, Moirangthem Okendra Kumbi began turning a Duranta hedge plant into a giant topiary. The plant, which he calls "Sweetheart," now stands a huge 61 ft (19 m) tall in Manipur, India. He spends five hours a day clipping, feeding, and watering his creation.

Battery-powered

Scientists at Japan's Tokyo Institute of Technology have invented an airplane powered solely by 160 tiny AA batteries. The 97-lb (44-kg) plane, with a 100-ft (30-m) wingspan, flew 1,283 ft (391 m) in one minute during tests in 2006 in what was thought to be the world's first household battery-powered takeoff.

Steam Gramophone

Music-lover and steam-train enthusiast Geoff Hudspith from Dorset, England, has created what he claims is the world's first steam-powered gramophone... just so that he could play his collection of old 78 rpm records. It took him four years to build, but cost him less than $200 because he used scrap metal.

Mini Masters

At the Smithsonian Institute in Washington, D.C., a mini art exhibition featured 1,122 tiny artworks measuring an average of 3 x 4 in (7.6 x 10 cm).

Chamber Music

An American firm has invented a new iPod accessory that combines the portable music player with a toilet-roll holder so you can enjoy your favorite tunes while in the bathroom.

PLASTIC WRAPPER

People walking the streets of Washington, D.C., never know what they're going to find next.

It could be a parking meter dressed as a lollipop, a baby up a tree, a translucent dog on the shore, or a man buried head first in a utility box. These and many other strange sculptures that have cropped up around the city are the work of local street artist Mark Jenkins. Mark works primarily in packing tape and plastic wrap to create clear, lifelike molds. He first tried the technique at school when he covered a pencil in plastic wrap and tape, made an incision, and removed the pencil.

Twenty years later, in 2003, in a moment of boredom, he made a ball from clear tape. He went on to wrap the contents of his apartment before making a cast of his own body, which he placed in a dumpster.

Moving to Washington, his tape men soon began to spring up all over the city. Sometimes they were transparent, other times he would dress them in old clothes for added realism.

He has also created tape babies and animals, and has perched them in trees, on monuments, and with abandoned shopping carts.

Balloon Sculpture

New York balloon artists Larry Moss and Royal Sorell used 40,781 oblong balloons to create a huge soccer-related sculpture in which the goal, the players, and even the grass were all made of balloons! It took 640 man-hours to make. The players were 40 ft (12 m) tall and dressed in the colors of the national teams of Belgium and The Netherlands, the host nations for the 2000 European Soccer Championships.

Jet Chair

Giuseppe Cannela of Bedfordshire, England, successfully attached a jet engine to the back of his mother-in-law's wheelchair to reach speeds in excess of 60 mph (97 km/h)!

Branching Out

British artist Tim Knowles encourages trees to draw! He attaches pens to a thin branch, places a blank canvas at the end, and allows the wind to do the work.

Dog on Display

For Vancouver's first Sculpture Biennale exhibition in 2006, passersby were encouraged to deposit random artistic items on shelves around the city. The objects placed included feathers, shoes, tree branches, and, briefly, a Chihuahua!

Snow Show

At the National Screen Institute Film Festival held in Winnipeg, Manitoba, Canada, the audience sat outside in −22°F (−30°C) weather watching movies projected onto a giant block of snow!

Cement Boat

A group of students from the University of Nevada spent a year working on an eight-man canoe made out of cement. The boat actually floats!

Metal Cheese

Los Angeles sculptor Bruce Gray created a slice of cheese measuring 25 x 43 x 29 in (64 x 110 x 74 cm) in welded aluminum! "The Big Cheese," which has metal bubbles of various sizes, featured in HBO's *Six Feet Under*.

Top Mosaic

In celebration of the town's 950th anniversary in 2005, artists from Landesbergen, Germany, used more than 2.25 million bottle tops to create a mosaic that measured 325 x 209 ft (100 x 64 m). The mosaic was so big it had to be laid out on a soccer field.

Cheese Church

In Edam, The Netherlands, there is a 1:10 scale model of the town's great church made out of 10,000 balls of Edam cheese.

Fish Art

Artist Carol Hepper of South Dakota creates sculptures using up to 200 dried fish skins! She collects the skins from fishing trips and fish-processing facilities.

Pub Pitch

Pub landlord James Banbury is so keen on soccer that he covered the interior of the Old Swan at Kibworth, Leicestershire, England, with turf for the 2006 World Cup. He laid turf on one of the bars, painted pitch markings on the grass, and turned the fireplace into a goal, complete with chalk-drawn goalposts and crossbar.

Larger than Life

London-based Australian Sculptor Ron Mueck creates hyper-real sculptures of human figures on a mind-blowing scale. This work is part of his 2006 exhibition at the Royal Scottish Academy in Edinburgh, Scotland, entitled "A Girl." Before becoming a sculptor, Mueck had a 20-year career as a puppet-maker and puppeteer in Australia.

243

Ripley's— Believe It or Not!®

Mud Art

Artist Angela Findlay from London, England, certainly gets her hands dirty in the name of art. She paints pictures with mud taken from the banks of England's Severn River. Angela collects mud in buckets before taking it back to her studio to mix with sand and acrylic paints. She then paints onto large canvases using her hands and fingernails.

244

Hot Ice

Scott Wilson of Cary, North Carolina, has created an ice cream that is made with three kinds of peppers and two types of hot sauce. The product, Cold Sweat, is so hot that customers must sign a waiver before tasting it.

Replica Ark

Inspired by the biblical story of Noah, Dutchman Johan Huibers spent 15 months building a wooden ark 230 ft (70 m) in length that he planned to fill with farmyard animals, and sail to several cities in The Netherlands.

Robot Conductor

In 2004, a humanoid robot standing 23 in (58 cm) tall conducted the Tokyo Philharmonic Orchestra in a performance of Beethoven's "5th Symphony."

Chopper Mower

C.G. Mouch of Brusly, Los Angeles, fitted the front end of a 750cc Honda motorcycle to the rear end of a lawn mower to create a "chopper mower" so that he could mow in style at speeds of up to 10 mph (16 km/h)!

Origami Expert

Devin Balkcom, a student at Carnegie Mellon University in Pittsburgh, Pennsylvania, developed a robot that can do origami, the ancient Japanese art of paper sculpture.

Junk Creations

Freeman Loughridge of Ardmore, Oklahoma, uses discarded junk to create quirky sculptures. Bicycle parts and springs form the basis for a flowering garden trellis, while an old army helmet has been converted into a flamingo! Loughridge says of his whimsical creations: "I'm very serious about not being serious."

Flower Power

In September 2005, a bouquet of more than 150,000 roses was created at a shopping mall in Frankfurt, Germany.

Robotic Taster

Japanese engineers claim to have developed a robotic wine taster capable of distinguishing between 30 different varieties of grape!

Chin Power

Owen Orthmann of Minnesota, paralyzed from the neck down, modified a crossbow so that it can be easily loaded, aimed, and fired without the use of arms or legs. Instead he fires it with his chin.

Snow Village

A group of 200 Swiss enthusiasts built an igloo village 200 ft (60 m) wide, complete with snow church and piazza, on a frozen lake in 2006. Led by Lars Kienitz, they took 12 hours to build 100 igloos, many with kitchens, fireplaces, and ice sofas.

Soap Statue

New York artist Gary Sussman carved a scale replica of the Statue of Liberty, 12 ft (3.7 m) tall—out of soap. Sussman has also made a giant sculpture of Uncle Sam from a 5,000-lb (2,270-kg) block of soap.

Cockroach Brooch

A new creepy fashion accessory now on sale is the giant Madagascar hissing cockroach. About 3 in (7.6 cm) in length, it is adorned with colored crystals that are glued in place on its hard outer shell. A small clasp attached to a silver chain allows the insect to roam around the wearer.

Long Cigar

Cigar makers in Tampa, Florida, have rolled a cigar that is 101 ft (31 m) long and weighs 53 lb (24 kg). It took Wallace and Margarita Reyes and their workers more than 75 man-hours over several weeks to craft the supersized smoke.

Stamp Heavy

In June 2006, artists Dmitry Shagin and Maksim Isayev delivered a postcard in St. Petersburg, Russia, that was 50 ft (15 m) long, weighed more than 123 lb (56 kg), and bore no fewer than 198 stamps!

Tapagami Town

Daniel Schieble is a "Tapagami" artist from California, an art form that uses only masking tape and painter's tape as its tools. In 2007, he created this vast masking tape city entitled "Atlas Losing his Grip on the World" that grows by the day. After only a few years in creation and using approximately 14 mi (23 km) of masking tape, the city now measures around 2,000 sq ft (186 sq m). He refers to his art as a self-regenerating sculpture as he spends nearly every night adding to it.

Fitting Forms

Britt Savage, a singer from Nashville, Tennessee, used mostly pink Child and Dependent Care 1040A forms and Individual Tax forms to create this fashionable dress in 2009. Her band had a gig on "tax day"—infamous for being a depressing day—so to cheer up her fans she spent a month creating this stylish tax dress to wear on stage. Using a shredder to create the thin strips, she then wove them together to make the center of the dress and glued them to the bottom to create the skirt. Britt plans to sell the dress on-line and give the money to charity.

Guido's Handicraft

Italian artist Guido Daniele has given a new meaning to finger-painting. Instead of working on canvas, he uses pencil and watercolors on human hands to create incredible portraits of animals and birds such as cheetahs, elephants, crocodiles, and toucans. Daniele, who used to paint human bodies for advertising campaigns, takes up to ten hours to produce his handicraft. This means that his models not only need big hands but a lot of patience as well.

Petite Picasso

Phoenix Perego of Ormond Beach, Florida, sees her paintings sell for anything between $50 and $100. And that's no mean feat considering she is only 2½ years old! She has created more than 15 works and, according to her father, who is himself a professional artist, she likes to paint in her diaper.

Feminine Roadster

Anita Dugat-Greene of Belton, Texas, has turned her 1997 Ford Taurus into a monument to women. The car is covered in thousands of buttons, numerous images of the Virgin Mary, and multicultural Barbie dolls.

Car Coffin

Jose Gomez of Ilhavo, Portugal, built a wooden replica of his Mercedes 220 CDI car. He plans to be buried in it!

Card Sign

In July 2006, Bryan Berg of Spirit Lake, Iowa, used 500 decks of playing cards, 1,800 poker chips, 800 dice, and several tubes of Superglue to build a replica of the "Welcome to Las Vegas" sign. It took him 450 hours—that's nearly 19 days.

Great Ball of Stamps!

Fred W. Miller from Newark, New Jersey, made this 8½-lb (3.8-kg) ball from 75,000 used U.S. stamps in the 1940s. It measured an impressive 8 ft 9 in (2.7 m) in circumference.

Bread Statue

Chilean artist Constanza Puente made a life-size statue of herself out of bread. When she placed the sculpture on a Santiago park bench in 2006, it quickly proved popular with pigeons.

Carton Cartographer

Skip Hunsaker of Coos Bay, Oregon, created a topographical map of his home county using cigarette cartons! A specialist in sculpting unusual materials, he also made miniature poodle figures from myrtlewood nuts.

Car Mail

A car owned by E.G. Hadley from Casper, Wyoming, was covered with 37,770 foreign stamps, from 60 different countries.

Straw Church

Farmers Will Morris and his son Tim spent two days creating a straw replica of an English village church in 2006, only for vandals to burn it down. The model of St. Mary's Priory Church in Deerhurst, Gloucestershire, stood 40 ft (12.2 m) tall, weighed 30 tons, and was made from 110 bales of straw.

Heavy Egg

Twenty-six chocolate makers took eight days and used 50,000 chocolate bars to make an edible chocolate egg that measured 27 ft 3 in (8.3 m) tall, 21 ft (6.4 m) wide and weighed 4,299 lb (1,950 kg). Metal scaffolding with wooden panels was used to create a "shell" to support the egg, which went on display at Englewood Cliffs, New Jersey.

Fallen House

There is something strange on the roof of Austria's Viennese Museum of Modern Art—an upside-down house. In fact it is a sculpture by Erwin Wurm and, although it is supposed to look as if the house has fallen from the sky and landed on the museum, it actually took two large cranes to lift it into place.

Ice Tower

Using 45 tons of ice, ten carvers spent 1,440 man-hours creating an ice sculpture that measured 40 ft (12.2 m) tall in Dubai in 2006. The sculpture is a mini version of the Burj Al Alam, that, completed in 2009, will be one of the world's tallest commercial towers.

Popcorn Mickey

Sculptors have created a giant model of Mickey Mouse as the Sorcerer's Apprentice... out of popcorn. The model, which stands 19 ft 8½ in (6 m) tall, was created at Disneyland's California Adventure Theme Park using prefabricated blocks of popcorn that were glued together.

Colorful Sari

A silk sari made in India has no fewer than 164,492 colors. The Seven Wonders of the World were brought to life on the border of the sari, which took 15 weavers more than 45 days to complete.

UV Tattoos

This ultraviolet tattoo is the handiwork of Richie Streate, a Californian tattoo artist who specializes in UV tattoos. The tattoos are completely invisible in regular light, once the scarring heals after about a year, but come to life under UV light used in clubs and bars.

Note Hunters

Davy Rothbart of Ann Arbor, Michigan, is the editor of the magazine *Found*, which prints letters, photos, drawings, and notes that he and others have found on the ground.

Hopping Mad

A company in Los Angeles developed a motorized pogo stick powered by a single two-cycle engine that gets 30,000 hops to the gallon.

Beach Sculpture

In 1991, a sand sculpture an astonishing 16½ mi (26.4 km) long was built by more than 10,000 volunteers at Myrtle Beach, South Carolina.

Recycled Purses

Saroj Welch of Louisiana crochets recycled plastic grocery bags into purses, then donates the proceeds to charity.

Small Writing

A.B. Rajbansh of India handwrote the U.S. Constitution in a 124-page book that measures only ¾ in (2 cm) in height.

Plane Lamps

Designer John Erik of Montréal, Canada, makes furniture and lamps out of discarded airplane parts, including engine turbines.

Waste Man

British sculptor Antony Gormley has created a sculpture 82 ft (25 m) high called Waste Man in Margate, England. The figure is made entirely from waste materials, including chairs, wardrobes, pictures, old rope, and toilet seats.

Salvage Ship

The U.S.S. *New York,* a transport ship, is being built with 24 tons of steel salvaged from New York City's World Trade Center buildings.

Mini Mobile

Jan Krutewicz of Munster, Illinois, built a working telephone that is smaller than a human thumb.

Stonehenge Replica

When he died, Al Sheppard of Hunt, Texas, was cremated and had his ashes spread about the half-size replica of Stonehenge that he had built on his property.

Rome Recreated

Using 10,000 tons of special river sand imported from The Netherlands, 60 artists created sand sculptures depicting the glory of Ancient Rome. Among the 200 sculptures at the exhibition, which opened in Brighton, England, in summer 2006, were the Pantheon, the Colosseum, and Emperor Augustus.

Tiny Gun

Mark Koscielski, a gunshop owner in Minneapolis, Minnesota, has created a double-barrel shotgun the size of a credit card.

Sweet Car

The tastiest sight at the 2006 Baton Rouge, Louisiana, Art Car Parade was Amy James's OREO Speedwagon. It was a Ford Contour decorated with 30 bags of Oreo cookies.

Cold Comfort

A company in Alabama has developed a talking refrigerator magnet that berates dieters when they open the fridge to snack!

Shiny Shoes

Talented Berlin artist Cihangir Gumustukmen uses recycled tin cans to make shoes. Whether they are slippers, sandals, stilettoes, or platform shoes, he can create them to form works of art.

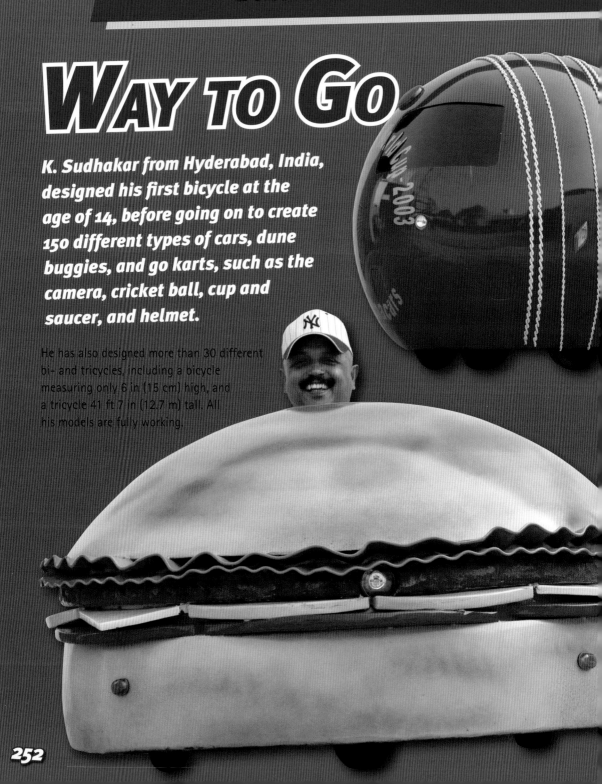

WAY TO GO

K. Sudhakar from Hyderabad, India, designed his first bicycle at the age of 14, before going on to create 150 different types of cars, dune buggies, and go karts, such as the camera, cricket ball, cup and saucer, and helmet.

He has also designed more than 30 different bi- and tricycles, including a bicycle measuring only 6 in (15 cm) high, and a tricycle 41 ft 7 in (12.7 m) tall. All his models are fully working.

Ghost Ship

When a 29-ft (8.8-m) yacht sailed from Fair Isle, Shetland, to Newcastle upon Tyne, England, in July 2005 (a journey of 330 mi/530 km), there was something missing—a crew. For this was the *Ghost Ship*, the brainchild of Boston, Massachusetts, artist Chris Burden, who wanted to create a crewless, self-navigating yacht. Built in Southampton, England, the boat was controlled via onboard computers but, in case it ran into trouble, was shadowed by an accompanying support vessel throughout the five-day voyage.

Chocolate Bust

New York artist Janine Antoni made a series of self-portrait busts in soap and chocolate. For her chocolate creations, she chisels cubes of chocolate with her teeth. Antoni once used the brainwave signals recorded while she dreamed at night as a pattern for weaving a blanket the following morning. And for a 1992 exhibition she washed her long hair and then mopped the floor of an art gallery in London, England, with it!

Paper Ship

Jared Shipman of Roseville, California, built a 320,000-piece model, 9 ft (2.7-m) long, of the U.S.S. *Nimitz* out of paper.

Fake Collection

Christophe Petyt of Paris, France, founded L'Art du Faux, a collection of more than 3,500 fake masterpieces. He has 82 artists working for him re-creating old masters. Visitors to Petyt's exhibitions have included Arnold Schwarzenegger, Frank Sinatra, and La Toya Jackson.

Amphibious Trailer

From 1989, Rick Dobbertin of Syracuse, New York, spent 4½ years (14,000 man-hours) turning an old milk trailer into a 32-ft (10-m) long stainless steel amphibious craft in which he hoped to circumnavigate the Earth over land and sea. He didn't quite achieve his objective, but he did manage to travel more than 33,000 mi (53,100 km) on land and a further 3,000 mi (4,828 km) on the ocean, tackling seas that swelled up to heights of 18 ft (5.5 m) in the process.

Mighty Mural

Since the 1970s, thousands of artists have contributed to a huge mural on the banks of a river at Pueblo, Colorado. The mural, which officially measures 2 mi (3.2 km) long and 58 ft (18 m) high, contains portraits of the likes of Elvis Presley, Andy Warhol, and Bob Marley, and contributors are invited to add to it each year.

Empty Feeling

British artist David Hensel was surprised when his sculpture was rejected by a leading art show—and even more so when its empty plinth was accepted and displayed on its own! The judges at the Royal Academy's Summer Exhibition thought the statue—a laughing head—and plinth were separate works. And they much preferred the plinth, complete with its piece of wood sticking up that was meant to keep the head in place.

Pavement Picasso

British artist Julian Beever creates incredible 3-D chalk drawings on flat city sidewalks. Known as the "Pavement Picasso," he has chalked pictures in America, Europe, and Australia, including a swimming pool so lifelike that shoppers swerved to avoid it and Coca-Cola bottles that appear to spring out of the ground. In a street in London, England, in 2006, the artist starred in his own work by posing against a wall (perched on a ledge he had drawn), while waiting to be rescued from a burning building by Batman and Robin!

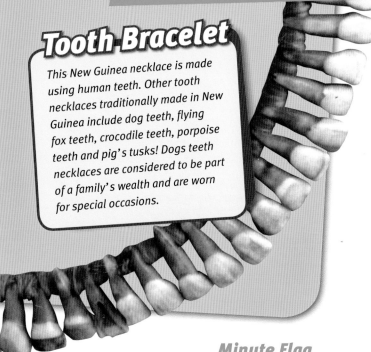

Tooth Bracelet

This New Guinea necklace is made using human teeth. Other tooth necklaces traditionally made in New Guinea include dog teeth, flying fox teeth, crocodile teeth, porpoise teeth and pig's tusks! Dogs teeth necklaces are considered to be part of a family's wealth and are worn for special occasions.

Hornet Mountain

In 1999, Yoshikuni Shiozawa of Nagano, Japan, created a model of Mount Fuji 12 ft (3.6 m) high by joining together 160 hornet nests. The finished sculpture contained no fewer than 160,000 hornets.

Sand Painting

In September 2005, more than 200 people made a sand painting measuring 46 x 52 ft (14 x 16 m) of "Fun in the Sun" at Jersey, Channel Islands, U.K. Half a ton of sand was mixed with poster paint to create 17 different colors. The dyed sand was then sprinkled onto hardwood sheets over areas of the design that had been covered with glue.

Minute Flag

Jang-Bae Jeon and Carlo Foresca, students at the University of Texas in Dallas, have created a likeness of the U.S. flag so small it would take 14 of them to span the width of a human hair. Using nanotechnology, they made an image of the flag—complete with all 50 stars and 13 stripes—that is just seven microns tall, compared to the 100-micron width of a human hair.

Saved Disks

Artist Tom Dukich of Spokane, Washington, saved on-line software disks for 10 years—enough to fill a 30-gal (115-l) garbage can—then created a giant sculpture out of them.

Human Exhibit

A student in Yorkshire, England, turned her own grandmother into an art exhibit in 2006! Janis Rafailidous flew 80-year-old Athena over from her home in Greece and placed her in a mocked-up kitchen in a Leeds art gallery as a living sculpture. There, visitors watched Athena tidying up, preparing food, and even doing some knitting.

Barbie Mutilator

There is a good reason why San Francisco artist Sue Wandell is known as the "Barbie Mutilator." Wandell produces works of art by chopping off the heads of Barbie dolls and replacing them with household objects. Among her creations are "Hammerhead Barbie" (where the doll's head is replaced by that of a metal hammer), "Vanity Barbie" (who has a mirror for a head), and "Bar Fly Barbie" (whose head is a removable pouring top for bottles of alcohol).

Ash Forest

As part of a degree show at Camberwell College of Arts in London, England, student Emma Fenelon glazed five ceramic trees with human ashes. She had advertised on the Internet for volunteers to donate the remains of their loved ones for the project.

Eyeball Mouse

Chinese high-school student Zhou Chen of Nanjing has invented a special computer that can be operated by the user simply moving his or her eyeballs. The "eyeball mouse," as he calls it, enables users to click and, for example, open a website just by looking at the screen and moving their eyes.

Eggsclusive Art

Many years of training have enabled Wang Jinyi from Tianjin, China, to develop his amazing skill in egg carving. He has carved a variety of subjects ranging from characters in ancient Chinese legends to the mascots for the Beijing 2008 Olympics.

Scrabble Sculpture

Scottish artist David Mach created a sculpture of a woman 8 ft (2.4 m) tall from 4,200 regular Scrabble tiles. The sculpture, entitled "Myslexia," was displayed in Sussex, England, in 2006 and the letters on the tiles were calculated to be worth more than 76,000 points!

Eagle-eyed

Nuclear scientist Bob Gibb and engineer Tom Chapman of New Brunswick, Canada, have developed special sunglasses that help golfers locate their lost golf balls.

Mighty Mousetrap

Students at the Art Institute in Fort Lauderdale, Florida, built a mousetrap 12 ft (3.6 m) long and weighing more than 600 lb (270 kg).

State Painter

Artist Scott Hagan of Belmont County, Ohio, traveled 65,000 mi (105,000 km) through the state using 645 gal (2,445 l) of paint and 100 brushes to paint the logo on 88 different barns. The feat was to celebrate the Ohio bicentennial.

Shedboatshed

British artist Simon Starling won the 2005 Turner Prize for converting a shed into a working boat and then back into a shed! He found his wooden shack in the Swiss town of Schweizerhalle and, after turning it into a boat, he paddled 7 mi (11 km) down the Rhine River to Basel, where he rebuilt it. In a previous artwork he used the waste water produced by a self-built electric bicycle during a ride across a Spanish desert to create a cactus painting.

Illuminated Slippers

Trips to the refrigerator for a middle-of-the-night snack could be safer thanks to U.S. inventor Doug Vick who has devised a pair of slippers with lights. The slippers have powerful flashlights in the toes that shine a beam of light for distances of up to 25 ft (7.6 m). When the slippers are removed, a timer means that the light stays on long enough to enable the wearer to climb back into bed!

CARTOON MANIA

Cartoon mania has gripped many Ripley's fans over the years. At the height of their enormous popularity in the 1930s, Robert Ripley's Believe It Or Not! cartoons had more than 80 million readers daily.

Frank S. Naroki from Cleveland, Ohio, collected enough Believe It Or Not! cartoons from 1929 to 1932 to wallpaper his entire bedroom. The last thing he saw at night and the first thing when he awoke, his collection of Believe It Or Not! cartoons undoubtedly gave him a new topic of conversation over breakfast every morning!

THE MOON NEVER SHINES!

EARL BEEBE Jr (12 years old) YAWNED SO WIDE THAT HE DISLOCATED HIS NECK Tulsa

UNDER THE SOIL THE OLD FISH DO LIE — 20 YRS he lived and then DID DIE

A GRAVESTONE TO A WAS ERECTED BY M © 1929, King Features Syndicate,

Unbelievable Dummy

Walter Cunningham, seen here in 1944, made his ventriloquist's dummy out of papier-mâchéd Ripley's Believe It or Not! cartoons, and used the dummy in his act for more than 30 years.

"DENVER" DARLING WALKS ABOUT A FREE HIGH STANDING UNSUPPORTED LADDER

W. SHOTT — of Cleveland PITCHED A NINE INNING GAME WITHOUT ALLOWING A HIT, OR A WALK, OR A MAN TO REACH FIRST — AND HIS TEAM MADE NO ERRORS ' YET HE LOST; 1—0 HOW? Suggested by Russell Ecklund — of Cleveland AGED 12

A BUNCH OF 502 BANANAS ON ONE STEM
— United Fruit Co. Puerto Castilla Honduras

Lieut. Frank Luke Jr. American Ace who shot down 14 German balloons and 4 airplanes — WAS RECOMMENDED for Court Martial AND THE Distinguished Service Cross AT THE SAME TIME AND BY THE SAME OFFICER

THE GOOD SHIP — "VENAYAGASOWPAKIALETCHEMY" — OF THE PORT OF JAFFNA

CONTRADICTING PROVERBS
"...S OF GREAT MEN RUN IN THE SAME CHANNEL"
"...FOOLS THINK ALIKE"

THE TRAITOR— ...EDICT ARNOLD ...SO A HERO ...OLUTIONARY WAR. ...s Washington's ...and ablest General

Chapter 1

ORIGINAL MANUSCRIPT OF "ALICE IN WONDERLAND" SOLD FOR $75,259.00 owned by DR. A.W ROSENBACH, Philadelphia

ABU SERIAH of ZOUBAIR, PERSIA 120 YRS. OLD AND

THE LARGEST CAKE EVER BAKED !

Cart Rescuer

British sculptor Ptolemy Elrington rescues supermarket carts that have been dumped in rivers and lakes and turns them into beautiful water wildlife creations. He saws up the carts and welds them into new shapes at his Brighton studio. Each sculpture takes him up to three weeks to complete. Among his works are a frog with bulging eyes (made from the cart's wheels), a dragonfly with a 6-ft 1.8-m) wingspan, and a kingfisher perched on top of a discarded cart.

Robot Barman

Students from the Technical University of Darmstadt in The Netherlands have created a robot that they claim can pour the perfect pint of beer! The robot, Hermann, is designed to pour the frothy German wheat beer at exactly the right angle.

Arctic Beer

A brewery in Greenland is producing beer by using water melted from the Arctic ice cap. Owners of the Inuit brewery—situated in Narsaq, a settlement 390 mi (628 km) south of the Arctic Circle—claim that the water is 2,000 years old and free from minerals and pollutants. The first consignment of the beer (which has 5.5 percent alcohol) is bound for the Danish market.

Bead Waterfall

To depict the annual salmon spawning, Bill and Clarissa Hudson constructed a cascading waterfall made from around 180,000 glass and crystal beads. The waterfall, which took two months to make, first went on display at Juneau, Alaska, in 1998.

Having a Ball

Danny O'Connor, an artist from Lexington, Massachusetts, creates art using recycled objects, including Scotch tape and old record albums. But his favorite medium is a ball and over the years he has amassed no fewer than 22,000 discarded balls. One of his exhibits featured 17,000 found balls—tennis balls, footballs, squash balls, golf balls, beach balls, basketballs, and soccer balls—all arranged in a circle.

Car-covered Car

Installation artist James Robert Ford, based in London, England, spent three years creating this eye-catching car, which he completed in October 2006. For the work, James covered a Ford Capri with no less than 4,500 Matchbox® toy cars. He named it "General Carbuncle."

Barking Bell

Gerrit Bruintjes of Oldenzaal, The Netherlands, has a doorbell that barks like a dog in memory of the family's German Shepherd that died a few years ago. It is so realistic that tax inspectors have twice ordered Bruintjes to get a dog licence because they think he has a dog in the house!

Converted Trough

A 14-year-old Swiss boy has built a functioning submarine out of an old pig trough and other bits of farm equipment. Aaron Kreier has been working on the pedal-powered craft for four years and in July 2006 took it on a successful 15-minute maiden voyage.

TV Tree

Lithuanian artist Gintaras Karosas has built a sculpture from around 3,000 old TV sets donated by the public. The sculpture, which looks like a tree when viewed from above, spans an area of 33,745 sq ft (3,135 sq m) and used 64,583 sq ft (6,000 sq m) of polythene, 7,535 sq ft (700 sq m) of bitumen cover, 3,178 cu ft (90 cu m) of wood, and 132 gal (500 l) of paint.

Paper Houses

Sherry Browne, an artist in Charleston, South Carolina, makes sculptures of houses and historical forts out of toilet paper!

Pumpkin Carver

Hugh McMahon of New York City makes his living sculpting fruits and vegetables. He charges $1,000 for a carved pumpkin or watermelon.

Chain Reaction

People are amazed when they see Wayne Simmons' ornate wooden carvings of eagles, bears, and pelicans. All the more so when they learn that whereas other artists choose more delicate methods of working, Simmons of Louisa County, Virginia, carves his sculptures of animals and birds using a chainsaw!

Meat Art

A 2006 exhibition in Ghent, Belgium, featured a coat made of beef steaks, along with a tent of bacon, and sleeping bags made from steaks. Artist Jan Fabre worked through the night to turn 220 lb (100 kg) of steak, 33 lb (15 kg) of minced meat, and a few miles of Parma bacon into art for his "Temples of Meat" exhibition. But the exhibit could be displayed for only three days before it began to rot. It was not the first time that Fabre had worked with meat. In 2000, he covered the columns of Ghent University in strips of bacon.

Memorable Kisses

Artist Tino Sehgal created a show at the Art Gallery of Ontario in Toronto, Canada, in 2006 where pairs of dancers copied great kisses from the history of art. Visitors came into the gallery to find the dancers performing kisses as depicted by the likes of Rodin, Munch, and Klimt.

Butt Painting

Stan Murmer, an artist from Virginia, is the pioneer of "butt painting," which involves him sitting in paint and stamping his butt on a canvas to create images. He has created butt-print tulips, butterflies, and parrots by this method, among other things, and, believe it or not, he has actually sold some of his work.

Ashes to Art

Derek Collins from England uses human ashes to create artworks for bereaved relatives to hang in their homes. He uses a "flaming" technique to create these unusual paintings out of resins, liquids, powders, and the deceased's ashes, which are then set on fire.

Sudoku Paper

A British company has catered for the craze in Japanese Sudoku numerical puzzles by producing special toilet paper with individual puzzles on each sheet!

Baby Bottles

Steve Klein of Encino, California, produces hand-blown miniature wine bottles that are just over 1 in (2.5 cm) high. Each bottle is filled with 0.025 fl oz (0.75 ml) of wine, then corked, sealed, and labeled.

Flashy Earrings

Inventors in California have developed earrings that flash in time to the wearer's heartbeat.

Tiny Testament

Using microlithography, three scientists at the Massachusetts Institute of Technology created a Bible measuring less than 0.2 sq in (1.3 sq cm) on a silicon tablet.

Paints Pants

Rachel Kice, an artist from Nashville, Tennessee, has made a career out of painting other people's pants. Kice gives the pants highly individual designs to transform ordinary clothes into fine-art pieces.

TURBO BEETLE

Ron Patrick wasn't content with quietly customizing his Volkswagen Beetle. He wanted something more dramatic, more explosive.

The 49-year-old California-based car computer designer wanted the wildest street-legal ride possible and spent four years making his creation safe to drive. He made several versions out of Styrofoam to get the layout and lighting right. The car has two engines—the production gasoline engine in the front driving the front wheels and the jet engine in the back. He says: "The idea is that you drive around legally on the gasoline engine and when you want to have some fun, you spin up the jet and get on the burner." The jet shoots the VW's speed from 80 to 140 mph (129 to 225 km/h) in less than four seconds! He chose a Beetle "because it looks cool with the jet." The air for the jet enters through the two side windows and the sunroof, prompting Patrick to concede: "It's a little windy inside but not unbearable." In fact, he is so pleased with his design that he is currently planning to add two jet engines to his wife's 40 mph (64 km/h) scooter.

The Beetle retains its original 90 horsepower engine in the front of the vehicle, but has a 1,350-horsepower jet engine fixed to the rear.

The jet burner is particularly eye-catching late at night, which is usually when Ron tries it out.

Tiny Field

Using nanotechnology, a German scientist has created a soccer field so tiny that 20,000 of them could be put onto the tip of a single human hair! The minute creation even has all the details and markings of a real field.

Plastic Fantastic

In a 2006 contest to make ingenious items from Tupperware, Evelyn Tabaniag of the Philippines designed a blue Tupperware evening bag, complete with lace lining and beaded bracelets for handles. And Stella Filippou from Greece created a Formula One race car entirely out of Tupperware items. The wheels were made from jello molds and potato mashers.

Dual Purpose

John and Julie Giljam of South Carolina made an amphibious motor home. The diesel-powered Terra Wind can reach speeds of more than 80 mph (129 km/h) on land and seven knots on the open water.

Long Bible

A Bible written on a piece of silk 16,427 ft (5,007 m) long—that's about 3 mi (4.8 km)—was exhibited in Beijing, China, in 2006. The longest Bible in the world, it consists of 50 volumes written in 900,000 Chinese characters and is perfect in every detail.

Light Aircraft

Alexander van de Rostyne created the Pixelito, a tiny helicopter that is controlled by infrared light. The invention, which was displayed in Brussels, Belgium, weighs a mere ¼ oz (6.9 g).

Cow Parade

A 2006 Cow Parade in Lisbon, Portugal, featured a herd of life-size fiberglass cows over which artists painted colorful, individual designs.

Commute Suit

To counter the heat wave that swept England in the summer of 2006, performance artist Liam Yeates invented a "commute suit" to make travel on the London Underground more bearable. The suit had colored spring-mounted balls to keep fellow commuters at least 6 in (15 cm) away, and a bowler hat with a flashing yellow light on top. Yeates also incorporated various gadgets useful for subway travel, including a fan in a briefcase, a built-in water bottle, and perfume bottles sewn into the shoulder pads of the suit to hide the smell of sweat on a particularly hot day.

Fried Flags

Art student William Gentry of Clarksville, Tennessee, staged an exhibit of dozens of deep-fried U.S. flags to protest against obesity. The flags were fried in peanut oil, egg batter, flour, and black pepper.

Tractor Art

Australian artist Ando, who was trained as a mining engineer, has created a vast artwork of a smiling stockman that covers 1½ sq mi (4 sq km) of the Mundi Mundi Plains in New South Wales. Using a tractor to expose the red earth, it took Ando a year to create the artwork. The portrait is visible 1.2 mi (2 km) from above.

Duct Love

Something to Do, a band in Waukesha, Wisconsin, won $2,500 in a songwriting contest by writing a love song about duct tape!

Penny Pile

Artist Gerald Ferguson created a work of art at a gallery in Halifax, Nova Scotia, Canada, that consisted of a pile of one million pennies worth $10,000.

Cardboard Piano

Researchers in a Swedish packaging company have made a working grand piano out of cardboard.

Pipe Music

Mike Silverman of Walnut Creek, California, makes music playing a galvanized steel pipe that is 7 ft (2.1 m) long and fitted with a bass and cello string.

Gingerbread House

A gingerbread house standing more than 67 ft (20.4 m) tall was designed by Roger Pelcher in Bloomington, Minnesota, in 2006. It took a team of builders nine days to create the cookie domicile, which contains 14,250 lb (6,464 kg) of gingerbread, 4,750 lb (2,155 kg) of icing, and more than one ton in candy embellishments.

Potato Longhouse

Over a layer of glue and cardboard, Washington State artist Marilyn Jones created an authentic-looking model of a longhouse from steak fries, shoe-string potatoes, hashbrowns, and instant mashed potato.

Secret Heart

A heart-warming surprise greeted loggers (and their young helper) when they cut down this tree to find a perfect heart within its trunk.

Heart-shaped Tree

This romantically shaped tree was photographed growing out of solid rock in Manitoba, Canada.

PICK OF THE BUNCH

San-Franciscan artist Steven J. Backman goes through more than 10,000 toothpicks a year creating his world-renowned sculptures.

Where did your fascination with toothpicks come from?

When I was about five years old, I made a DNA molecule from beans and toothpicks for a science project. I have a lot of patience when I work now, but I didn't back then—I got frustrated and hit it, and got a toothpick lodged in my hand. That's where it all began!

What is the most famous thing you have made?

An exact replica of San Francisco's Golden Gate Bridge, made 20 years ago. It's 13 ft long, and took 30,000 toothpicks, perfectly suspended without any cable or wire. It even lights up! It took about 2½ years.

Do you have any other favorites?

My replicas of San Francisco cable cars, my abstract sculptures of masterworks such as the Mona Lisa or public figures such as President Bush... but above all, a 4½-ft-long radio-controlled yacht, covered with fiberglass resin for water resistance so it actually floats in water. It's my pride and joy—it was valued at $25,000, but I wouldn't sell it for a million dollars.

How does your work differ from that of other model makers?

Some people create big objects, but I create fine art. People don't always take it seriously because I use toothpicks and not bronze or plaster, but I want to create pieces—like my 2,330-toothpick interpretation of Rodin's "The Thinker"—that can be compared to Picasso or Rembrandt!

Do you wake up every morning and think: "Toothpick"!

I'm most creative when I'm asleep! I dream about things, and often get up in the middle of the night and start working on them.

What helps you to concentrate while you are working?
I used to work 24 hours straight without a break. These days I do about eight or ten hours a day. I work in total silence, not even a radio or a phone. I like to be alone.

What kinds of toothpicks do you use—and do they cost you a fortune?
I have a contract with a supplier—each piece I make generally requires at least 400 to 1,000 toothpicks. I use mainly blanks, which don't have the tapered ends. They're stronger. And lots of glue!

What toothpick challenge awaits you?
The hardest piece I made was the Empire State Building, with 7,470 toothpicks, because it was hollow. But the biggest challenge would be to make something life-sized. I want to make a car that will actually operate.

You have a motto—what is it?
It's "The Essence of Patience"—to sit for hours on end you need extreme patience. Ironically, outside my work, I'm the most impatient person in the world—I don't even like to wait in line!

Floral Sculpture

A floral sculpture measuring 249 x 86 ft (75 x 26 m) and resembling a strip of Aspirin tablets was constructed in one week by nearly 2,000 people in Jakarta, Indonesia, in 1999.

Floating Bed

Dutch architect Janjaap Ruijssenaars has spent six years developing a floating bed that hovers 15¾ in (40 cm) above the ground through magnetic force. Magnets built into the floor and into the bed repel each other, pushing the bed up into the air. Thin steel cables tether the bed in place. The bed, which was inspired by the cult film *2001: A Space Odyssey*, has a price tag of around $1,500,000!

Fizzy Monster

At the 2006 Kentucky Art Car Weekend, Lewis Meyer decorated the front of his Nissan truck with a sea monster made out of soda bottle caps.

Cheesy Perfume

The British makers of the pungent Stilton blue cheese have launched their own perfume, Eau de Stilton. It claims to "re-create the earthy and fruity aroma" of the cheese "in an eminently wearable perfume."

Varnished Gourds

Larry Ray of Gulfport, Mississippi, paints and sculpts gourds. His beautifully decorated creations are finished with two coats of varnish and one coat of paste wax.

Gingerbread Town

Sven Grumbach re-created the town of Rostock, Germany, out of gingerbread. The model measured 4,300 sq ft (400 sq m) and was made using 1,760 lb (800 kg) of flour, 705 lb (320 kg) of honey, 880 lb (400 kg) of almonds, 175 lb (80 kg) of raisins, and 2,400 eggs.

The Candy Man

Jason Mecier is a celebrity portrait artist with a difference. Whereas other artists depict the rich and famous in traditional paints, San Francisco-based Mecier creates celebrity mosaics from household odds and ends or food products. Starting out with beans and noodles, he has progressed to doing candy portraits of, among others, Pamela Anderson, Christina Aguilera, Dolly Parton, and the Spice Girls. He has re-created Martha Stewart entirely out of vegetables, Demi Moore from dog food, Marilyn Manson in yarn, Mariah Carey in her favorite make-up, Billy Bob Thornton out of cigarette cartons, and Sigmund Freud from tablets and pills.

Inverted Church

Visitors to Vancouver, Canada, in the summer of 2006 were stunned to see an upside-down church buried in the ground on its spire. Measuring 20 x 22 x 9 ft (6 x 6.7 x 2.7 m), it was made from steel, glass, and aluminum, and is called "Device to Root Out Evil." It is the work of New-York-based sculptor Dennis Oppenheim.

Favorite View

Artist William A. Bixler of Anderson, Indiana, created 5,000 paintings—all of the same scene, a swimming spot on the Brandyvine River.

Gum Artist

In 2004, German artist Heidi Hesse made a life-sized Humvee sculpture 16 ft (5 m) long from gum balls!

Big Boot

Igor Ridanovic of Los Angeles, California, has created the "Mono Boot," an extra-wide ski boot that holds both feet!

Cuddly Car

Art student Lauren Porter has created a sports car you could pull over very smartly in—a Ferrari knitted from wool! Lauren, from Hampshire, England, spent ten months making the full-size replica for her honors degree project using 12 mi (19 km) of yarn. Supported by a steel frame, the red bodywork consists of 250 squares of garter stitch. The windows are V-shaped stocking stitch and the Ferrari horse badge is hand-embroidered.

Eight-mile Scarf

Helped by more than 1,000 volunteers, German woman Elfriede Blees knitted a scarf 8 mi (13 km) long to commemorate the 2006 World Cup. The scarf, which featured the flags of all 32 nations competing in the soccer tournament, used some 70,000 balls of wool worth around $30,000.

Butter Figures

For an exhibition at the Pennsylvania Farm Show, sculptor Jim Victor spent a week in a refrigerator carving 900 lb (400 kg) of butter into models of two life-size cows and the late chocolate magnate Milton Hershey! Victor, from Conshohocken, Pennsylvania, has also made pigs, a tractor, and a Harley-Davidson from chocolate, and dinosaurs and cars from cheese.

Auto Robot

Blacksmith Sage Werbock from Hulmeville, Pennsylvania, has built a robot made entirely of welded car parts. The arms are made from shock absorbers, the chest from a speaker, and the feet from brake pads. The robot weighs more than 200 lb (90 kg) and is 6 ft 9 in (2 m) tall. Werbock used his own body as a template, holding pieces of metal up to his arms and legs to get the proper ratios for his used-car droid.

Secret Gardening

Members of the Guerilla Gardening Movement in England secretly plant gardens and shrubbery in run-down urban areas under cover of darkness.

Tree Messages

Artist Antje Krueger held an exhibition in Berlin, Germany, that consisted of notes and messages that had been put up on trees and lampposts in her neighborhood.

Leonardo da Vinci in Nails

Albanian artist Samir Strati, 40, spent almost a month creating a huge 3-D nail mosaic portrait of Leonardo da Vinci using some 500,000 industrial nails. His work, measuring an impressive 86 sq ft (8 sq m), was displayed at the International Center of Culture in the Albanian capital Tirana, in August 2006.

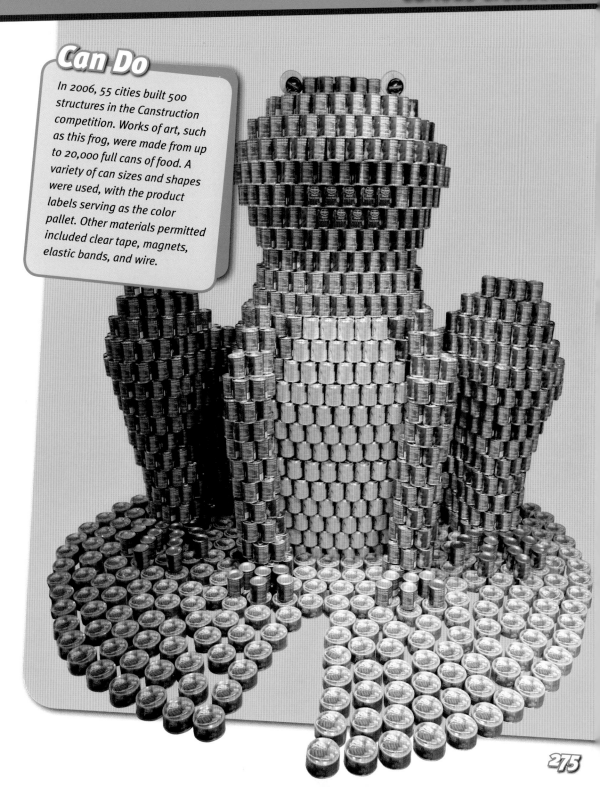

Can Do

In 2006, 55 cities built 500 structures in the Canstruction competition. Works of art, such as this frog, were made from up to 20,000 full cans of food. A variety of can sizes and shapes were used, with the product labels serving as the color pallet. Other materials permitted included clear tape, magnets, elastic bands, and wire.

EXTRAORDINARY ENDEAVORS!

MAN IN A BUBBLE

Having previously spent 61 hours inside a block of ice, balanced on top of a 90-ft (27-m) pillar, for 35 hours, and fasted for 44 days in a plastic box, illusionist David Blaine embarked on yet another amazing feat in May 2006—to spend seven days in a gigantic water-filled bubble and then hold his breath for nine minutes, handcuffed to 150 lb (68 kg) of metal chains.

Blaine prepared for the stunt by training with U.S. Navy Seals and shedding 50 lb (23 kg) in body weight over the previous few months to improve the efficiency with which his body used oxygen. In the week before the challenge, he practiced holding his breath and refrained from eating any solid foods so that he wouldn't need the bathroom while inside the 8-ft (2.4-m) acrylic sphere.

Hundreds of people turned out to see Blaine lowered into the tank at the Lincoln Center for the Performing Arts in New York City, wearing trousers, rubber shoes, and a special diving mask. Tubes fed him oxygen and liquid nutrition to keep him alive, and the water inside his "human aquarium" was maintained at around 97°F (36°C). He said he would try to sleep whenever possible during the week-long performance.

But the final challenge proved beyond Blaine. Two minutes short of his nine-minute goal, after appearing to release his hands successfully, he began struggling to free his feet from the chains and divers had to pull him from the water. Looking shaken and weak, and his skin peeling, he thanked his supporters and headed straight for hospital where doctors tested his physical health. Prolonged submersion in water brings with it a number of hazards, including nerve damage and blackouts, but Blaine's main complaint was a feeling of skin pain "like constant pins and needles."

"My only fear is the unknown," said Blaine, before descending into his water-filled sphere.

Blaine said afterward that the ordeal in the big goldfish bowl was "horrific in many, many ways. Every muscle doesn't just ache, it feels like a sharp, shooting pain—like a knife being stabbed."

279

Seven Up!

By reaching the top of Mount Everest in 2005, Danielle Fisher had climbed the highest peaks on all seven continents. And she was still only 20! The Washington State University student, who is 5 ft 7 in (1.7 m) tall and weighs 130 lb (59 kg), started climbing at the age of 15 when her father took her to climb Mount Baker in northwest Washington. She began the Seven Summits circuit in January 2003 by scaling Mount Aconcagua in Argentina, following that up with Mount Kilimanjaro in Tanzania, Mount Elbrus on the Russia–Georgia border, Mount Kosciusko in Australia, Mount McKinley in Alaska, Mount Vinson Massif in Antarctica, and finally Mount Everest.

Reverse Running

Swiss runner Rinaldo Inäbnit, 28, was the proud winner of a 7-mi (11-km) run in the Swiss Alps in 2006, but, unusually, he ran the distance backward. The new sport of "retro-running" is gathering pace in several European countries, with athletes retraining their brains to accommodate their back-to-front coordination. Inäbnit won the race with the aid of a rearview mirror, and told reporters afterward that his motto is: "Don' t look back in anger. We have to move forward backward."

Cross-country Ride

A group of about 30 cyclists completed an eight-week cross-country ride from Providence, Rhode Island, to Seattle, Washington, in August 2006 to raise funds for affordable housing. They averaged about 75 mi (121 km) a day on the grueling 3,800-mi (6,115-km) westward journey.

Junior Scientist

Maya Kaczorowski of Hamilton, Ontario, Canada, wrote a research paper on headaches caused by ice cream. When she was only 13 years old it was published in the British Medical Journal!

Kayak Karen

Karen Richardson of Florida traveled 1,750 mi (2,816 km) to Nashuam, New Hampshire, by paddling a kayak.

Deep Dive

In the Red Sea in 2005, Nuno Gomes, a 53-year-old civil engineer from Johannesburg, South Africa, made a scuba dive to a depth of 1,044 ft (318 m), which is the same height as the Eiffel Tower, including the aerial on top. "I went very close to what was physically impossible," he said. "I knew that I couldn't go another meter deeper. If I'd gone any deeper, it would have meant my death."

Panda Portrait

Using a single rabbit hair as a paintbrush, Jin Yin Hua took ten days to create a picture of a giant panda on a strand of human hair. His artwork is so tiny that visitors to the Chinese gallery where it was on display had to view it through a microscope. The New York micro-painter also creates portraits of people on single strands of hair. He has carved portraits of the King of Brunei and silent movie star Charlie Chaplin on lengths of white hair.

Sentimental Journey

In 2005, British artist Shelley Jacobs embarked on a journey to visit all 288 streets in the U.K. bearing the name "Shelley." She traveled thousands of miles to photograph the signs. She plans to expand her quest to other countries.

Never Too Old

Edward Nelson of Jacksonville, Florida, aged 67, does pull-ups with a 45-lb (20-kg) plate tied to his waist.

Carriage Pull

In 2006, a man worried about reaching the age of 60 pulled a carriage 430 mi (692 km) across Hungary in a bid to prove he was still as strong as when he was younger. Fifty-nine-year-old Laszlo Aranyi dragged the 924-lb (419-kg) carriage from Zahony, on the country's eastern border, to Szombathely in the west in 22 days.

Monster Drive

Wade Goldberg can drive a golf ball 411 yards (376 m)—and he's only 17. The East Texas teenager produced his monster drive— longer than four football fields—at a junior long driving competition in 2006.

Alpine Gift

Keizo Miura of Japan celebrated his 99th birthday by skiing down the 12,600-ft (3,840-m) high Mont Blanc along with his 70-year-old son Yuichiro.

Birthday Jump

To celebrate her 90th birthday, Britain's Mary Armstrong chose to jump out of a plane at 12,000 ft (3,660 m). The great-grandmother of nine made her first parachute jump when she was 87 and hopes to be doing it when she is 100.

Balearics Swimmer

Spanish long-distance swimmer David Meca arrives at San Antonio, Ibiza, on January 5, 2006, after a 21½-hour nonstop crossing from the Spanish mainland town of Javea—a 64-mi (103-km) odyssey, during which he overcame bouts of vomiting and swarms of jellyfish.

Playing the High Notes

Conservationists cleaning the U.K.'s highest mountain in May 2006 were astounded to find a piano weighing 226 lb (103 kg) on the summit! And it turned out that the piano had been on the 4,409-ft-high (1,344-m) Ben Nevis in Scotland for 35 years, having been carried there by strongman Kenny Campbell in 1971.

Legless Hero

A New Zealander who lost both legs to frostbite climbed to the top of Mount Everest in 2006. Mark Inglis, 47, reached the summit of the world's highest mountain in 40 days even though one of his carbon legs broke during the climb and he had to repair it. Fortunately, he had taken a spare set of limbs and parts in case of an accident. Inglis had lost his real legs below the knees when he was trapped by a storm while climbing New Zealand's highest peak, Mount Cook, in 1982.

Blind Faith

South African Hein Wagner completed a 24-mi (40-km) cycle race in 2006—even though he is blind. By following a friend with a noise-making device attached to the back of his bicycle, Wagner finished the arduous Construction du Cap Ninety Niner race around Durbanville in under two hours.

Step Master

Indianapolis fireman Jim Campbell climbed more than 106,000 steps on a step mill in 24 hours in August 2006. The feat is equivalent to completing a half-marathon vertically or climbing the steps of the Empire State Building 56 times.

AIRBED SPECTACULAR

The waters off Coogee Beach in Sydney, Australia, were the venue in 2006 for a lineup of 863 hot-pink airbeds, all in the shape of giant flip-flops!

The event took place on Australia Day (January 26), and flip-flops (or thongs) were chosen as the shape of the airbeds in homage to their status as an Australian fashion staple. In addition, participants maneuvered the enormous line of airbeds to form an outline of Australia.

Hair-raising Feat

Chinese artist Tseng Hai Sun and his partner Brigit enjoy a cup of tea above the harbor in Hamburg, Germany, while hanging from a crane hook by their hair. They were promoting their circus show, which featured the ancient Chinese art of braid hanging—exponents of which were hung by their hair to demonstrate courage.

Karate Demolition

Fifteen members of the Aurora Karate Club in Ontario, Canada, demolished an entire house in 3 hours 6 minutes 50 seconds!

Skateboard Trek

In August 2006, two months after skateboarding the length of Britain—some 900 mi (1,448 km)—Welshman Dave Cornwaithe set off for an even more daunting challenge—to skateboard 3,000 mi (4,828 km) across Australia. The 27-year-old graphic designer's trek from Perth in Western Australia to Brisbane, Queensland, on the country's east coast took him across hundreds of miles of scorching desert and lasted 90 days. Arriving in Brisbane in January 2007, he said that he mostly skates early in the morning because it's far too hot during the day to do anything.

Keep Fit

At age 91, Ervin Ashley of Springfield, Oregon, climbed 2,000 steps every day, five days a week, to keep in shape!

Table Toppers

Sharon Linter, Lorraine Jones, Steve Hammond, and Rhian Jones played nonstop table soccer in aid of a charity for the homeless for an impressive 33 hours 35 minutes at Swansea, Wales, in 2006.

Teenage Pilot

Inglewood, California, resident Jonathan Strickland is already an accomplished pilot—even though he is only 14. In June 2006, Jonathan, who has been training to fly since 2003, was flown to Canada, where youngsters can obtain a pilot's licence at 14, compared to 16 in the U.S.A. There, he achieved the unique distinction for someone his age of flying solo both an airplane and a helicopter on the same day.

Sharp Art

Monks from the Shaolin Temple in China's Henan Province are famous for their combination of Zen Buddhism and martial arts. One of their "mind-over-matter" skills is shown here being exhibited at a martial arts show in the city of Xining in Qinghai province, China, in August 2006.

String Stunt

A Chinese stuntman pulls a rope out of his nose that has passed through his mouth, into his throat, and through his nasal passages.

Base Jumper

Thrill-seeker Roger Holmes rode a mountain bike off cliffs 360 ft (110 m) in height in Sussex, England, in 2006—and survived. Holmes, a 37-year-old BASE jumper, was in freefall for two seconds before opening his parachute and landing on the beach 12 seconds later. The term "BASE" jumping is an acronym of the objects jumped from—building, antenna, span, and earth—and Holmes has completed more than 250 jumps in ten countries.

Young Buck

John Jordan "Buck" O'Neil, who died in October 2006, played in a minor-league baseball game in July 2006— at the age of 94! He had signed a one-day contract to play for the Kansas City T-Bones, the first time he had swung a bat in a game since 1955. A former player and coach, O'Neil said afterward: "I've been in baseball 70 years—this is how I made my living. And here I am at 94 with a bat in my hand!"

Cutting Edge

American magician Matthew J. Cassiere (also known as Matt the Knife) is a skilled fire eater. He can escape from a pair of handcuffs in five seconds and has escaped from a straitjacket in fewer than 19 seconds.

Stunt Kid

In July 2006, 12-year-old Australian motorcyclist Tyrone Gilks landed a jump of 169 ft (51.5 m) on his 85cc bike during a celebration in Butte, Montana, honoring U.S. stunt legend Evel Knievel.

Balancing Act

In 1934, Robert Ripley himself asked a contact in India to look for performers who might come to the U.S.A. to appear at his Chicago Odditorium (a museum), and this is one of the photographs he received.

Strange Journey

In 2006, Roz Gordon traveled the length of Britain using 73 different types of transport! The 35-year-old landscape photographer from Suffolk took six weeks to make the 1,162-mi (1,870-km) trip from John O'Groats in Scotland to Land's End, Cornwall, England, in 183 stages. Her modes of transport included dog sled, pogo stick, space hopper, camel, unicycle, go-kart, ambulance, catamaran, lawn mower, golf cart, canoe, luggage trolley, pedalo, quad bike, skateboard, tricycle, rickshaw, wheelbarrow, and stilts. She used each method for at least 328 ft (100 m) and a maximum of 50 mi (80 km) and finished the journey with a piggyback from her brother Phil.

High Mileage

Irvin Gordon of Long Island, New York, has driven more than 2.5 million mi (4,023,360 km) in his 1966 Volvo car!

Kayak Marathon

In May 2006, 34-year-old Brandon Nelson kayaked more than 146 mi (235 km) in 24 hours on a 2-mi (3-km) course near Lakewood, Washington State. On the way he battled strong winds, broke his custom-made boat, and had to paddle a slower boat for more than 5½ hours until his was repaired.

Hang Ups

Johnnie Reick was able to eat and drink while hanging upside down for 1 hour 57½ minutes in Ocean Park, California, in 1930.

Fire Eater

When his eldest brother suffered serious burns, George McArthur of Bakersfield, California, overcame his fear of fire by eating it! He is a regular fire eater on the sideshow circuit, where he also swallows swords and devours insects. And at 7-ft 3-in (2.2-m), he lives up to his nickname "The Giant."

Snow Wonder

Austrian army officer Josef Resnik, 52, skied the Schorshi piste for 240 consecutive hours over ten days in the winter of 2005, taking only short breaks to go to the toilet, eat, and take a warming shower.

Diamond Formation

A team of 85 skydivers teamed up to form a giant diamond in the sky above Lake Wales, Florida, in November 2005. Dropped from an altitude of 24,000 ft (7,315 m), members of the canopy formation branch of skydiving (in which fliers team up to form geometric shapes in the air) quickly assumed their designated positions as their formation descended at a speed of 1,000 ft (300 m) a minute. The skydivers were able to secure themselves to each other by wrapping their feet around the lines of the parachute below them.

Swim Strokes

Italian painter and long-distance swimmer Alberto Cristini has combined his two passions in life to create the art of "swim painting." Since 1997, Cristini has swum acoss lakes, bays, and seas around the world, including Lake Garda and the Strait of Messina in Italy, English Bay in Vancouver, British Columbia, Canada, and San Francisco Bay, California, painting all the while on a specially created floating easel, which he guides with his right hand and paints on with his left. Cristini says: "I tried to make a fusion between what I do so I invented swim painting."

Nationwide Read

On August 24, 2006, more than 150,000 students right across the U.S.A. read the same book on the same day. The literary event attracted more than 1,200 groups, meeting everywhere from schools to coffeehouses to read the 77-year-old classic *The Little Engine that Could* about a small locomotive that struggles to gets its train over a daunting hill.

Cracking Finale

For the closing show at the 2006 Pyrotechnics Guild International Convention near Kaukauna, Wisconsin, Dave Carlson pushed a button to detonate 9.8 million firecrackers!

Wheelchair Thrills

Tyler Deith of Muskoka, Ontario, Canada, goes to extremes in his quest for thrills—even though he has been confined to a wheelchair since a motorcycle accident in 2002. He once traveled at 50 mph (80 km/h) in his wheelchair while hanging off the back of a friend's car and has also hung on to the back of moving buses. By way of a change, he rides skateboard ramps on his manual wheelchair, performing a variety of daring stunts.

Fair Challenge

Grover and Gamet Castro of Stow, Ohio, have visited every County Fair in the state of Ohio—that's 88 fairs!

Trial by T-shirt

David Alexander got a little hot under the collar in 2006, when he put on an incredible 121 T-shirts one on top of another. His friend, Will Sharp, spent almost two hours helping David into the garments, which ranged in size from small to 8XL. Despite sweating profusely in the 93 °F (34 °C) heat, by the end of the exercise David tipped the scales at 285 lb (130 kg), 75 lb (34 kg) over his usual weight.

Autograph Hunters

Akram Marufshonow and Musadshon Chornidow, two soccer fans from Uzbekistan, cycled 4,000 mi (6,437 km) across Europe for three months in 2006 to get the autograph of their favorite player—German national team goalkeeper Oliver Kahn.

Desert Jump

Jumping from a ramp 39 ft (12 m) long and 10 ft (3 m) high, 24-year-old Nathan Rennie cleared over 121 ft (37 m) on his mountain bike in the Painted Desert, South Australia, in November 2005.

LIVING ROBOTS

A U.S. company has devised robots that behave like living creatures. They are capable of mimicking human emotions and facial expressions, eye contact, face recognition, and even conversation.

One such robot, created by David Hanson of the University of Texas, can make 28 different facial movements, including smiling, sneering, frowning, and arching its eyebrows.

Flying JCB

The usual function of a JCB engine is powering a lumbering mechanical digger, but in August 2006 a turbocharged version of the same thing propelled a racing car to speeds of over 350 mph (563 km/h) at Bonneville Salt Flats, Utah. The British JCB Dieselmax, driven by Wing Commander Andy Green, has six gears and reaches 110 mph (177 km/h) in first. It shifts into third gear at 270 mph (435 km/h) and is fitted with a parachute to help it slow down.

Ball Juggler

An 11-year-old Hungarian boy, Bence Kollar, juggled a soccer ball an impressive 2,214 times in a Budapest bar in 2006 without the ball once touching the ground.

Concorde Tug

British strongman Dave Gauder once pulled a 101-ton Concorde aircraft a distance of 40 ft (12 m) along the runway at Heathrow Airport, London. He also held back two Piper Cherokee 180 aircraft, one with each arm, to prevent them taking off, and on another occasion he lifted a Volvo estate car weighing 4,180 lb (1,896 kg) off all four wheels.

Net Buster

Tom Waite reeled in no fewer than 42 trout in seven minutes while fishing at the State Fair Park in Milwaukee, Wisconsin, in 2006. That means he caught a fish approximately every ten seconds.

Watermelon Eaters

Whoever manages to swallow the greatest amount of watermelon in a set time wins this eating contest held in the Chinese city of Zhengzhou.

Kite Crossing

Despite failing to cross the Antarctic by kite-powered buggy when he was becalmed by a lack of wind, Britain's Brian Cunningham refused to give up on his quest for adventure. In September 2004, joined by Kieron Bradley and Peter Ash, he crossed the hostile Gobi Desert in Mongolia in a kite buggy, traveling at speeds of 40 mph (64 km/h). The three men made the 625-mi (1,006-km) crossing in 17 days.

Long Marriage

In 2006, Bill and Eluned Jones of Slough, Berkshire, England, celebrated their 83rd wedding anniversary! Mr Jones was 105 and his wife was 102.

Eyelash Lifter

Ashok Verma of Agra, India, can lift heavy objects—using only his eyelashes. He has lifted three 50 fl oz (1.5 l) bottles of Coca Cola with a string attached to his eyelashes and says he can lift an 80-lb (36-kg) stone by the same method. His ultimate goal is to pull a car using his eyelashes.

Shrimp Supper

The winner of the seafood-eating contest in China in August 2005 gobbled up 18 meaty mantis shrimps.

Mango Munch

The only rule of entry for the mango-eating contest is an ability to eat 6 lb 10 oz (3 kg) of mangoes in 3 minutes!

Sure Touch

Carl Celella of North Greenbush, New York, can easily find any of the 70,000 items in the plumbing department he manages for Home Depot—despite the fact that he is completely blind.

Nottingham Quest

Alex Picker from the city of Nottingham, England, embarked on a six-week trip in 2006 to visit 14 other Nottinghams around the world. He began with Nottingham, in Saskatchewan, Canada, and then visited 11 Nottinghams in the U.S.A.—two each in Alabama, Ohio, and Pennsylvania, and one each in Virginia, Maryland, New Jersey, New Hampshire, and Indiana. Then he flew to South Africa where he paid a visit to the Nottingham Road Village. He also called in on two Nottinghams in Scotland, although both turned out to be just farms.

Mass Dribble

More than 1,000 students dribbled a basketball simultaneously at a college in Bendigo, Australia, in 2006. A total of 1,111 people took part, the biggest problem being to find enough balls for them all!

Hudson Swim

On July 28, 2004, Christopher Swain of Portland, Oregon, became the first person to swim the 315-mi (507-km) Hudson River. It took him eight weeks to complete the swim.

Wing Walker

An 85-year-old Englishman has developed an unlikely interest—wing walking on an airplane! Grandad Tom Lackey of Solihull, Warwickshire, took up the sport in 2000 following the death of his wife, and in 2006 completed his 14th wing-walk when he was strapped to the upper wing of a biplane as it performed a loop and a roll 2,000 ft (610 m) above ground.

Robot Breath

This robot, built by U.S. firm Westinghouse in 1932, was able to inflate a balloon with its mouth. Westinghouse later created breathing apparatus machines, of which this may have been the forerunner.

Balloon Buffoon

Danish clown Lars Lottrup performed his eye-catching act at the International Clown Festival in Copenhagen, Denmark, in August 2006. A crowd favorite, Lottrup manages to get himself sucked gradually into a giant orange balloon.

Speed Cyclist

"Fast" Freddy Markham has designed a bicycle that can travel in excess of 50 mph (80 km/h) over a sustained period of time. The former Olympic cyclist from Soquel, California, covered more than 53 mi (85 km) in one hour at a special challenge in July 2006 in his recumbent bicycle, Easy Racer, and won $18,000 in prize money as a result.

Giant Cabbage

A gardener from County Durham, England, grew a cabbage almost as tall as him! Frank Watson's prize cabbage was 5 ft (1.5 m) tall and 16 ft (4.9 m) round and had more than 100 leaves.

Daring Dive

SCUBA divers Mark Brimble and Jan Burt from the Aloha Dive Center in Limassol, Cyprus, spent 24 hours underwater in 2006 without coming up for any surface breaks.

INTERNET TRADER

It took Canadian Kyle MacDonald, 27, exactly a year to turn a red paperclip into a house of his own on Main Street, Kipling in Saskatchewan—simply by making 14 trades over the Internet.

Starting with a simple on-line offer on July 12, 2005, two women from Vancouver snapped up the big red paper clip in exchange for a wooden fish pen that one of them had found on a camping trip. MacDonald made swift progress until followers of his adventure despaired when he traded an afternoon with rock star Alice Cooper for a snow globe featuring the band Kiss. But MacDonald knew

that Hollywood director Corbin Bernsen was an avid snow globe collector and, sure enough, Bernsen was happy to add the globe to his 6,500-strong collection, in return offering MacDonald a role in his next movie *Donna on Demand.* Finally, the town of Kipling offered to trade a 1920s house for the movie role, which it planned to auction off to promote the area.

camping stove

doorknob

electric generator

fish pen

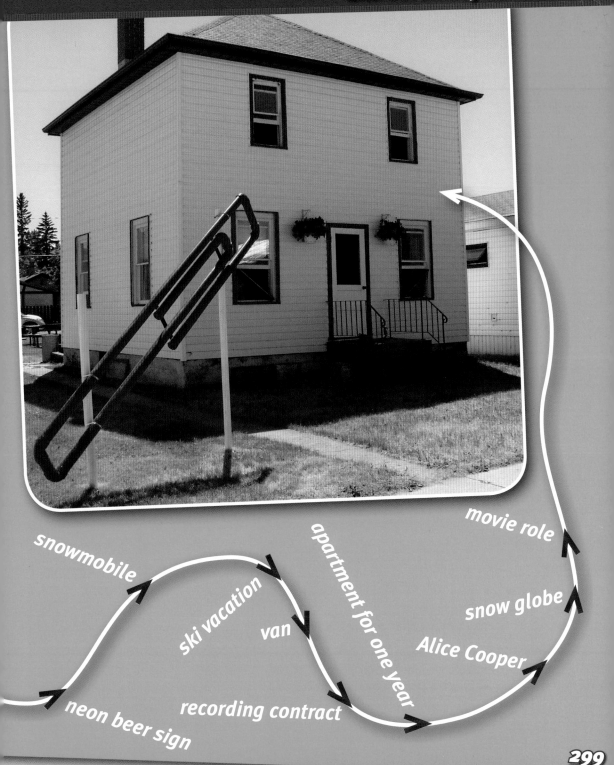

snowmobile

ski vacation

van

apartment for one year

movie role

snow globe

Alice Cooper

recording contract

neon beer sign

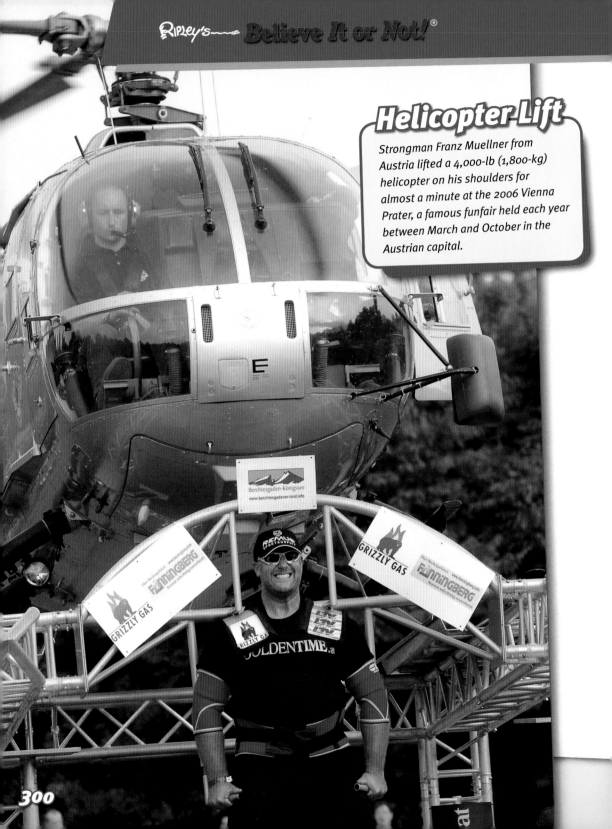

Helicopter Lift

Strongman Franz Muellner from Austria lifted a 4,000-lb (1,800-kg) helicopter on his shoulders for almost a minute at the 2006 Vienna Prater, a famous funfair held each year between March and October in the Austrian capital.

Roaming Pigeon

When Judy the homing pigeon set off from Bourges, France, on July 7, 2006, she was expected to fly the 596 mi (959 m) back to her owner John Stewart in Northumberland, England, in 48 hours. But she never made it home. Instead, seven weeks later she turned up 5,000 mi (8,047 km) away on the Caribbean island of St. Eustatius in the Dutch Antilles! It is thought that she was blown off course and hitched a ride on a passing ship.

Sitting Target

Angelo del Monaco of West New York, New Jersey, allowed 128 motorcycles, each weighing up to 800 lb (363 kg), to run over his body in 2006. He lay on the pavement under a 150-lb (68-kg) board, while 13 bikes took turns running over him, one by one, for seven minutes. He said it was the most dangerous stunt he had ever done. "When you jump over cars, you have control. ... But I can do nothing here—my life depends on the motorcycle riders."

Pulling Teeth

In summer 2006, Wang Xiaobei, a 72-year-old Chinese grandmother, pulled a 4-ton truck, loaded with people, for more than 30 ft (10 m)—with her teeth! In the winter of 2005, Wang had pulled two cars, also with her teeth.

One-armed Golfer

Ask golfer Lee Norton his handicap and he'll tell you straight: He can only play with one arm. But Norton, of Greeneville, Tennessee, can hit a golf ball farther with one arm than most people can hit it with two. He lost the use of his right arm in a motorcycle crash in 1987, but refused to be deterred from playing his favorite sport. And in August 2006 he drove a golf ball, one-armed, an amazing 296 yd (271 m).

Fast Mover

Furniture mover and former wrestler James Clark of Edina, Minnesota, reeled off an incredible 751 push-ups in 30 minutes in August 2006.

Tricycle Trek

Dan Prince of Joseph, Oregon, traveled an amazing distance of 4,250 mi (6,840 km) across the U.S.A. on a 27-speed tricycle to raise awareness of the benefits of gas-free travel.

Phil the Flipper

Show Phil Pfister a car and the chances are he will want to flip it over! Pfister, born in Charleston, West Virginia, is 6 ft 6 in (2 m) tall, weighs 325-lb (147-kg), and has been named the strongest man in the U.S.A., so flipping cars or pulling two huge 18-wheelers comes naturally.

SCUBA Relay

Six men and a woman swam the English Channel in 2006 in an underwater SCUBA relay. The British team completed the 21-mi (34-km) journey from Dover, England, to Cap Gris Nez, France, in just over 12 hours. Their biggest worry was huge passenger ferries. Organizer Colin Osbourne said: "When you're under water, you don't know where they're coming from and you think, it's going to hit me!"

Double Ace

A golfer playing in a weekend tournament at Lubbock, Texas, in July 2006 followed up his first-ever hole in one with another— on the same hole and using the same club. What's more, Danny Leake, a 53-year-old insurance agent with a 14 handicap, aced the sixth hole with a five-iron on consecutive days.

Bullet Bike

In 2006, Ironman competitor Greg Kolodziejzyk of Calgary, Alberta, Canada, traveled 650 mi (1,046 km) in 24 hours on his bullet-shaped bicycle called Critical Power. Riding around the track at Eureka, California, he averaged more than 27 mph (43 km/h) on his two-wheeled recumbent bike and didn't get out of the vehicle once during the 24 hours.

Overcame Pain

In January 2005, a British escape artist who calls himself David Straitjacket escaped from a special high-security straitjacket in Manchester, England. The jacket had loops and buckles designed to be inoperable from inside the jacket, but David managed to extract himself from it in 81.24 seconds, dislocating his right shoulder in the process!

Bike Jump

In October 2005, motorcycle stuntman Ryan Capes of Seattle, Washington, became the first person to jump more than 300 ft (91 m) on a bike when he leaped a colossal 310 ft 4 in (95 m). At Ohio Bike Week in June 2006, Capes achieved another landmark jump when he cleared 120 Harley-Davidson bikes. Ramp-to-ramp, this jump measured 187 ft (57 m).

Everest Landing

In 75 mph (121 km/h) winds, Frenchman Didier Delsalle touched a helicopter down on the summit of Mount Everest in 2005. To make it even more hazardous, Delsalle had no idea whether he was landing on snow-covered rock or merely a lump of brittle ice, which would have instantly given way beneath the helicopter.

Tractor Trek

In 2006, a group of 15 vintage tractors, each with a top speed of 30 mph (48 km/h), crossed the width of Australia from Perth, Western Australia, to Cape York, Queensland—that's an epic journey of more than 3,400 mi (5,472 km).

Amputee Pilot

Despite suffering 40 percent third-degree burns and losing his left leg in a 1989 fighter aircraft accident, Commander Uday K. Sondhi of the Indian Navy has retrained as a helicopter pilot. To date, he has flown nearly 2,000 hours.

Blind Team

The Seeing Ice Dogs are a hockey team located in Calgary, Canada. The team is so named in honor of the fact that the majority of the players are blind. They use a metal puck with ball bearings inside so that they can follow its sound.

Pretty as a Picture

A woman and two children walk in between a painting made by 800 children in Bucharest, Romania, on November 18, 2006. It stretched for an amazing 2.2 mi (3.6 km).

Coast to Coast

In 2006, Ginny Bowman from Rochester, Vermont, teamed up with her 13-year-old son and two of her teenage nieces to cycle across the U.S.A. from California on the west coast to Connecticut in the northeast to raise money for diabetes research. Despite facing temperatures of up to 118°F (47.8°C) and several arduous mountain climbs, they managed to cover an average of 65 mi (105 km) every day.

Step Climb

Medical student Jonathan Hague climbed the 242 steps of Australian landmark Jacob's Ladder no less than 269 times in the space of 24 hours in 2006. Climbing the Perth beauty spot 215 times equates to climbing the height of Mount Everest.

India Walk

In an incredible feat of endurance, Sabalsinh Vala of Toronto, Ontario, Canada, walked a total distance of 6,200 mi (9,978 km) across India.

Yearly Dip

Between 1928 and 2003, Ivy Granstrom of Vancouver, British Columbia, Canada, took a swim in the ocean near English Bay every year on New Year's Day—that's 76 years running!

Ski Fanatic

When he swept down Oregon's Timberline ski area on July 27, 2006, Rainer Hertrich reached the milestone of 1,000 consecutive days of skiing. Since November 1, 2003, Hertrich, from Boulder, Colorado, skied somewhere every day, clocking up 34 million vertical feet (10,363,200 m) in the process. On an average day, he skied 33,000 vertical feet (10,058 m)—that's higher than Mount Everest. He battled through cold, frostbite, rain, and illness, and once hiked up an active volcano in Chile, because it had more snow to ski down than neighboring mountains!

Great Adventurer

Singapore's Khoo Swee Chiow is one of the world's great adventurers. He has scaled Mount Everest twice, climbed a 26,335-ft (8,027-m) peak in Tibet without any oxygen, skied to both the North and the South Pole, broken SCUBA diving records, cycled from Singapore to Beijing, and climbed the highest peaks in seven continents.

One Man went to Mow

On July 4, 2006, Bobby Cleveland of Locust Grove, Georgia, roared along the Bonneville Salt Flats at a speed of more than 80 mph (130 km/h)... on a lawnmower! The eight-time National Lawnmower Racing Series champion, Cleveland built the specially modified mower from scratch over a period of six months.

Wheelchair Stunt

Trevair Snowden of Gardnerville, Nevada, performs daring stunts in a gas-powered wheelchair. Trevair, who has been in a wheelchair since breaking his back in a snowboarding accident in 1997, races his four-wheeler up a 5-ft (1.5-m) ramp, vaults through the air, lands on a flaming rail, and travels 12 ft (3.6 m) down it on the slide plate—a piece of metal at the bottom of his vehicle. He describes himself as being "like Evel Knievel in a wheelchair."

MAGNETIC PERSONALITY

Known as "Mr Magnet," 78-year-old Liew has performed amazing feats with what appear to be special magnetic powers. He can make up to 2 kg (4lb 6 oz) of metal objects stay on his skin without any aid.

His biggest feat yet was in 2006 when using only his body's magnetism he pulled a 10.6 ton bus. He placed a steel contraption under his armpit, hooked it to a chain, then tied it to a bus. In less than a minute he had pulled the bus 11.2 ft (3.4 m).

Bizarrely the trait appears to be genetic as Liew's three sons and two grandchildren have a similar magnetism. Investigators have concluded that Liew's skin has a special suction effect that helps metal stick to it, not a magnetic field, making him a scientific mystery.

Veteran Pilot

Jonas Blanton of Battle Creek, Michigan, is a daredevil glider pilot—even at the age of 84. Blanton has specialized in aerial stunts for more than 60 years and in June 2006, at Whitewater, Wisconsin, he piloted a glider that was towed by a small plane to an altitude of 11,050 ft (3,368 m).

Economy Drive

In 2006, John and Helen Taylor of Melbourne, Australia, drove a Volkswagen Golf 18,100 mi (29,129 km) around the world in just 78 days and on less than 24 tanks of fuel. They attributed their achievement to their "relaxed and measured" driving styles.

Superior Crossing

Although he nearly drowned as a child and didn't learn to swim until his late twenties, Jim Dreyer of Grand Rapids, Michigan, is now one of the world's foremost endurance swimmers. In 2005, towing a supply dinghy, he completed a 60-hour solo swim across Lake Superior, battling storms, 15-ft (4.6-m) swells, and powerful rip currents that pushed him off course and increased the distance of his swim from 55-mi (89-km) to 70 mi (113 km). His success meant that he had finally achieved his goal of swimming all five Great Lakes.

Teeth Statues

Russian dentist Igor Tsarik has a collection of mini-statuettes made out of human teeth. He makes these faces by grinding out the shapes from teeth that he has taken out of the mouths of his patients!

Great Escapes

Chicago escape artist and magician Thomas Solomon has escaped from maximum security jails in the U.S.A. and the U.K., from a locked, burglar-proof, titanium steel bank safe under 30 ft (9 m) of water, and from a 20-lb (9-kg) ball and chain at the bottom of the Hudson River. He has also escaped from more than 1,000 pairs of handcuffs and various types of straitjacket.

Bridge Jumper

In July 2006, Oregon National Guard captain Dan Schilling made 201 BASE jumps in 24 hours off a bridge 486 ft (148 m) above the Snake River Canyon near Twin Falls, Idaho. And the 43-year-old kept jumping even after fracturing his wrist. The feat required the assistance of 15 parachute packers and 25 other personnel, and Schilling admitted: "The difference between life and death on every jump is about two seconds."

Walking on Eggshells

In 2005, Zhang Xingquan from northeast China's Jilin Province not only managed to pull along a family car using his ear, but achieved his astonishing feat while walking on clutches of raw eggs, none of which broke during the exercise!

Mini Marvel

Lu Di won admiration at a kung fu school in Songshan, China, in July 2006 by performing 10,000 push-ups in 3 hours 20 minutes. But what really astounded onlookers was the fact that he was just six years old! The school's president, Shi Yongdi, was so impressed that he decided to waive the boy's tuition fees for the next ten years.

Music Degree

Tammie Willis of Richmond, Virginia, received a master's degree in music from Virginia Commonwealth University—the first deaf student ever to earn a music degree there.

Bike Ride

Gary Eagan traveled 5,632 mi (9,064 km) from Alaska to Florida by motorcycle in 101 hours, setting a new record certified by the "Iron Butt Association."

Tight Fit

Wu Xizi, a Chinese contortionist, squeezes his 67⅜-in (1.71-m) frame into a box measuring 23⅝ in (60 cm) long, 11¾ in (30 cm) wide, and 15¾ in (40 cm) high in Nanjing in eastern China on May 22, 2006.

Backsack Run

With a backsack weighing a staggering 40 lb (18 kg) strapped to his back, U.S. soldier Jake Truex of Albany, Oregon, ran 5,468 yd (5,000 m) in just 22 minutes 20 seconds in Hanau, Germany, in February 2006.

Skating Away

Peggy Gray spent a lot of time walking or roller skating upside down near her home in Plainfield, New Jersey, in the 1920s and 30s.

Double Backflip

Riding up a ramp, 23-year-old Travis Pastrana of Annapolis, Maryland, soared into the air on his 200-lb (90-kg) motorcycle and made two complete revolutions to land a double backflip at the 2006 X Games—the first time such a stunt had been performed successfully in X Games competition.

Tree Planting

In an attempt to improve air quality in the Philippines, volunteers simultaneously planted more than 500,000 trees on 2,137 mi (3,439 km) of road across the archipelago in August, 2006.

Water Balloon Fight

In April 2006, a crowd of 2,921 people launched a staggering 55,000 water balloons at each other during a massive water fight that took place on a beach in Sydney, Australia.

Unrattled

On November 9, 2006, American Jackie Bibby, alias "The Texas Snakeman," held a frightening ten western diamondback rattlesnakes 2½ ft (76 cm) long in his mouth for 12.5 seconds!

Bikers' Burnout

By scorching their rear tires simultaneously, more than 260 motorcycle riders staged a mass burnout at Maryville, Tennessee, in August 2006. The bikers performed the burnout by locking their front brakes, gunning the throttle, releasing the clutch, and letting the rear tire spin against the asphalt.

Mechanical Marvel

In 2006, a British mechanic was still working full-time—at the age of 100. Buster Martin actually retired at 97, but three months later he applied for the job maintaining a fleet of plumbing vans, because he found retirement too boring.

DIFFERENT STROKES

London-based long-distance swimmer Lewis Gordon Pugh has conquered the coldest and roughest stretches of water in the world. Known as the "Ice Bear," he can control his own body temperature to battle the elements.

What made you want to swim in extreme conditions?

My father was an Admiral in the Royal Navy, and he used to read me stories about Captain Cook, Lord Nelson, and Captain Scott. When I was ten we moved to South Africa and at 17 I had my first swimming lesson—one month later I swam the 7 km from Robben Island to Cape Town and barely made it.

You're the first person to complete long-distance swims in all five oceans of the world. What was your longest swim?

The longest continuous one was the English Channel at 35 km. The longest "staged" one, where I swim for a day, sleep, then carry on the next morning, was down the River Thames which was 350 km—I swam the equivalent of half the Channel each day for 21 days. At least the pleasure barges avoided me—but there were lots of jelly fish at the mouth of the river!

Which were the most dangerous?

Round the Cape of Good Hope because of the sharks, or inside Deception Island, a flooded volcano in the Southern Ocean. The temperature was 2°C and I swam for 30 minutes —the longest Polar swim ever completed.

What are some of the worst obstacles you have encountered on a swim?

My "big five" predators are the Great White shark, the hippopotamus, the crocodile, the polar bear, and the leopard seal. The least intimidating are actually the Great Whites—they can come along and look at you, and then speed off!

How do you prepare for a swim?

I train physically for power and endurance, but the battle is not in the arms, it's between the ears. I use techniques to turn all my doubt into certainty, so when I stand on the edge of an iceberg and prepare to dive in, I have no doubt that I will get to the other side.

Is it true you can control your body temperature?

It's done subconsciously. I don't tell myself to start heating up—we believe it's a Pavlovian response to many years of cold swimming. I swim in just trunks, cap, and goggles—no wetsuits. I stand on the edge and look at the cold, and my core body temperature rises from 37°C to 38.4°C, which is the difference between life and death.

Have you received any serious injuries on a swim?

So far no. We watch for predators before a swim—I don't get in the water near a penguin because they are the diet of a leopard seal. We've also designed an anti-shark device, which creates a pulse around our boat.

How will you top your achievements so far?

I never do the same swim twice—the next one has always got to be bigger, longer, harder, colder, rougher! And it has to be a first—I'm a pioneer swimmer. There is better to come!

Big Mouth

Marco Hort from Switzerland stuffed an impressive 264 brightly colored drinking straws into his mouth, beating his earlier best of 259 straws, in Vienna, Austria, in 2006. Marco dislocates his jaw in a painful but necessary maneuver in order to achieve his feat.

Bowled Over

In June 2006, 40-year-old Dave Wilson of Mason, Ohio, bowled continuously for 102 hours—a period of four days and nights.

Epic Walk

Canadian Jean Béliveau is halfway through his epic 12-year walk around the world, covering 47,224 mi (76,000 km). The former neon-sign salesman set off from Montréal on August 18, 2000. Traveling alone with a three-wheeled stroller containing food, clothing, a first aid kit, a small tent, and a sleeping bag, he walked through North America to South America before crossing the Atlantic to South Africa and then walking up to Europe. August 2006 found him in Britain. The remainder of his journey takes him through the Middle East, Asia, Australia, and New Zealand until he finally comes back to Canada by 2012. His accommodation has varied from using the tent, staying with friendly families, or sleeping at local police stations and churches. His wife Luce visits him every Christmas... wherever he is in the world.

Young Kicker

Laudon Wilson of Herrin, Illinois, could kick field goals over regulation goal posts at the age of three!

Fair Crossing

Linda Fair crossed Canada from coast to coast over a period of four years using a dog team and a customized adult-sized tricycle.

Caught Shark

Melissa Ciolek, 15, of Orleans, Massachusetts, landed an 11-ft (3-m) blue shark, weighing 364 lb (165 kg), single-handedly in 40 minutes off Martha's Vineyard in 2006.

Mobile Thrower

Finland's Lassi Etelatalo won the gold medal at the 2006 Mobile Phone Throwing World Championships by hurling a scrapped Nokia unit nearly 300 ft (91 m). Around 100 throwers from as far afield as Canada, Russia, and Belgium converged on the competition held in Finland.

Charity Ride

A nine-year-old boy from Calgary, Alberta, Canada, completed a 205-mi (330-km) charity cycle ride to Edmonton over two days in August 2006. Noah Epp learned to ride a bicycle at the age of three and has been going on 10-mi (16-km) rides since he was six years old.

Two Aces

Marva Ged of Boynton Beach, Florida, beat odds of 67 million-to-one by hitting two holes in one in a single round of golf.

Loyal Employee

After more than 75 years working for public transit agencies, Arthur Winston retired from the Los Angeles Transportation Authority in March 2006—on his 100th birthday. In his entire career he missed only one day's work—in 1988 when his wife died.

Puzzle Expert

Californian Leyan Lo solved a Rubik's Cube in 11.13 seconds in San Francisco, California, in January 2006. He has even solved the cube blindfolded in less than 1½ hours!

Jet Ski Journey

In June 2006, South Africans Adriaan Marais and Marinus Du Plessis set off on jet skis from Anchorage, Alaska, on a 13,000-mi (20,921-km) trip to Miami, Florida. Their route took them down the west coast of the U.S.A., then through the Panama Canal to the east coast. Three years earlier they made a 5,000-mi (8,047-km) jet-ski trip along Africa's east coast.

Push-up King

John Morrow of Ottumwa, Iowa, was sitting in a waiting room at the doctor's office when he read a magazine article about great feats of strength. He immediately set out to surpass those feats and in May 2006 completed an amazing 123 backward-hands push-ups (where the wrist is at a 90-degree angle) in one minute. Morrow says the key to his success is a 40-day fast that he takes each spring.

Motorcycle Marvel

Motorcross legend Mike "The Godfather" Metzger executed an incredible 125-ft (38-m) motorcycle jump, which included a backflip, over the top of a fountain at Caesars Palace in Las Vegas, Nevada, in 2006.

Long Journey

This 1919 Studebaker touring car was driven an incredible 520,000 mi (836,859 km) in just 5½ years in the early 1920s. For part of this time, it was owned by a transit company and was driven 400 mi (645 km) daily on routes in California.

Miracle Arrow

Anne Rohner of New Haven, Indiana, shot an arrow that pierced the brackets of an 8-ft (2.4-m) fluorescent tube and came to rest inside the light—all without breaking the glass exterior of the bulb!

Ace at Last

After 77 years of playing golf, Vivian Barr of Vancouver, British Columbia, Canada, made her first-ever hole in one in 2006—aged 95! Barr, who is also a regular ten-pin bowler, hit her ace with a seven-iron on Point Grey's 114-yd (104-m) second hole.

Sporting Granny

Spectators at the 2006 World Veteran Table Tennis Championships in Bremen, Germany, were expecting some elderly players, but no one as old as sprightly British grandmother Dorothy de Low—aged 95! Known as "Dotty," she has been playing table tennis for 40 years and has won a number of medals in seniors' competitions.

Towed Trailers

John Atkinson, aged 70, towed more than 100 trailers for nearly 328 ft (100 m) in Clifton, Queensland, Australia, in February 2006. He hitched his Mack prime mover up to 112 loaded trailers, with a total length of 4,837 ft (1,474 m).

Free Formation

A total of 400 skydivers from 31 countries held hands to shape a spectacular midair free-fall formation over Thailand in February 2006.

Woman Caged

A 25-year-old Chinese woman spent a week living in a cage with 300 birds in the spring of 2006. The cage, suspended 12 ft (3.6 m) above the ground, was equipped with a bed and a computer. The woman said she hoped to increase her awareness of conservation by experiencing a caged bird's pain.

Outran Train

Despite navigating heavy morning traffic along the 1½-mi (2.4-km) highway, marathon runner Steve Moneghetti outran a commuter train in Sydney, Australia, in June 2006!

Courageous Climber

Despite being paralyzed in a mountain climbing accident, Mark Wellman of Truckee, California, has made ascents of the sheer granite faces of El Capitan and Half Dome in Yosemite National Park. A talented wheelchair athlete, he was also the first paraplegic to sit-ski unassisted across the Sierra Nevada Mountain Range.

Mini Monster

British rally champion Stefan Attart has given his Smart forfun2 vehicle an upgrade, transforming it into an impressive all-terrain 4WD. The chassis has been jacked up to 145 in (368 cm), supported by 26-in (66-cm) wheel rims with a diameter of 55 in (140 cm), achieving a total vehicle height of 12 ft (3.6 m). A massive six-cylinder diesel 5,675cc engine provides the necessary oomph.

OVER THE TOP!

JET MAN

Yves Rossy really does fly like a bird. The former Swiss military pilot is able to swoop and soar through the skies like a falcon by wearing a pair of kerosene-powered metal and fiberglass wings strapped to his back.

He jumps from a plane at an altitude of around 7,750 ft (2,360 m) and, as his 10-ft (3-m) wings unfold electronically, he becomes a human glider. Then when his four engines are turned on, he is transformed into a jetplane. Not only does he maintain altitude, he can even gain height at the rate of several hundred feet a minute.

In December 2006, Rossy achieved horizontal flight for more than four minutes at a speed of 115 mph (185 km/h). He steers the contraption by shifting the weight of his body and, when the fuel runs out, he lands by parachute. "It is an amazingly good feeling," he says, "like in a dream."

Rossy's "Flying Man" project takes him soaring high above western Switzerland.

The jetplane is powered by four kerosene engines, each of which develops 49 lb (22 kg) of thrust.

Store Dweller

Skyler Bartels, a student from Drake University, Iowa, spent two days in 2006 living inside a Wal-Mart store. He wandered the Iowa supercenter for 41 hours, day and night, existing solely on Wal-Mart products. He even managed to get a few minutes' sleep, either in a restroom stall or in a chair in the lawn and garden section.

Highs and Lows

Fran Capo, the world's fastest-talking female, has become the first person to do a book signing at the wreck of the Titanic, 12,400 ft (3,780 m) below the sea, some 380 mi (612 km) off the coast of Newfoundland. Fran has previously done a book signing on the top of Africa's Mount Kilimanjaro.

Juggling Priest

At Fargo, North Dakota, in August 2006, student priest Zach Warren of Charleston, South Carolina, rode a unicycle a mile in just under four minutes while juggling, achieving an average speed of 15½ mph (25 km/h).

Converse Collector

Joshua Mueller from Lakewood, Washington, started collecting Converse shoes in 1991 at the age of 13. He is now the proud owner of more than 400 pairs, none of which is identical, and he wears at least one or two different pairs every day.

Special Delivery

Steve Knight from Essex, England, has been collecting old British postboxes for ten years. A true aficionado, he lovingly restores the damaged boxes, and has a collection of more than 80, some dating back to the reign of Queen Victoria.

Stücke in the Saddle

Since 1962, Germany's Heinz Stücke has ridden more than 335,000 mi (539,130 km) through at least 211 countries and territories on a bicycle he bought at the beginning of his journey.

Caged Writer

French playwright Norbert Aboudarham lived for a week in a cage at Amiens Zoo while writing a drama about a panda! Composing the play on his laptop, which was hooked up to his cell phone, he sat in a cage furnished with straw and a log, alongside neighbors that included raccoons and wolves. During his stay, he refused to talk to the public, communicating solely via messages passed through the bars.

Turtle Total

Richard Ogust of New York City has a collection of more than 100 species of turtle in his Manhattan loft—that's more than the Bronx Zoo.

Lachance in Luck

After meeting a Belgian woman named Sabine on holiday in Cuba, Marc Lachance of Canada realized he did not have her full name and address. So he wrote to 3,700 Belgian women named Sabine. Eventually, her brother heard about Lachance's search on Belgian radio and, in 2006, the sweethearts were reunited.

Club Addiction

Mike MacDougall of North Palm Beach, Florida, fell more than $100,000 into debt by collecting rarely used one-iron golf clubs.

Big Noise

Believe it or not, a company called Hornblasters from Tampa, Florida, installs 140-decibel train horns in cars.

Polar Elvis

Three British Elvis impersonators walked and skied to the top of the world in 2006. Alex Tate, Jonny Clayton, and Steve Goodair trekked 368 mi (592 km) from Cornwallis Island, off Northern Canada, to the Magnetic North Pole in Elvis-style survival suits, complete with thermal insulation and rhinestones.

Mousetrap Mansion

Tim Evans of Brownsburg, Indiana, has a collection of more than 1,000 mousetraps in his home.

Quiet Wedding

Daisy and John Franko of Springfield, Ohio, were married on February 14, 2006—at the funeral home where they first met!

Amazing Brace

U.S. manufacturer Hasbro has marketed a toothbrush that plays pop songs while you brush your teeth—by transmitting the sound waves along the bristles, through your teeth and jawbone to your ear. The music is stored in a microchip in the brush's handle and plays on a mini-computer at the push of a button.

Polish Floatathon

Andrzej Szopinski-Wisla drifted on water for 2 hours 5 minutes 18 seconds near Warsaw, Poland, in 2006. And throughout his marathon float he kept his hands behind his head and his toes above the water's surface.

Mature Cake

Morgan Ford of Tecumseh, Michigan, still has a fruitcake that was made by his great-grandmother, Fidelia Bates, over 120 years ago!

Victorian Cake

When Vera Howarth of Devon, England, celebrated her 98th birthday in 2006, the cake was even older than she was! The seven-tier fruitcake was made in 1895 (when Queen Victoria was still on the throne) for the wedding of Vera's parents, and the top tier has been kept in the family ever since, to be brought out on special occasions. The cake had yellowed slightly in the intervening 111 years, but still smelled beautiful.

Pipe Major

Nick Hudson, a student at Carnegie-Mellon University in Pittsburgh, Pennsylvania, is the only person in the U.S.A. with Bagpipes as his college major.

Theatrical Delights

Dedicated theatergoer Roy Burtenshaw from the city of Bath in Somerset, England, has visited his local playhouse more than a thousand times over a period spanning more than 50 years, and has the theater programs to prove it. A retired printer, Roy has been visiting the Theatre Royal in Bath ever since his father took him to a Christmas pantomime there when he was six years old. At the age of 26, Roy wooed his wife-to-be Sonia (also pictured here) with romantic dates at the theater, and he has seen every show performed there at least once ever since, always sitting in the same seat in the stalls. His favorite shows include Joseph, Blood Brothers, Cats, and Les Misérables.

Let it Snow!

Josef Kardinal from Nuremberg, Germany, is the proud owner of a vast collection of snow globes that have been gathered from across the world. Currently standing at more than 7,500 globes, Josef's collection includes some of the first snow globes ever produced, made in Austria at the end of the 19th century.

Male Kindergarten

A man tries out a new compass saw at a special kindergarten for men in Hamburg. Women can now leave their partners on weekend shopping trips at the Saturday afternoon men's crèche "Maennergarten" at the Nox Bar. Equipped with tables, couches, comics, games, cards, remote-controlled cars, and plastic toys, men are given a name badge on arrival and for 10 euros can get two beers, a hot meal, and nonstop televised sport.

Mobile Doctor

A New York doctor has opened for consultation in the world's smallest doctor's office—his car. Dr. Safwan Sweidan has installed a desktop computer, a lamp, an Oriental rug, and even fake plants in the front seat of his Chrysler convertible and spends two or three hours every night in the heart of Manhattan dispensing medical advice to passersby.

Stick Man

You can't beat Peter Lavinger's collection of drumsticks. Ever since he caught a drumstick at a concert in 1980, the New Yorker has been collecting famous drummers' sticks. He has attended thousands of concerts—including The Rolling Stones, R.E.M., and U2—and has built up a collection of more than 1,300 celebrity sticks, nearly all of which are autographed. Each one is valued at more than $700.

Chop Shop

Customers at Szabolcs Bodnar's barber shop in Budapest, Hungary, no longer expect the traditional scissors and comb. Instead, they have their hair cut with such implements as axes, swords, vacuum cleaners, and irons. Bodnar's chosen method of cutting hair is to place it on a chopping board and strike it with an ax. The hair is then styled using a vacuum cleaner or straightened with an iron. For more energetic customers there is also the option of hanging upside down while Bodnar hacks away with a Samurai sword at such speed that the entire haircut can be finished in seconds!

Old Coach

Former Welsh international Ivor Powell worked as assistant coach for British soccer club Team Bath in 2006—even though he was 90 years old.

Peel's Privies

There's never any shortage of somewhere to sit in Janie Peel's backyard. The real-estate broker from Appling, Georgia, rescues old outhouses that would otherwise have been demolished. Among her growing collection is an ancient two-holer with a tin roof and a metal side that is peppered with shotgun pellets—right where the occupants would have been sitting!

Rock Artist

On September 3, 2006, artist Bryony Graham created a beach sculpture from 30,000 sticks of edible rock candy. It took four hours to assemble the one-ton artwork into a circular mound 20 ft (6 m) across and 2 ft (60 cm) high on the beach at Felixstowe in Suffolk, England. Graham was relieved that it didn't rain for fear the rock would have dissolved into a sugary mess.

Cotton Statues

Since 1987, Indian sculptor Anant Khairnar has made hundreds of statues of Lord Ganesha, famous personalities, abstract objects, and birds—all from cotton. He uses special chemicals to toughen the cotton so that his statues last for at least ten years.

Tapestry of Love

A woman from London, England, has single-handedly re-created the famous Bayeux Tapestry in a labor of love that has spanned more than 20 years. Annette Banks developed her talent for embroidery as a child. She also loved English history, so her father suggested that she make a replica of the Bayeux Tapestry. When Annette eventually finished her tapestry, it was 51 ft (15.5 m) long and 23 in (58 cm) wide. After visiting the real tapestry in Bayeux, France, Annette decided to add another 5 ft (1.5 m) to her version, and to make up her own ending.

Blood Money

In October 2004, businessman Stephen Son of Los Angeles, California, promised to pay back a finanacial investor with a contract—written in his own blood!

Prison Painter

Donny Johnson, a prisoner serving a life sentence in California, paints as a hobby, using dye leached from candies to make paints and his own hair to make brushes. Twenty of his paintings have sold for $500 each.

Hidden Sheep

Since 1995, James Hartman of Burlingame, California, and his family have hidden over 2,000 tiny plaster sheep all around the world at locations ranging from the Eiffel Tower, Paris, to London's Big Ben to India's Ganges River.

Colorful Diet

Soccer fan Scott Campbell took his devotion to new heights in 2006 by vowing to eat food that came only in his club's colors for the whole nine-month season. The Glasgow Celtic club supporter went on a strict diet of green and white foods—mainly chicken, fish, and vegetables.

Bag Man

Since 1975, Germany's Heinz Schmidt-Bachem has collected 150,000 plastic and paper bags. He feared that these everyday items would otherwise be lost.

Golden Cocktail

Spectators at the 2006 Kentucky Derby were able to order a $1,000 mint julep cocktail—with mint from Morocco, ice from the Arctic, and sugar from the South Pacific, served in a golden cup with a sterling silver straw.

Wrong Numbers

The Pierce family of Salt Lake City, Utah, have answered more than 25,000 misdialed phone calls during the past 14 years. They enjoy chatting with each caller and keep a log of each call!

Penny Pile

John Trembo of Plymouth, Michigan, has a collection of more than one million pennies, weighing more than three tons.

Golf Line

Ted Hoz of Baton Rouge, Louisiana, has collected nearly 70,000 golf balls since 1986. If you lined them up side by side, they would stretch almost two miles.

Small Read

Neale Albert of New York has a collection of more than 3,000 miniature books. A former corporate lawyer, he began seeking out the books to fill the tiny shelves of the historic dolls' houses that he collected at the time. Among his miniatures is a 30-page edition of Anton Chekhov's *The Chameleon* with miniscule dimensions of $1/24 \times 1/24 \times 1/24$ in (1 x 1 x 1 mm), which is about the size of a single grain of salt.

Identity Crisis

A Chinese woman had a mole removed from her leg and grafted on to her face to avoid being mistaken for her twin sister. Xiao Ai from Xiamen City said that after her confused brother-in-law tried to kiss her, she and her sister marked their faces each day so their husbands could tell them apart. Then they decided that the mole relocation would be a more permanent solution.

Swim Truck

Don Underwood of Louisville, Kentucky, owns a 1954 fire truck with a built-in swimming pool that was originally installed to provide mobile swimming lessons for children.

Toilet Theater

Dennis Neale of Worcestershire, England, is the proprietor of a theater with a difference. A puppeteer by trade, he has converted a Victorian public lavatory that he bought in 1999 into a tiny arts venue. The once bleak building now has colorful background scenes on the walls, the urinals have been replaced by a small stage, and the toilet cubicles have made way for 12 audience seats. The wedge-shaped theater measures just 16 x 9 x 6 ft (4.8 x 2.7 x 1.8 m), but has still managed to host drama, puppetry, poetry, music, and even a day of opera. Unsurprisingly, perhaps, the theater is almost always sold out.

GREAT DANE

American runner Dane Rauschenberg ran a marathon every weekend for a whole year to raise money for charity—even organizing his own race to complete the "Fiddy 2" challenge.

Why 26.2 miles every weekend?

My brother dared me to do an event where you run 15 km and then 5 km in one day, and then a marathon the following day. I ended up winning the event! I realized that I needed only a short recovery time between runs—so I decided to set up 'Fiddy 2' and do 52 in 2006.

Where were the races?

They were all across North America, from Disney World, Orlando, to the Cayman Islands, and a lot near where I live in Virginia. The second-to-last weekend of the year, I couldn't find a race because it was Christmas—so I had to organize my own one in Pennsylvania.

How did you choose them, and how did you get to them?

I had to finance my travel myself, so many were close to home. But I still completed 85,000 miles of flying and changed time zones 62 times in order to run my 1362.4 marathon miles.

Which was the hardest marathon to run?

No question—the one in Leadville, Colorado. My average time is around 3 hours 20 minutes— my fastest was Niagara Falls at 2 hours 59 minutes—but Leadville took 5 hours 17 minutes. There was over 12,000 feet of vertical ascension in that race—it was an uphill war.

Have you always liked running?

I actually don't consider myself a marathon runner—I'm a frustrated swimmer who can't find a pool! I started running in law school because there wasn't a pool nearby.

Did you train between races?

No. I work about 60 hours a week in patent licensing. Nobody else has ever done this while holding down a full-time job.

So how are you able to run marathons so close together?

People say to leave a few months between marathons, but I think,

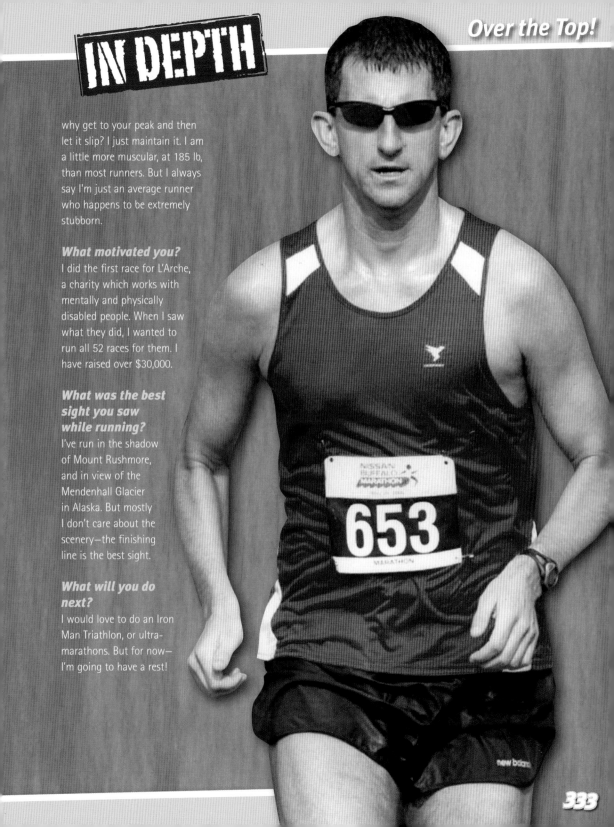

why get to your peak and then let it slip? I just maintain it. I am a little more muscular, at 185 lb, than most runners. But I always say I'm just an average runner who happens to be extremely stubborn.

What motivated you?

I did the first race for L'Arche, a charity which works with mentally and physically disabled people. When I saw what they did, I wanted to run all 52 races for them. I have raised over $30,000.

What was the best sight you saw while running?

I've run in the shadow of Mount Rushmore, and in view of the Mendenhall Glacier in Alaska. But mostly I don't care about the scenery—the finishing line is the best sight.

What will you do next?

I would love to do an Iron Man Triathlon, or ultra-marathons. But for now—I'm going to have a rest!

Fish Food

Visitors to the Kowakien Yunessun spa resort in Hakone, Japan, are offered an unusual treatment for the removal of old or dead skin from their feet. They bathe their feet in a Turkish bath that is filled with Garra rufa fish (also known as Doctor fish or Nibble fish), and the fish happily munch away on the old or dead skin and any other unwanted detritus, to leave the feet clean, refreshed, and revitalized!

Spell it Out

Lovestruck Serbian Vujadin Stojkovic hired a fleet of taxi drivers to propose to girlfriend Ivana Novakovic in 2006. He paid each of the 12 cab drivers to paint a single letter of "*udaj se za mene*," which means "marry me" in Serbian, on the side of their vehicles and then pull up outside Ivana's house. She was so touched by the romantic gesture that, naturally, she accepted.

Monkey Business

Ron Warren of New York City has a collection of around 1,800 sock monkeys.

Cheesy Whiff

In one year, Alex Johnson, a 17-year-old student at Munising High School in Michigan, collected 3,500 empty bags of cheese-flavored snacks in his locker.

Scary Guy

With tattoos covering 85 percent of his body and many piercings, Earl Kenneth Kaufmann had his name legally changed in 1998 to "The Scary Guy!" Although he spreads a message of peace, he has been banned from two U.S. cities because of the way he looks.

Fiat Jam

More than 750 owners of little Fiat 500 cars positioned their vehicles to form a huge single-model traffic jam at an Italian racetrack in 2006.

Luxury Facial

At a New York City beauty salon, you can get a $270 facial that promises to firm up facial skin by coating it with a layer of caviar.

Baseball Collector

John Baker of Gosport, Indiana, has a collection of more than 1,000 old baseball gloves.

Cash Compilation

Larry Beebe of the U.S.A. has collected banknotes from more than 200 different countries.

Game Grandma

Ohio grandmother Barbara St. Hilaire, 70, who works as a video-game correspondent for MTV, earned her nickname "Old Grandma Hardcore" from playing video games for up to ten hours a day.

Match This

A total of 6,300 matches were balanced on top of this beer bottle without any artificial supports in the 1930s by a group of friends from Pittsburgh, Pennsylvania.

Card Dealer

Walter Cavanagh of Santa Clara, California, has nearly 1,500 valid credit cards, with total credit worth more than $1.7 million. His wallet stretches 250 ft (76 m), weighs about 38 lb (17 kg), and can hold 800 cards. He keeps the remainder in bank safety-deposit boxes. The idea began in the late 1960s when he and a friend made a bet whereby whoever could collect the most credit cards by the end of the year would win dinner. Cavanagh won with 143. He says: "I have a nearly perfect credit score. I only use one card and I pay it off at the end of the month. But you should see the length of my credit report!"

Huge Appetizer

A group of 20 Palestinian chefs spent 20 hours in June 2006 preparing a plate of tabbouleh, a Lebanese appetizer, that was 13 x 13 ft (4 x 4 m). The plate of chopped parsley, onion, lemon, tomato, and olive oil weighed over a ton.

Self Tribute

British millionaire Scott Alexander has bought an entire town in Bulgaria and plans to rename it after himself.

Favorite Food

Brenda Lashley of Kenosha, Wisconsin, named her newborn baby Edward Allen Frank after her favorite brand of sauerkraut!

$100 Burger

Diners at the Old Homestead Steak House in Boca Raton, Florida, can pay $100 for a hamburger made of beef from three different countries. Owner Marc Sherry has created a burger made from cows raised in Colorado, Argentina, and Japan.

Flame Face

H.H. Getty from Edmonton, Alberta, Canada, was known as "The Fireproof Man" because flames did not pain or blister him. He discovered his "talent" by accident when working on a construction site in the 1930s.

Believe it or Knot!

December 2005 saw workers in the city of Harbin in northeast China take the art of Chinese Knotting to a new level. Exponents of this traditional handicraft make decorative knots as auspicious household ornaments to symbolize such values as happiness and unity—but they are usually no more than a few inches square. However, this gigantic red knot, made to celebrate a snow carving expo in the city, measured an incredible 120 x 80 ft (37 x 24 m) and weighed a colossal 6,175 lb (2,800 kg).

337

Skater Boys

In 2005, Moshe Arazi, Aaron Lyon, and David Micley of Newton, Massachusetts, made a skateboard that measured a staggering 30 ft 1 in (9.17 m) in length.

Weird Tradition

Since 1952, fans of ice hockey team Detroit Red Wings have traditionally thrown octopuses on to the rink at the beginning of the play-offs.

Antique Sleighs

Retired teacher Bill Engel of Denver, Missouri, has a collection of more than 80 horse-drawn sleighs, most of them at least 100 years old.

Foot Funeral

Antonio Magistro of Gioiosa Marea, Sicily, held a funeral service for his amputated left foot before burying it in a coffin at the city cemetery.

Expensive Taste

New York City's Algonquin Hotel offers a martini cocktail with a diamond garnish at a cost of $10,000.

Code Buster

David Rosdeitcher of Boulder, Colorado, also known as "The Zip Code Man," can identify the location of any U.S. town based on its zip code. He has memorized all 48,000 zip codes in the U.S.A.

Deafening Digits

When Bob Hatch of Pasadena, California, snaps his fingers, the sound that he makes registers at 108 decibels—that's equal to the sound from a jackhammer or a race car.

Airplane Modeler

John Kalusa hand-carved 5,829 model wooden airplanes up to his death in 2003, each built to a scale of 1/18 in to 1 ft (1.3 mm to 30 cm). His collection is housed in an aeronautical university library at Prescott, Arizona.

Baseball Coffins

Thanks to a Michigan company, U.S. baseball fans will be able to stay close to their favorite teams in the afterlife. Eternal Image announced in 2006 that it would be reproducing the names and logos of all 30 U.S. major league baseball teams on a range of coffins and urns, priced from $600 to $3,500.

Naked Ride

Hundreds of cyclists in some 50 cities around the world staged a naked bike ride on June 10, 2006, to protest against pollution caused by cars. Wearing nothing but their helmets, they paraded through venues such as Toronto, Los Angeles, Madrid, Barcelona, Prague, London, Milan, Seattle, San Francisco, and Vancouver.

Long Brows

Leonard Traenkenschuh of Port Townsend, Washington, has eyebrows that are 3½ in (9 cm) long.

Bar Towel Bob

Robert Begley has the best collection in Chambersburg, Pennsylvania—bar none. Starting out in 1990, Begley (known to his friends as "Bar Towel Bob") has managed to collect more than 2,300 bar towels, from 27 different countries.

Chopping Board Belly

This Chinese chef is seen here displaying great dexterity with two meat cleavers by chopping meat on his stomach in the city of Nanjing in eastern China.

KNITTED GARDEN

In some gardens the emphasis is on trees and shrubs, with others the accent is on flowers. However, in a newly unveiled English garden, the overriding theme is wool.

That's because, with the help of more than 300 volunteers, Jane Bolsover of Surrey, England, has knitted a life-size English garden.

The garden, which is sponsored by the British Hand Knitting Confederation, measures 15 x 10 ft (4.5 x 3 m) and took six months to create. Jane estimates her team made four million individual stitches in that time, knitting together 50 mi (80 km) of wool.

Everything in the garden is hand-knitted (including the wall, pond, and waterfall) and the attention to detail is extraordinary, right down to the flowers, insects, and toadstools, and even the worms and carrots in the vegetable patch.

There is a knitted picnic laid out on a rug on a knitted lawn, next to a knitted path. Among the woolen wildlife are a red squirrel, a robin, a mole emerging from a molehill, a bird at a nesting box, a frog, and a snail. Elsewhere, a woolen dog plays with a woolen ball to the backdrop of "music" from a woolen radio.

It was only when the project was complete that Jane made a startling admission. "I'm one of the world's worst knitters," she said.

A knitted deckchair provides the centerpiece to this amazing woolen garden.

Early Bird

Jeff Twieden of Seattle, Washington, began waiting in line for *Star Wars: Episode III* at the cinema 22 weeks before the movie's 2005 release!

Weight Loss

Thai policemen with waistlines larger than 40 in (102 cm) were ordered to lose weight in 2005 so that they looked good while directing traffic. As a result, more than 80 overweight officers underwent a one-month fitness regime in Bangkok.

Diary Enthusiast

James Cummings of Knapp, Wisconsin, has a collection of 16,000 diaries, including works by John Quincy Adams, Winston Churchill, and Benjamin Franklin.

Fast-food Diet

For his documentary film, *Supersize Me*, U.S. director Morgan Spurlock ate nothing but McDonald's fast food for breakfast, lunch, and dinner over the course of 30 days.

Bottle Fireplace

Eric Rayner's family home, near the Russian River in California, has an outdoor fireplace made from hundreds of old bottles.

Nail Clippers

Andre Ludwick of Parys, South Africa, has a collection of more than 500 different kinds of nail clippers from around the world. His favorite was handmade by a blacksmith in 1935. The collection started after a visit to Israel in 1971, where Ludwick acquired two nail clippers as souvenirs.

Channel Paddle

In the space of nine days in 2006, Michael O'Shaughnessy of Ponce Inlet, Florida, completed a 64-mi (103-km) paddleboard marathon that took in four countries. First the 49-year-old real-estate broker paddled his way across the English Channel in just over five hours, then he made a 3.00 a.m. start to cross Scotland's Loch Ness in 5 hours 49 minutes, and finally, in a nod to his Irish roots, he crossed the Irish Sea in 2 hours 37 minutes.

$3,000 Takeaway

A group of curry-mad England soccer fans paid over $3,000 to have a takeout dinner flown out from home to the 2006 World Cup in Germany. Bath restaurant Bombay Nights flew out the meal in an insulated bag to the fans' hotel in Munich.

Egg Launch

The Aerospace Industries Association of America runs a contest for students to build a model rocket that can fly to a height of 850 ft (259 m) while towing two raw eggs, and then parachute the eggs back down to earth—unbroken.

Colorful Coffins

Artist Alfred Opiolka offers an unusual service to the bereaved and their families in the town of Wertach in southern Germany. He paints coffins in bright colors, often with floral motifs and sometimes decorated with butterfly ornaments, and says that people often find funerals easier to bear when the deceased is lying in a cheerful, brightly painted casket.

Tricky Track

In 2006, Steve Shanyaski and Richard Connolly created a model racing car track that was enough to drive you round the bend—all 724 of them. Laid out on an airfield in Kent, England, the track had 2,683 straights as well as the 724 curves to make a total length of 3,625 ft (1,105 m). Placed vertically in a straight line, it would be taller than Mount Snowdon, the highest mountain in England and Wales. The track was so long that each lap took 25 minutes.

Giant Rocker

When Tom Doxey put his Penrose, Colorado, restaurant up for sale in 2006, it came with an unusual accessory out front—a 9,100-lb (4,130-kg) rocking chair. The rocker stands 21 ft (6.4 m) high and 14 ft (4.3 m) wide, and was built from 12 Douglas fir logs, 25 tubes of caulk, and six gallons of glue by woodworker Dwayne Simmons back in 1990.

Golden Sum

Cosmetics magnate Ronald Lauder, co-founder of the Neue Galerie, New York, paid an unprecedented $135 million for a painting in 2006. He forked out the staggering sum for Austrian artist Gustav Klimt's 1907 oil-and-gold-encrusted portrait of Adele Bloch-Bauer, the wife of a sugar industrialist.

Lego Aircraft Carrier

Malle Hawking from Munich, Germany, has made a massive scale model of the U.S.S. Harry S Truman aircraft carrier, out of lego. Using more than 300,000 bricks, Malle spent more than a year creating his masterpiece, which boasts electric lights on the flight deck as well as inside the individual aircraft on the deck. It also features movable elevators and radar dishes. The ship's measurements are a whopping 14 ft 10 in (4.52 m) long, 4 ft 6 in (1.37 m) wide, and 3 ft 11 in tall (1.2 m), and it weighs more than 353 lb (160 kg).

Wiggly Feast

Eating a handful of worms might not be everyone's idea of a tasty snack, but this man in Madras, India, is loving them! He ate an astonishing 200 worms in a fraction over 20 seconds at a worm-swallowing contest in 2003.

In the Pink

In 2007, 57-year-old Reverend Wendy Saunders of London, England, went entirely pink to raise her profile. First she dyed her hair pink, then added a pink jacket, pink trousers, and a pink shirt below her conventional dog collar. To complete the effect, she bought a pink Nissan Micra car. No wonder she is known locally as "The Pink One."

Arrow Birthmark

Adrian Volcu of Richmond Hill, Ontario, Canada, has an arrow birthmark in the iris of his eye.

Underwater Ironing

A keen exponent of the sport of extreme ironing, whereby competitors press clothing in dangerous environments, Louise Trewavas of London, England, plunged to new depths in August 2006 by taking an ironing board and iron to 452 ft (138 m) underwater at the Red Sea resort of Dahab. After ironing a T-shirt, she had to spend almost another three hours in the water carrying out decompression stops in order to avoid the sickness known as the bends.

Family Tattoo

Father-of-20 Mike Holpin from New Tredegar, Wales, has his family tree tattooed on his back. He started the tree in 1997, adding to it whenever another baby was born—and there's still room for more!

Bath Friends

Valli Hammer of Farmer City, Illinois, is never short of company in the bath... because she owns around 2,500 rubber ducks. She began collecting them in 2000 to keep her young son happy at bathtime and now she has rubber ducks from all 50 U.S. states and several foreign countries.

Sweet on Sugar

Phill Miller of Greenfield, Indiana, has a collection of more than 6,000 sugar packets from around the world.

King of Cards

LeRoy Gensemer of Exeter, Michigan, has collected more than 1.4 million different business cards. To celebrate reaching the million mark in 2002, naturally he had a commemorative business card printed.

Strong Shoulders

In the 1940s, Joe Jirgles from Grand Rapids, Michigan, could hold a 1-gal (3.8-l) can of varnish between his shoulder blades. He could also use his shoulder blades to attach himself to a fence so firmly that he could hang in place.

Going Loco

A total of 1,740 students at the University of Guelph in Ontario, Canada, welcomed the new school year in September 2006 by simultaneously doing "The Locomotion."

Basketball Marathon

Two teams of students and teachers from Japan took part in a basketball game that lasted two and a half days in June 2006. Miyazaki International College beat Miyazaki Municipal University by 5,493 points to 5,432 in the 60-hour marathon.

Road Fork

Steve Schreiber planted a sculpture of a 31-ft (9.5-m) high silver fork at the intersection of two roads in Rock City, New York.

Fearless Grandma

A 92-year-old British great-grandmother rappelcd (abseiled) 220 ft (67 m) down the side of an apartment building in June 2006. Doris Long of Hayling Island, Hampshire, completed the daredevil feat in the nearby city of Portsmouth. She said afterward: "I was swinging like a pendulum. People inside must have thought I was dropping in for tea."

Supersize Soccer

Fans warm up with a full-size soccer ball on a giant table soccer game in Berlin, Germany, in 2005. Created to promote the Confederation Cup, which Germany hosted in 2005, the game featured players in the shape of the Berlin Bear—the city's mascot for more than 700 years.

24-hour Ride

Mark Brown managed to cover a distance of 580 mi (933 km) on a little 50cc scooter at Australia's Le Minz 24-Hour Scooterthon in 2005.

Noisy Rejects

Believe it or not, China's army turns away recruits that snore too loudly!

Sturdy Bike

Cyclist Reg Blease is still pedaling the streets on his first bike—58 years after he bought it. In that period, the 74-year-old from Greater Manchester, England, has notched up more than 300,000 mi (482,800 km)—equivalent to cycling around the world 12 times. The bike has no gears, just one brake, and is built from heavy steel.

DOMINO DAY

A team of 87 builders from 13 different countries took around two months to set up an intricate domino course—and then saw more than four million dominoes toppled in a matter of minutes.

The "Domino Day" challenge took place in the city of Leeuwarden, in the Netherlands, on November 17, 2006. It was created by Weijers Domino Productions, who had designers working on the Domino Day project for almost the entire year. The course comprised 4,400,000 dominoes, took five months to produce, and weighed a total of 77,600 lb (35,200 kg).

Four special builders' challenges were included in the course whereby pairs of builders had to complete key areas of the display while the dominoes were already falling. By the end of the event, 4,079,381 of the 4,400,000 dominoes that had been set up were toppled successfully.

The theme for Domino Day 2006 was "Music in Motion" and nine musical genres, including rock, classical, disco, and hip-hop were represented. The set-up included famous figures, such as Mozart and Britney Spears, as well as pictures, and even a "domino city."

One of the most spectacular sections of the design was devoted to Michael Jackson. A mechanical figure that was part of the display did a moonwalk and, while the soundtrack to "Billie Jean" was played, the dominoes fell to form three impressive figures of Jackson.

A member of the international team of builders carefully sets up a part of the course.

More than 250 varieties of dominoes, some with stickers and some painted, were used in the course.

Crazy Eric

An electrician from France calling himself "Crazy Eric" carries 1,300 objects including screwdrivers, a shaving kit, a fold-up umbrella, spare batteries, and paint brushes in his specially designed outfit.

Sick Bags

Feel queasy on airplane flights? Go and see Sweden's Rune Tapper who has 1,079 different airsickness bags from 448 airlines in 131 countries!

Cabin Collector

James Grisley of Pittsburgh, Illinois, has a collection of around 28 full-size log cabins, ranging from small sheds to large barns, all built in the mid to late 1800s. His interest began in 1976 when a neighbor gave him an old, rundown cabin to use as a toolshed.

Disco Ball

In Johannesburg, South Africa, in September 2006, the Citizen newspaper built an operational disco ball measuring about 12 ft (3.6 m) in diameter and weighing two tons!

Busy Balloon

Ralf Schüler from Dessau, Germany, must be really popular at children's parties, because, believe it or not, he has managed to squeeze 23 people inside a latex balloon.

Britney Sandwich

In 2006, a sandwich half-eaten by Britney Spears was sold for more than $500. The egg salad sandwich was collected by a waiter after an awards ceremony and put up for sale on eBay. It was bought by on-line gaming company Golden Palace, who also purchased the remains of a corndog that was being eaten by Britney's now ex-husband Kevin Federline.

16,000 Ties

Derryl Ogden of the U.S.A. has a collection of more than 16,000 neckties that he has amassed since 1934.

Seaweed Wine

Marine biologists in Germany make seaweed wine, which sells for $28 a bottle.

Tag Quilt

Diana Douglas of Higdon, Alabama, made a giant quilt using 2,591 shirt tags.

Fish Fan

In 2006, 98-year-old Constance Brown of Pembroke, Wales, revealed that the secret of her long life was eating nothing but fish and chips. "That's all I eat. I don't eat any vegetables at all," says Constance, who has been frying fish and chips for a living for 80 years.

Plane Auction

An African charter airline bought a Gulfstream jet for $4.9 million... on the Internet auction site eBay.

Relaxed Reptiles

These lizards have been dressed up and placed in this tableau after being deeply relaxed and hypnotized by a ten-year-old girl in Florida. Lily Capehart discovered her uncanny ability to "hypnotize" lizards when she was just two years old, and has been doing it ever since. Maintaining that all of her lizards are handled with the greatest care and respect, Lily and her parents have created the world of "Lizard-Ville"—a series of images showing the lizards dressed up and placed in whimsical lizard-sized scenes.

Mole Man

For nearly half a century, 75-year-old William Lyttle of London, England, has been digging burrows beneath his 20-room Victorian house. Known locally as the "Mole Man," it is estimated that, using a shovel and a homemade pulley, he has scooped 120 sq yd (100 sq m) of earth to hollow out a network of tunnels and caverns, some 26 ft (8 m) deep, and spreading up to 60 ft (18 m) in every direction from his house.

FIRST AID KIT

Runaway Bride

Kate Austin and Gordon Fryer had a wedding with a difference when they were married while running the 2006 London Marathon.

Out of this World

Russian-born American Ekaterina Dmitriev poses with a life-size cutout of her bridegroom Russian cosmonaut Yuri Malenchenko following her satellite wedding to the Commander of the International Space Station in Texas in 2003. Texan law allows weddings where one party is absent, but this does not usually mean they are in orbit 240 mi (385 km) above the Earth.

Cake Capers

In New York's Times Square in June 2005m 20 brides-to-be dressed in wedding gowns dived into a giant wedding cake to find a $50,000 prize as part of a promotion for a cable TV series *Bridezilla*.

Weighty Wedding Dress

In August 2006, Josephine Doherty from Surrey, England, got married in a dress that weighed a colossal 392 lb (178 kg)! The bride who took two hours to get into the dress, and its 60-ft (18-m) train took five bridesmaids and eight best men to carry it.

Yo, Eddy!

Canadian "Fast Eddy" McDonald is a speedy yo-yo performer who has managed to perform an astonishing 35 separate yo-yo tricks in a single minute, and a dizzying 8,437 loops in one hour.

Cool Wedding

A couple adopted drastic methods to avoid getting married in a heat wave that struck southern Italy in 1995. Domenico Manchia from Italy and his French bride Marlene Mulet were wed 18 ft (6 m) under the sea in front of the town of Tavolara in Sardinia.

Mud Muncher

For the past 12 years, Bao Bao from Zhengzhou in central China has had a strange compulsion to eat mud. It started when, at the age of seven, she was walking along a river bank and thought how she would like to try some mud, and has eaten it ever since. Yellow mud is her favorite. She is estimated to have eaten more than 1.5 tons of mud to date.

SPOON RACER

This automotive achievement is the creation of Chuck Weedman from Beaver Dam, Kentucky. Chuck has welded more than 1,800 ruby red spoons to the frame of this motorbike to create a reptilian lizard-skin look.

Curry Bath

A Japanese health spa is offering the unusual specialty of a communal curry bath to its patrons. The bath, which resembles a green soup, contains a blend of curry spices, including turmeric and red pepper, and is said to improve blood flow, help boost the metabolism, and produce beautiful skin in all who bathe in it.

Twine Ball

Since 1979, James Frank Kotera of Lake Nebagamon, Wisconsin, has been creating a huge ball of twine. Using leftover twine from a neighbor's bales of hay and working up to four hours a day, he has assembled the "Mr JFK Twine Ball." It weighs more than 19,000 lb (8,600 kg), stands as tall as a person, and is twice as long.

Healthy Hobby

Huang Chunyi, 94, of Taiwan credits his longevity to his 20-year hobby—collecting photos of beautiful women!

Jewel Box

By 2000, Carol McFadden of Oil City, Pennsylvania, had accumulated a collection of more than 30,000 different pairs of earrings.

Tinned Treat

Les and Beryl Lailey of Manchester, England, celebrated their wedding anniversary in 2006 by eating a can of chicken that they had been given on their wedding day... 50 years earlier. They had vowed to keep the canned chicken, which was part of a wedding gift hamper, in their kitchen cupboard as a memento of their happy day in 1956 and promised that they would not eat it until their golden anniversary. And when they finally opened the can, the chicken tasted as good as new. Les said: "I had it with some potatoes and vegetables and it went down a treat."

I Do... I Do... I Do...

There is no secret to how David and Lauren Blair of Henderson, Tennessee, keep that newlywed feeling alive in their marriage—they simply keep getting married over and over again. In August 2006, the fortysomething couple staged their 90th wedding in 22 years of marriage! They actually had three weddings the first week they were married in 1984. The first was in Topanga Canyon, Los Angeles; the second was a traditional church wedding in Chicago; and the third was in Las Vegas after they picked up a coupon for a free wedding while on their honeymoon. And since then they've tied the knot on a regular basis, including being married in 11 Hard Rock Cafés.

Giant Gnome

Artist Maria Reidelbach is dwarfed by her latest creation—a concrete garden gnome that stands 13 ft 6 in (4 m) tall. Chomsky the gnome is part of Maria's Gnome on the Grange project, located near Accord, New York.

Top Table

In August 2006, 20 people carried a 630-lb (285-kg) pool table almost 3,000 ft (915 m) to the summit of the Brecon Beacons mountain range in Wales.

Deluxe Doggy Treats

Pampered pooches in Taiwan can enjoy top-notch treats in "Dr. Pro," an ice-cream parlor for dogs in the capital city Taipei. One of a host of speciality stores for pets that have opened recently in the city, Dr. Pro offers a full range of ice-cream flavors with scoops all beautifully presented.

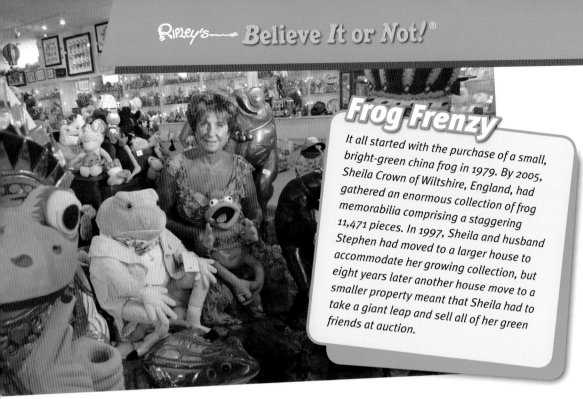

Frog Frenzy

It all started with the purchase of a small, bright-green china frog in 1979. By 2005, Sheila Crown of Wiltshire, England, had gathered an enormous collection of frog memorabilia comprising a staggering 11,471 pieces. In 1997, Sheila and husband Stephen had moved to a larger house to accommodate her growing collection, but eight years later another house move to a smaller property meant that Sheila had to take a giant leap and sell all of her green friends at auction.

Major Dachshund

An Internet website called "Pets In Uniform" gives you the chance to see your pet dressed as a U.S. Marine or a British General! You simply send a picture of your pet, and three days later a digital download of it in your chosen uniform will be available.

Junior DJ

Avante Price is a little kid with a big reputation—as a DJ in Chicago, Illinois. Avante started DJing in public in 2006, at just five years old. According to dad Johnny, Avante began scratching out the beats on their home turntables at the age of three, despite needing a piano bench to reach them.

Prayer Beads

Architect Jamal Sleeq of Kuwait has been collecting precious prayer beads, known in Arabic as *misbah*, since 1979. Today his collection numbers more than 2,000, the majority of which are made from amber. He has been known to fly all the way to Poland or Turkey just to collect one stone. In total he has 56,000 antiques and curios from all around the world, including some 14th-century silverware and 200-year-old carpets.

Duke Devotee

Jim Duncan of Brownsburg, Indiana, has a collection of more than 4,000 items devoted to the film actor John Wayne.

Final Cut

Peter Vita of Port Chester, New York, was 12 years old when he began cutting hair and, until his death in 2004, he had been working as a barber for 82 consecutive years.

March of the Undead

Every July, the village of Ribarteme in northwest Spain hosts a pilgrimage known as the "Procession of the Shrouds," whereby people who believe they have cheated death during the previous year are paraded through the streets lying in open coffins. This unusual custom, which dates back to the Middle Ages, symbolizes the penitents demonstrating their thanks to God for sparing their lives.

Black Belt

Raymond Wood of Hull, England, was given a top martial arts honor in 2006—at the age of 73. A former all-England jujitsu champion, he is one of just six people in the country to be given the coveted Tenth Dan black belt.

Bubble Keeper

Eiffel Plasterer of Huntingdon, Indiana, captured a soap bubble inside a mason jar and kept it intact for almost an entire year.

Barbie Girl

A collection of 4,000 Barbie dolls—the lifelong passion of late Dutch housewife Letje Raebel—was put up for sale in 2006. She bought her first Barbie for daughter Marina in the early 1960s, but Marina did not want to play with it and left it in the box. However, mom developed the collecting bug, inspired by Barbie's ever-changing wardrobe.

Bible Group

Retired Croatian bishop Marijan Oblak has a collection of almost 1,000 Bibles in 250 different languages. He has been collecting Bibles for 20 years and was given some in person by the late Pope John Paul II.

Bunny Bliss

Giant rabbits Roberto and Amy got married in Somerset, England, in April 2006. Both bride and groom weigh around 40 lb (18 kg) and are more than 3 ft (91 cm) in length.

Paper Boats

An Indian man has a collection of over 10,000 tiny, handmade paper boats. Shrinath Dixit from New Delhi carves the miniature boats in various colors with glaze and origami papers. They range in size from 7/8 in (2 mm) to 2 in (0.5 cm), so are best viewed under a magnifying glass.

Old Chocolate

A woman from Derbyshire, England, owns a chocolate bar that is 105 years old. Jane Marshall was given the bar, made to celebrate King Edward VII's 1902 coronation, by her grandfather when she was nine.

A Dog's Life

Eighteen-year-old Aija Gillman of Pinckneyville, Illinois, won a new car after she spent 13 days chained to a doghouse and wearing a dog collar in July 2006, as part of a competition to discourage dog owners from chaining up their pets. Her life was limited to the space accessible within the reach of the chain. She slept in her doghouse, battled boredom by playing in the mud and with her water bottle, and fought off sunburn by rubbing mud on her face. Hygiene was a porta-potty.

Brussels Bonanza

British office worker Richard Townsend was left feeling a little green when he tried to eat a colossal 44 Brussels sprouts in 60 seconds in December 2006. Using a wooden toothpick to transport the vegetables to his mouth, Richard managed a heroic 37 sprouts before he ran out of time. After his marathon attempt, Richard said that he couldn't face another sprout for a few days, but then popped another in his mouth, saying, "It's a shame to waste them."

Massive Mouth

At a whopping 11¾ in (30 cm) in circumference, the mouth of university student Gordon du Cane from Wiltshire, England, certainly is something to shout about. It is more than two inches bigger than a baseball, and Gordon can easily hold a whole apple in it, between his teeth.

Index

Index

Index

Index

Index

Index

Index

Index

Index

Acknowledgments

FRONT COVER AND TITLE PAGE (l) Reuters/Marcelo Del Pozo, (r) AFP Photo/Saeed Khan; 10 Courtesy of Todd Day; 12—13 (dp) Courtesy of Juan Cabana 14—15 Courtesy of Juan Cabana; 16—17 PA Photos; 18 2daymedia; 20 Dr Matthew Cobb, The University of Manchester; 21 Stewart Cook/Rex Features; 22 Nils Jorgensen/Rex Features; 22—23 Rex Features; 24—25 Reuters/Francois Lenoir; 26—27 Reuters/Stringer India; 30 Stan Honda/AFP/Getty Images; 31 Matt Cardy/Getty Images; 33 Reuters/Rupak De Chowdhuri; 35 Peter Lawson/Rex Features; 41 Jamie Hanso/Newspix/Rex Features; 43 Camera Press/Wu Fang/ChinaFotoPress/Gamma; 45 Davison Design and Development www.inventionland.com; 46 Chris Jackson/Getty Images; 46—47 Rex Features; 48 (l) Camera Press/Yang Wanjiang/Phototex, (bl) Mark Clifford/Barcroft Media; 49 Jamie Jones/Rex Features; 50—51 Reuters/Stephen Hird; 52 Reuters/China Daily China Daily Information Corp – CDIC; 55 PA Photos; 56 Roderick Russell/CNY Medical Center; 58—59 Spectrum Multi-Media Ltd Kent Hart - Hart Images www.AlwaysEscaping.com; 61 Reuters/Sean Yong; 64 Feature China/Barcroft Media; 68—69 Roderick Russell/ CNY Medical Center; 73 Reuters/Alexandra Beier; 74—75 Reuters/Frank Polich; 76—77 Reuters/Sergio Moraes; 78—79 Courtesy of David Straitjacket; 83 PA Photos; 84—85 Richard Bouhet/AFP/Getty Images; 86 Reuters/Kamal Kishore; 87 Camera Press/Zhang Xiangyang/Phototex; 94 PA Photos; 96 Reuters/Alex Grimm; 97 (c) Reuters/ Mohamed Azakir, (tr) Reuters/Daniel Aguilar, (cr) Reuters/China Photos, (br) PA Photos; 98—99 Duan Renhu/Phototex/Camera Press London; 100—101 (dp) T.Falise/Gamma; 102 Reuters/Heino Kalis; 103 Reuters/Albert Gea; 104 Kazuhiro Nogi/AFP/Getty Images; 105 R.Gaillarde/Gamma; 106—107 Reuters/Pawel Kopczynski; 108—109 2daymedia; 110—111 Rafa Rivas/AFP/Getty Images; 114 Mark Clifford/Barcroft Media; 115 Reuters/Paul Yeung; 116—117 Benjamin Stansall/Rex Features; 119 Reuters/China Daily China Daily Information Corp – CDIC; 120 Reuters/David Gray; 121 PA Photos; 124—125 Chris Hellier/Rex Features; 126 Sam Barcroft/Barcroft Media; 129 Jeff J Mitchell/ Getty Images; 130—131 Daniel Graves/Rex Features; 132—133 William Thomas Cain/Getty Images; 134—135 Benguc Ozerdem/Rex Features; 136—137 Junko Kimura/ Getty Images; 139 Reuters/Bogdan Cristel; 140—141 Saverkin Alexsander/UPPA/Photoshot; 142—143 T.Falise/Gamma; 145 Renee Chambers www.ArtistisaHorse.com 146—147 Camera Press London; 148 Top Photo Group/Rex Features; 153 Toby Zerna/Newspix/Rex Features; 154—155 Renee Chambers www.ArtistisaHorse.com; 157 Wenn; 159 Courtesy of Karl Beznoska; 161 Reuters/Richard Chung; 162—163 Frederic Neema/Gamma/Camera Press London; 164 PA Photos; 166 Hydestile Wildlife Hospital/Rex Features; 167 Chris Martin Bahr/Rex Features; 168—169 Drew Gardener www.drew.it; 170—171 swns.com; 172 Courtesy of David C Steele; 173 PA Photos; 174 Reuters/ Herb Swanson; 176 David Burner/Rex Features; 179 PA Photos; 180 PA Photos; 181(t) Reuters/China Daily China Daily Information Corp – CDIC, (b) PA Photos; 182 Sam Barcroft/Barcroft Media; 183 Daniel Rushall/Rex Features; 185 Feature China/Barcroft Media; 186—187 Courtesy of Janice Wolf; 190 (b) PA Photos, (t) ChinaFotoPress/ Getty Images; 191 (b) PA Photos, (t) ChinaFotoPress/Getty Images; 192—193 PA Photos; 194—195 PA Photos; 198 De Ville/Rex Features; 199 swns.com; 200 Mark Mirko/ Rex Features; 202—203 Passionate Productions/Getty Images; 205 Reuters/Str Old; 208—209 Reuters/Nir Elias; 210 PA Photos; 212—213 Reuters/Pilar Olivares; 214 Reuters/ STR New; 217 Reuters/Victor Ruiz; 219 Rex Features; 220 PA Photos; 224—225 www.sunderlandbodyart.com; 226 Wenn; 228 PA Photos; 230 (l) Denis Charlet/AFP/Getty Images, (r) CHU Amiens via Getty Images; 231 Wang Xiaocun/CQCB/ChinaFotoPress/Getty Images; 232 www.ronpatrickstuff.com; 233 Mark Jenkins; 234—235 Heather Jansch; 236—237 (bl/br) ChinaFotoPress/Getty Images; 238 Courtesy of private collector; 240—241 Mark Jenkins; 243 Jeff J Mitchell/Getty Images; 244 2daymedia; 246 "Danny Scheible Masking Tape City" www.dannyscheible.com; 247 Britt Savage/Senor Mcguire; 250 Richie Streate – The Dungeon Inc. USA, 251 UPPA/Photoshot; 252—253 Stephen Boitano/Barcroft Media; 255 (t) Wenn, (b) PA Photos; 257 UPPA/Photoshot; 260—261 Ben Phillips/Barcroft Media; 262 Murmur, Stan. Sittin' Pretty (Anthropometric Monotype, Ashley Barlow) 2005; 263 2daymedia; 264—265 www.ronpatrickstuff.com; 267 Mundi Man created by Ando Art (ANDO along with Christini Righetti) AndoArt.com; 270—271 www.toothpickart.com; 273 2daymedia; 274 Reuters/Arben Celi; 275 PA Photos; 276 Courtesy of David Hanson 277 Terje Eegum; 279 Reuters/Brendan McDermid; 280 Urs Flueeler/epa/Corbis; 281 PA Photos; 282 Reuters/Gustau Nacarino; 283 Sandy Maxwell/John Muir Trust. The John Muir Trust acquired Ben Nevis Estate which includes Britain's highest point at Ben Nevis summit (1334m) in June 2000. www.jmt.org; 284—285 Ian Waldie/Getty Images; 286 Kay Nietfeld/AFP/Getty images; 287 Reuters/Sean Yong; 290 Giovanni Zardinoni www.studioartezj.net; 291 Wenn; 292—293 Courtesy of David Hanson 294 Reuters/ Stringer Shanghai, 295 (t) Reuters/China Daily China Daily Information Corp – CDIC, (b) Reuters/Adnan Abidi; 297 PA Photos; 298—299 Courtesy of kyle MacDonald; 300 Vladimir Kmet/AFP/Getty Images; 302—303 Reuters/Bogdan Cristel; 304 www.goldeagle.com; 305 Courtesy of Trevor Andre Snowden; 306—307 Reuters/Bazuki Muhammad; 309 Reuters/China Daily China Daily Information Corp – CDIC; 310 Ian Waldie/Getty Images; 311 Timothy A. Clary/AFP/Getty Images; 312 Investec Asset Management; 313 Terje Eegum; 314 PA Photos; 316 Ethan Miller/Getty Images; 318—319 Rex Features; 322—323 Reuters/Yves Rossy; 325 Philippe Hays/Rex Features; 326 swns.com; 327 Timm Schamberger/AFP/Getty Images; 328 (tl) Reuters/Christian Charisius; 328—331 (b) Ben Phillips/Barcroft Media; 331 (r) Daniel Graves/Rex Features; 332—333 Courtesy of Dane E Rauschenberg; 334 Sutton-Hibbert/Rex Features; 336—337 (b) Gamma/Camera Press London/ChinaFotoPress; 338—339 Shao Dan/Photocome/ UPPA/Photoshot; 340—341 ICHF www.ichf.co.uk; 342—243 Reuters/Michaela Rehle; 344—345 Malle Hawking; 346 Reuters/Stringer India; 349 Reuters/Fabrizio Bensch; 350—351 Weijers Domino Productions www.dominodomain.com/www.mrdomino.com; 353 Camera Press/ED/DW; 354 John Gichigi/Getty Images; 355 Reuters/Richard Carson; 358 Reuters/Yuriko Nakao; 359 Reuters/Richard Chung; 360 Solent News/Rex Features; 361 PA Photos; 362 PA Photos; 363 Solent News/Rex Features.

Key: t = top, b = bottom, c = center, l = left, r = right, sp = single page, dp = double page

All other photos are from Ripley's Entertainment Inc.

Every attempt has been made to acknowledge correctly and contact copyright holders and we apologize in advance for any unintentional errors or omissions, which will be corrected in future editions.